THE AMUSEMENT PARK GUIDE

"Whether you are a carousel or coaster enthusiast, or just out for family fun, *The Amusement Park Guide* is loaded with tips, hints, facts, and trivia that will take you through the labyrinth of North America's greatest amusement parks . . . I had no idea there were so many . . . It is sure to help you get the most out of your amusement park outings . . . What a great book."
— William Manns, author of *Painted Ponies, American Carousel Art*

"Tim has provided the tips on the dips, the moods, the food and all that's good at North America's amusement parks From large to small, it's all here . . . everything you need to know for making your visit a great memory."
— Dennis L. Speigel, President, International Theme Park Services, Inc.

THE AMUSEMENT PARK GUIDE

Fun for the Whole Family
at More Than 250 Amusement Parks
from Coast to Coast

by Tim O'Brien

A Voyager Book

The Globe Pequot Press

Chester, Connecticut

Photo Credits: Pp. xxii, 136: courtesy of Cedar Point; pp. 8, 181: courtesy of Kings Dominion; p. 15: courtesy of Great America, Santa Clara; pp. 26, 147: copyright © 1988 Universal City Studios, Inc.; p. 45: courtesy of Dollywood; pp. 53, 187: courtesy of Busch Gardens, The Old Country; pp. 63, 74: Tim O'Brien; pp. 85, 118: copyright © 1991 Knott's Berry Farm; p. 95: courtesy of Six Flags Over Mid-America; p. 110: courtesy of Old Tucson Studios; p. 128: courtesy of Carowinds Amusement Park; p. 158: copyright © 1990 Sea World Florida; p. 172: courtesy of Astroworld; p. 195: courtesy of Six Flags Magic Mountain.
Cover photo of the Cyclone wooden roller coaster at Lakeside Park, Denver, Colorado, by Mark Wyatt.

Library of Congress Cataloging-in-Publication Data

O'Brien, Tim.
    The amusement park guide: fun for the whole family at more than 250 amusement parks from coast to coast / by Tim O'Brien. — 1st ed.
        p.   cm.
    "A voyager book."
    Includes index.
    ISBN 0-87106-300-x
    1. Amusement parks—United States—Directories. 2. Amusement parks—Canada—Directories. I. Title.
GV1853.2.025   1991
791'.06'87—dc20
                                                        91-7421
                                                        CIP

Manufactured in the United States of America
First Edition/Second Printing

 This text is printed on recycled paper.

Dedication

To my wife, Rosi, who kept the home fires burning
and the grass mowed while I was out researching
the amusement parks of North America. And to my
two daughters, Carrie and Molly, who unselfishly
volunteered to come with me and help out whenever possible.

Contents

Distribution of Amusement Parks
in the United States and Canada

Ontario

Quebec

New Brunswick

Wisconsin

Michigan

Vermont

Maine

Nova Scotia

New Hampshire
Massachusetts

New York

Rhode Island
Connecticut

Illinois

Ohio

Pennsylvania

New Jersey

Indiana

West Virginia

Delaware

Maryland

ssouri

Kentucky

Virginia

Tennessee

North Carolina

kansas

South Carolina

Mississippi

Alabama

Georgia

Louisiana

Florida

Enlargement of gray area appears on following page.

Detail of Eastern States

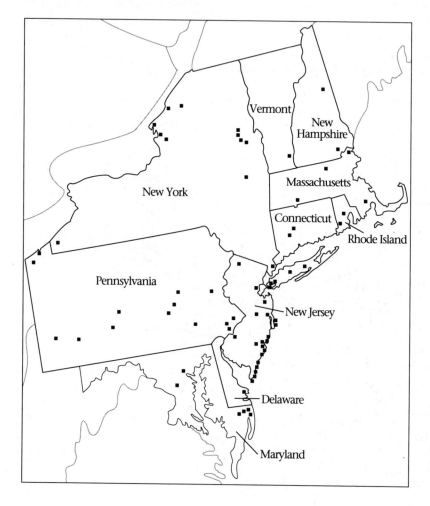

Acknowledgments

While researching this book, I found there were a lot of terrific people running the amusement parks of America and Canada—no wonder there are so many great parks! While compiling information, I talked with more than 250 people and they were all willing to share valuable time with me during their busy summer season. Thanks to everyone at the parks for so much help and insight into the industry.

Of the hundreds who helped me put this book together, Mark Wyatt, the editor of *Inside Track*, an amusement park newsletter, deserves special mention. He contributed his knowledge, his time, and part of his summer to this project.

Bill Manns, a carousel historian and the author of *Painted Ponies, American Carousel Art*, provided the list of the top park carousels.

My wife, Rosi, also helped with the research and saved me a good deal of time in doing so. I'd like to acknowledge her patience and understanding while I was married to this book. It's a lot easier to dedicate yourself to a major project like this when you know someone's out there supporting you; thanks!

Introduction

I don't know about you, but when I enter an amusement park, every one of my senses starts working overtime. The color, the excitement, the smells, and the sounds all join together to give me a feeling of total escape from the cares of the world.

I eat foods I normally wouldn't eat, I do silly things and play games, and if I'm lucky enough to win a prize, I feel like a youngster again as I carry that teddy bear along the midway.

Growing up in a resort area that had an amusement park, I was "hooked" at a very young age on the trappings of merriment that such establishments provide. Little could I guess that years later when I was a grown-up with a wife and children of my own, I would visit the world's finest amusement parks, ride the rides, eat the food and allow my senses to rejoice again . . . and get paid while doing so.

Well, that's what I now do as Southeast Editor of *Amusement Business*, a trade publication that covers the mass-entertainment industries, including amusement parks. Even on assignment, with a camera and notepad in hand, I still experience the thrill of being in a park.

It's great being a journalist who chronicles an industry in which the main purpose is to create an environment where people have fun. And amusement parks of all sizes are discovering new ways to help people of all ages do just that. As a result, amusement parks are more popular today than they've ever been. During the past few years, more than 250 million people have flipped the turnstiles of America's parks each year. Major league baseball's published gate attendance, including play-offs and the World Series, comes in at around 60 million yearly. Who says baseball is America's favorite pastime?

A Very Brief History of America's Amusement Parks

Most people today take for granted the sophisticated rides, shows, and attractions found in modern parks. With all the excitement a park has to offer, few people take the time to consider how the park or the rides came to be. Actually, the amusement park phenomenon has an interesting, albeit humble beginning.

During the nineteenth century, beach clubs were popular along the shores of New York. These clubs were gathering places to drink beer, play games, and socialize. By 1850, the Coney Island area of Brooklyn was becoming a popular resort area and thousands made their way to the beaches every weekend during the summer. There was a plethora of entertainment pavilions at which those city folks who didn't want to swim, could drink, socialize, and watch musical productions.

The first real "ride" didn't make it to the beach area until 1877, when a 300-foot-tall observatory from the Philadelphia Centennial Exposition was moved here and renamed the Iron Tower. Then in 1884, LaMarcus Thompson built a Switchback Railway ride, the forerunner of the roller coaster, in Coney Island. Others soon copied and improved on Thompson's railway idea. But it wasn't long until he was eager to enhance the concept even more. Two years later, in 1886, Thompson built a "real" roller coaster, and the success of that ride soon brought a steady stream of other amusement rides—and bigger crowds—to the beach.

While this activity was taking place in New York, folks in other parts of the country were enjoying their weekends and holidays at entertainment facilities built near their homes. Picnic parks with swimming pools and sports fields were springing up throughout America. As the crowds grew, so did the need for other activities.

Restaurants and dance halls were added for the adults, and pony rides were added for the kids. As mechanical rides became available, they were added, and before long, hundreds of amusement parks were in operation.

Many of those early parks were originally developed by a trolley or steamship company. They were built at the end of the line, or in a remote area served by the company, to help build weekend and holiday use of the transit system. These "trolley parks," as they are often called, were tremendously successful and prospered into the 1930s. Most survived the Great Depression, but by this time the automobile was increasing the scope of leisuretime opportunities available to the public. The smaller parks started losing their weekend guests, who could now drive to a larger park, or to the beach 50 or 60 miles away.

While many of the small parks closed, most of the strong, clean, well-run family operations continued to prosper. But by the early 1950s, only a small percentage of those early parks were still in operation, and many experts were writing death notices for the American amusement park. The parks couldn't compete, many thought, with motion pictures and television.

Along Came Walt

Then, in 1955, Walt Disney combined color, fantasy, and excitement with food, rides, and shows and put that combination into a safe, clean family environment. He called it Disneyland—and the theme park industry as we know it today was born.

The almost-immediate success of Disneyland paved the way for more corporate investments in the park industry, and soon other large, multi-million-dollar theme parks started showing up all over the country. These megaparks breathed new life into the entire industry. As a result, many of the smaller trolley parks were able to take advantage of America's new attitude toward amusement parks and began to grow and prosper once again.

Introduction

Although the large destination parks in the country today get most of the attention, the backbone of the industry is still the small, family-run park. On the whole, these parks are professional, well-run attractions but are unknown to most outside a small marketing area.

There are more of these small "traditional" parks, as they are called, than larger theme parks. Most often, though, they don't have themes and don't have many of the multimillion-dollar rides that are so abundant today. What they do have, however, is history, quaintness, and nostalgia. They are well-preserved examples of true Americana and provide visitors with great opportunities for low-key fun.

The Rides, Parks, and Other Things

Roller coasters are still the most popular ride in amusement parks, and the coaster resurgence of the late 1980s and early 1990s has left us with some mighty big, fast, and expensive thrill machines in the parks across America.

Right behind roller coasters in popularity are the water-oriented rides found in so many parks today. More log flumes, raging rapids, and spill-water raft rides are being added each year. Usually equipped with a warning sign that proclaims YOU WILL GET WET, PROBABLY SOAKED, these rides offer a way to cool off during a hot summer's day at the park.

In addition to regular rides that run in or over the water, several parks have been adding regular water-park elements to their lineup of attractions. Patrons must wear swimsuits to participate, and the parks have built bathhouses and locker rooms to accommodate the water lovers.

A more recent category of water rides is the the wet/dry slide. Although such rides resemble water-park flumes and slides, people in street clothes can ride them in small, raft-type boats. Instead of having its riders splash down into a deep pool, these rides have long run-outs at the bottom so that the raft ends up on dry land after skimming across a shallow pool of water.

Some parks charge extra for using the water-park elements, whereas others include such use in the general admission price.

Parks are Changing with the Times

A major concern of park owners and officials today is the declining number of youth in the marketplace and the so-called graying of America. As a result, park officials have been reevaluating their priorities and making their parks a more comfortable place for older people to visit.

Asphalt has been ripped up and replaced with brick paths, flower beds, and shaded rest areas graced by an ample supply of park benches. There are also more air-conditioned, table-service restaurants in parks today than there have ever been, and the quality of food has improved dramatically during the past few years. Many parks even provide a "healthy choice" menu.

Moreover, the entertainment package is also being seen as a way of giving adults a reason to rediscover amusement parks: Everything from indoor, Broadway-style revues to circus acts to world-class ice-skating shows are being produced and are usually included in the park admission fee.

Purpose of This Book

This book is intended to show off the parks of North America and to call attention to some of the great entertainment treasures hidden within our continent. Sure, you've probably heard of many of them, but unless you live in Minot, North Dakota, I'll bet you've never heard of Lucy's Amusement Park. And I'd wager that few people outside Little Rock, Arkansas, have ever heard of that city's War Memorial Amusement Park or Burns Park Funland.

You'll be amazed and delighted by what's out there.

Happy trails!

How to Use This Book

In an effort to be as thorough as possible and to paint a realistic picture of amusement and theme parks, I've listed not only the larger, better-known facilities but also the small, family-owned parks offering just a few rides. Thus, you will find two types of listings in this book, major and minor.

The Minor Listings

The minor listings are for those parks that I feel are special enough to be included but that don't necessarily have as much to offer as the major parks. Some of these parks have only three or four rides, but because of their setting, theme, attractions, or activities, I felt they should be included.

As you will discover, some of the neatest parks in the country have little more to offer than a few good rides and a great deal of atmosphere.

The Major Listings

Most of the major listings are self-evident, but for a better overview, here are a few additional comments:

■ If a park is not a year-round facility, most are usually open on a weekend-only basis prior to Memorial Day and after Labor Day. I have listed the first and last days of seasonal operation; unless the listing specifies otherwise, assume the park is open only on weekends in the spring and fall.

■ You will encounter three common types of admission policies. At pay-one-price parks, you'll pay one price at the gate; after that, almost every ride, show, and attraction is included.

   Parks that charge general admission require you to pay one fee, usually less than $5.00, and then pay extra for rides and attractions. Quite often, general admission permits you to enjoy most of the live shows and productions; usually, a pay-one-price ride ticket is available once you get into the park, or you can play on a pay-as-you-go basis.

   Parks that allow free admission charge nothing to get in; you pay for anything you want to do as you go. Again, pay-one-price ride tickets are often available.

■ Probably in no other business existent today do open hours fluctuate as much as in the amusement park business. In listing these hours, I've tried to be as exact as possible; nevertheless, to list some parks' hours would take an entire paragraph. So, if you plan to visit a park either early or late in the day, be sure to call first. Also, although the hours and admission fees listed in this guide were confirmed at press time, it's generally a good idea to call for the most current information before traveling.

Tim's Tips on How to Make Your Amusement Park Trip More Fun

Your trip to an amusement park ought to be fun for every member of your family, even if you have a bunch of kids in tow. Sure, you're probably there in the first place because the kids wanted to come. But with a little planning and common sense, the outing can be fun for everyone. Here are a few tips on how to make your trip to an amusement park fun, memorable, and maybe even relaxing.

1. Be kind to your feet. Wear comfortable sneakers. Although the park may look small, you'll probably circle it at least twice—plus, you'll be standing in lines.

2. Pick up a guidebook and entertainment schedule when you buy your ticket. It's wise to plan your day around the specific times of the shows you don't want to miss. Make a list of must-do's and plan your route so that you won't be doing a lot of time-consuming and tiring backtracking.

3. If you have kids old enough to go off on their own, give them a marked map or a sheet of paper with a meeting place and time well specified. In the excitement of the day, kids have a way of forgetting specific directions.

4. When entering the park, point out the facility's uniformed workers to your children. Tell them to report to one of those workers or to a police officer if they become lost or need help.

5. Make sure you're dressed for the day. Take along a rain parka or a folded-up trash bag to use in case of a sudden shower. It's also wise to take along sweaters or jackets and leave them in the car, just in case. A change of clothing is advisable as well, especially if you enjoy riding the wet rides.

6. Beat the lunch rush by eating before noon or after 2:30 P.M. Although parks have sufficient food-service staff and outlets most of the time, it seems everyone wants to eat during prime "lunch" hours. Don't waste your time in food lines. If you schedule your eating for non–prime times, you'll be able to ride the rides while everyone else stands in food lines.

7. Although most parks don't allow food to be brought onto the grounds, it still makes sense to take along an apple or two to tide you over until eating time. This guideline is especially important if you have children.

8. Don't eat a lot of high-sugar-content foods while you're in the park. Most parks today offer good alternatives in the way of food and drink. You don't need anyone in your group to be on a "sugar high" in addition to all the excitement of the park.

9. Plan to eat before a show, and not before that big ride on the roller coaster. Let your stomach rest awhile after eating or drinking.

10. If the day is hot and sunny, be sure to wear a hat, apply sunscreen, and drink lots of fluid. If you start feeling ill, report immediately to the park's first-aid station.

11. If you have medication that needs refrigeration, most first-aid stations should be able to keep it for you. If not, ask at the office. All parks with any sort of food service have large coolers.

12. Even if you don't have children with you, consider renting a stroller to hold your camera equipment, souvenirs, and so on. A camera bag gets awfully heavy by midafternoon.

13. Souvenirs are enjoyable, but don't buy them before you're ready to leave. Hauling around some breakable item or a large balloon or teddy bear all day isn't too much fun. Tell the children that each can pick out one thing to buy before leaving but not before then.

14. Most of the larger parks have rental lockers. If you want to take along a lot of stuff but don't want to leave it in your car, rent a locker.

15. Take your children to the bathroom *before* getting in a long waiting line for a ride. In addition, make sure the kids understand what the ride does and how it works *before* waiting in line—it's frustrating to finally reach the front of a line, only to have the little one get scared and refuse to ride.

16. Never force children to ride if they don't want to; doing so could turn them off to amusement rides for the rest of their lives. If your child does get on a ride, but you think he or she may chicken out once it begins, alert the ride operator. It is possible to signal the operator to stop the ride so as to allow your child to get off. And don't be shy—the operators are used to this situation.

17. In-park entertainment is very popular, and there is usually standing room only at most of the shows. Get there early and pick out a good (and shady) seat for yourself.

18. Your visit is not a marathon—plan a rest break during the hot afternoon. If you've rented a motel room nearby, go back and take a swim or a nap and then come back around 5:00 P.M., when most people are leaving for the day. If you have kids with you, not only will this kind of break help them physically, but they'll feel they've been to the park twice.

19. If you do leave the park, make sure that you have your parking receipt with you and that you won't have to pay to park again. Be sure, too, to get your hand stamped for readmittance. (And if your plans call for swimming while away from the park, try to protect the stamp.)

20. At larger parks, make sure you remember where you park your car. In the excitement of the day, it's all too easy to jump out of the car and head to the park without paying attention to your exact location. After a long day in the park, it's no fun to spend an hour hunting for your car.

21. Many larger parks sell their tickets off-premises at hotels, rental-car agencies, and the like. If you can buy your ticket before you reach the park, you'll eliminate one line right away.

22. When riding rides, make a mental note of the number of the car you're in. If after getting off the ride you realize that something fell out of your pocket or that you left your purse, you can tell the operator exactly where that item should be.

23. If you're lucky enough to win a lot of stuffed animals, you may have a hard time carrying all of them. Most of the plush toys found in parks have small loops attached. You can easily carry these toys by looping them over your belt.

24. Rules are usually made for safety reasons, so for your own safety, follow them. There are good reasons for not standing up on the roller coaster and for keeping your arms and hands inside the flume log. Nothing can ruin a day quicker than an unexpected injury, especially if it could have been prevented by using common sense. Don't lock your brain in the car.

25. Try to avoid visiting a park on the opening day of the season. Everyone has been waiting for that day, and most parks are packed. Moreover, lines tend to be slow at both food stands and rides while the new employees grow comfortable with their responsibilities.

Hold onto your lap bar! The first drop of Cedar Point's Magnum XL200 steel roller coaster, in Sandusky, Ohio, is 194 feet at an incredible 60-degree angle.

Author's Choices

Tim's Terrifying Top Ten Roller Coasters

1. **The Beast**, Kings Island, Kings Island, Ohio
2. **The Cyclone**, Astroland, Brooklyn, New York/Coney Island
3. **Phoenix**, Knoebel's Amusement Resort, Elysburg, Pennsylvania
4. **Magnum XL200**, Cedar Point, Sandusky, Ohio
5. **Giant Dipper**, Santa Cruz Boardwalk, Santa Cruz, California
6. **Thunder Run**, Kentucky Kingdom, Louisville, Kentucky
7. **Big Bad Wolf**, Busch Gardens, Williamsburg, Virginia
8. **Georgia Cyclone**, Six Flags Over Georgia, Atlanta, Georgia
9. **Thunderbolt**, Kennywood Park, West Mifflin, Pennsylvania
10. **Hercules**, Dorney Park, Allentown, Pennsylvania

Top Five Non–Roller Coaster Rides

1. **Slidewinder**, Dollywood, Pigeon Forge, Tennessee
   A fast, scary ride down a mountainside through a water trough in a six-passenger, foam-rubber boat. Next to the Beast roller coaster, this is the most exciting ride in the whole world!
2. **Derby Downs**, Cedar Point, Sandusky, Ohio
   A large, fast carousel whose horses move back and forth and actually race one another as the ride spins. One of only two such rides left in the country, this one was built in 1925; the other one can be found at Rye Playland, Rye, New York.
3. **Pirates of the Caribbean**, Disneyland, Anaheim, California/Walt Disney World, Lake Buena Vista, Florida
   A dark boat ride through the loud, crazy, and often-scary life of the pirate. It's nicely paced, nice and cool, and marked by a great theme song.
4. **Kongfrontation**, Universal Studios Florida, Orlando, Florida
   You board an aerial tram, and no sooner have you left the station, than you find out King Kong is loose and your life is in danger. He misses you the first time, but the second time, look out—he gets so close you can smell his banana breath.
5. **Skooters**, Knoebel's Amusement Resort, Elysburg, Pennsylvania
   There are two ways you can identify a quality bumper-car operation: First, you smell the graphite when you get within 20 feet of the place. Second, the cars must be the classic Lusse Skooter cars, in near-perfect condition. Knoebel's passes the test on both counts.

Top Six Favorite Foods and Where to Find the Best

1. **Chicken.** There's none better than that served at Mrs. Knott's Chicken Dinner Restaurant at Knott's Berry Farm, Buena Park, California.
2. **Popcorn.** The Disney parks—Disney World, Lake Buena Vista, Florida, and Disneyland, Anaheim, California—sell only Orville Redenbacher popcorn. They peddle it hot and fresh, for a good price from their mobile popcorn wagons.
3. **Pork barbecue.** Dollywood, in Pigeon Forge, Tennessee, serves up the best in the land. The meat is tender in texture and smoky in flavor and the sauces are fantastic. A smokehouse is right in the park.
4. **Chili.** Although it's franchised, there's none better than Skyline Chili, and to my knowledge the only park that serves it is Kings Island, near Cincinnati, Ohio. It's especially good for lunch on a hot day.
5. **Hot dog.** The original Nathan's hot-dog stand at Coney Island, near Astroland and Deno's Wonder Wheel Park, still sells the best dog in the country. Even other Nathan's locations can't match the taste.
6. **Milk shakes.** The ones made at the Prime Time Cafe in Walt Disney World's Disney–MGM Studios Theme Park in Orlando, Florida, can't be touched. The cafe's specialty is the Peanut Butter and Jelly milk shake—a marvelous concoction.

Top Antique Wooden Carousels Located in U.S. Amusement Parks

These listings, arranged in no particular order, were contributed by William Manns, a carousel historian.

1. **Hersheypark**, Hershey, Pennsylvania, circa-1919 Philadelphia Toboggan Company, no. 47. This is an extraordinary, four-row machine containing elaborate artistic carvings by John Zalar, one of the most noted artists in the field.
2. **Riverside Park**, Agawam, Massachusetts, created in 1909 by the Coney Island carver Marcus Illions. This ride has the finest and most flamboyant horses ever created that still operate on a carousel. The machine also features several menagerie (nonhorse) animals, including rare Illions carvings of a lion, a tiger and a deer.
3. **Dollywood**, Pigeon Forge, Tennessee, 1903 Gustav Dentzel Philadelphia-style carousel, with original factory paint. It features some of the rarest Dentzel animals, including a rooster and a dog, and operates with an antique band organ and a brass-ring dispenser.

4. **Six Flags Over Georgia**, Atlanta, circa-1908 Philadelphia Toboggan Company, no. 17. This is the largest antique merry-go-round in the country, with five rows.

5. **AstroWorld**, Houston, Texas, circa-1915 Dentzel, with the outer row carved by Daniel Muller, one of the premier carousel artists.

6. **Cedar Point**, Sandusky, Ohio, has three antique carousels, two by Dentzel and one by Muller. The one in Frontiertown has a Muller "ghost horse" and is the only haunted merry-go-round in the country.

7. **Elitch Gardens**, Denver, Colorado, circa-1920 Philadelphia Toboggan Company, no. 51, has four rows containing beautiful, floral-decorated chariot horses and a monogrammed, armored-style lead horse carved by John Zalar.

8. **Playland**, Rye, New York, has the finest surviving carvings by the Coney Island artist Charles Carmel. This circa-1928 ride features armored horses, and the horses on the outside row are laden with cherubs and eagles. Designated a National Historic Landmark in 1987.

9. **Disneyland**, Anaheim, California, has a hybrid machine with horses by Dentzel, Carmel, Stein and Goldstein, and Muller, on a Dentzel frame. Has some extremely fine horses not found anywhere else.

10. **Oaks Amusement Park**, Portland, Oregon, has a Spillman Engineering carousel built in 1921. It boasts a wonderful assortment of menagerie animals, including one of the rarest, a kangaroo.

THE PARKS

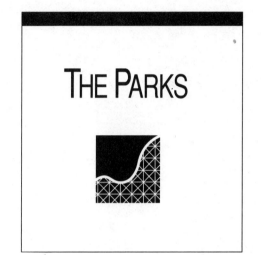

THE UNITED STATES

Alabama

Main Street Family Fun Park
25050 Canal Road, Highway 180E
Orange Beach, AL (205) 981–9849

The weather can't shut down this park—it has activities both in- and outside. A 30,000-square-foot building and 7½ acres, with a 1½-acre lake, offer fun and activities for the entire family.

The action includes an indoor train ride, kiddie rides, kiddie bounces and ball plunges, paddleboats, roller skating, go-carts, and live puppet and costumed character shows.

Admission is by a gate fee that includes some of the activities. Call for hours.

Alaska

Alaskaland
Airport Way and Peger Road
Fairbanks, AK (907) 452–4244

Founded in 1967 to celebrate the hundredth anniversary of the purchase of Alaska from Russia, this 44-acre historical theme park has a playground, a native village, a mining valley, an art gallery, and a miniature golf course. It also has 3 family rides, including the Crooked Creek and Whiskey Island Railroad train ride around the city, and an antique carousel.

Live entertainment includes demonstrations of games from the World's Eskimo Indian Olympics, a stampede show, and a saloon variety show. The park is home to the famous Alaska Salmon Bake, served daily.

Open daily from Memorial Day to Labor Day, 11:00 A.M. to 9:00 P.M. Call for admission prices.

Arizona

Golf N' Stuff
9445 Metro Parkway East
Phoenix, AZ (602) 997-7576

There's a lot more stuff than golf here. In fact, the city's only major per-manent roller coaster is located in this 7-acre complex, across from the huge Metrocenter regional mall.

In addition to the looping steel coaster, are a junior coaster, a log flume, a Sea Dragon and several kiddie rides, 4 miniature golf courses, bumper boats, and a Lil' Indy go-cart track.

The park is marked by a mammoth stucco castle with big blue fiberglass domes, housing the arcade games and a few other smaller attractions.

Open 365 days a year, from 10:00 A.M. to 11:00 P.M. or midnight. There is no admission fee; all attractions are on a pay-as-you-play basis. Free parking.

The above rides have recently been added as part of a major expan-sion. All should have been completed by the time this book went to press. You may, however, want to call first.

Metro Midway and Discovery Center
Indoors, Metrocenter Mall
9617 Metro Parkway West
Phoenix, AZ (602) 395-9915

Once you're inside the mall, a big neon sign points you to this action-filled family center. Besides the escalator ride down to the park, you'll find several family rides, including a 36-horse carousel, the Red Baron planes, and the Space Raiders video combat ride. You'll also find a handful of coin-operated kiddie rides and a midway featuring more than 30 games of skill.

The Learning Center is a separate facility, adjacent to the ride area, that offers 36 interactive and visual science displays.

Admission to the rides and game area is free, but there's a small charge for the Learning Center. Both areas open at 10:00 A.M. and close at various times during the week.

Old Tucson Studios
201 South Kinney Road
Tucson, AZ (602) 883-0100

Howdy, partner—welcome to the real West. This intriguing desert facil-ity was created in 1939 as the set for the film *Arizona*, and at that time was the largest film location ever built outside Hollywood; in fact, it was called Hollywood in the Desert. The park is Hollywood's version of what the Old West looked like, including Southwest adobe sets and an Old West Frontier Street. Filming still takes place here, and the enterprise has more than 200 film, TV, and commercial credits.

In addition to any film action taking place, you'll find numerous shows and 4 mechanical family rides.

Food service: Among the several restaurants are the Iron Door Cafe, serving pizza and taco salads, and Big Jake's Ramada, serving Buffalo Burgers and barbecued ribs and beef. Also on the premises are an ice-cream parlor and various snack and beverage operations. The famous Rattlesnake-brand beer is served here. Food may be brought into the facility.

Entertainment: 4 shows: a live gunfight, a special-effects western stunt show, saloon entertainment, and a sound-stage show.

Extras: Petting Corral, free. A horse-drawn stagecoach ride is available for extra charge. The performers hang around after their shows to talk with guests about filmmaking, and you might find one that will teach you how to fast draw.

Special events: Western Music Festival, November; Professional Rodeo Cowboy Association's circuit finals, January; intercollegiate rodeo competition, February, March and November.

Season: Year-round.

Operating hours: 9:00 A.M. to 9:00 P.M. Closed Thanksgiving and Christmas only.

Admission policy: Pay-one-price, under $10. Discount admission available after 5:00 P.M. Free parking.

Top rides: Iron Door Mine Ride, a ride-through fun house; A-Car, antique autos; a carousel; a narrow-gauge train ride that circles the facility and is narrated.

Plan to stay: 4½ hours.

Best way to avoid crowds: Come midweek. Peak season here is between Thanksgiving and Easter.

Directions: Take the Speedway Boulevard exit off I-10. Go west 12 miles. When Speedway dead-ends, take a left; the park is about ¼ mile on the left.

Nearby attractions: Sonora Desert Museum, a Southwest native museum; Reid Park Zoo; University of Arizona Museum of Art; Pima Air Museum. And you'll see the beautiful saguaro cactus everywhere you look around here.

Arkansas

Burns Park Funland
Funland Drive
North Little Rock, AR (501) 753–7307

Located in the heart of Burns Park, a 1,562-acre city park, Funland bills itself as the place to have "good old-fashioned fun."

With 14 rides, including 7 for kids, Funland is a shaded oasis set apart from the rest of the park activities.

Food service: 2 concession stands, serving hot dogs, corn dogs, cotton candy, and ice cream.

Extras: Miniature golf, extra charge.

Special events: Easter Egg Hunt, Easter Sunday; Summerfest, an arts-and-crafts festival on Labor Day weekend; Fireworks, July 4.

Season: March through mid-October.

Operating hours: 10:00 A.M. to 5:00 P.M. on weekdays; 12:30 to 8:00 P.M. on weekends.

Admission policy: Free gate; rides on a pay-as-you-go basis. Free parking.

Top rides: A mile-long train ride; a circa-1915, Allan Herschell carousel; Spook House, a dark ride.

Plan to stay: 2 hours.

Directions: Take the Burns Park exit off I-40; follow signs into the park and then to Funland.

Nearby attractions: Arkansas Arts Museum; Museum of Natural History; Arkansas Territorial Capitol Restoration, a restored village of 12 original buildings.

Dogpatch
Highway 7
Dogpatch, AR (800) 643–8213

"There it is—way down in the valley!" you'll exclaim. Like most mountain theme parks, Dogpatch requires that you take an incline to get to it, but then things are a bit different here. At Dogpatch, you park your car at the top of the mountain and take transportation down into the valley to the park.

The 16-ride park is home to Li'l Abner, Daisy Mae, and all their Dogpatch gang and is appropriately rustic and "hillbilly" looking. The characters' cabins have been reproduced throughout the 40 acres, and who knows which of the characters you'll run into during your stay.

Dogpatch is located on the site of a former rainbow-trout farm, and fishing is still a big draw here. Poles and bait are provided; you pay for the fish by the pound when you catch them. The fish will be either iced down for the trip home or taken over to the restaurant, cleaned, and cooked for you to eat right there!

TIM'S TRIVIA

Like fresh fish? You can catch your own trout in the pond at Dogpatch in Arkansas, and have the staff clean it, cook it, and serve it to you at the park's Fishtaurant, along with hush puppies and cole slaw.

Food service: 10 locations, including the Kountry Kitchen, featuring an all-you-can-eat, country breakfast buffet; the Fishtaurant, specializing in fresh trout and catfish dinners; and Daisy Mae's Ice Cream Parlor, offering some outstanding confections.

Entertainment: 5 shows, including puppet and magic presentations, bluegrass and country music shows, and a rainmaker. Top-name country entertainers are occasionally booked in.

Extras: Anteek, an antique car ride, is available for an extra fee. A great place for souvenir photos is Kissin' Rocks, a formation in the shape of human heads with puckered lips. The Gravity House is a walk-through with unbelievable illusions. Marble Falls, the largest falls in the Ozarks, is located at the end of the park; the waterwheel beneath the falls is thought to be the largest wooden waterwheel in North America.

Special events: Soap Opera Festival, Labor Day weekend; Children's Festival, late August.

Season: May through the first week of October.

Operating hours: 10:00 A.M. to 6:00 P.M.

Admission policy: Free gate; rides on a pay-as-you-go basis. Come in after 3:00 P.M., next day free. Free parking.

Top rides: Monsterous Mushroom Ride; Paratrooper; Whirlin Whiplash, flying swings; Wes Pok Chop Spechul, a scenic train ride through the park, over Marble Falls, and into the woods; Frustatin Flyer, a Mad Mouse compact steel roller coaster; paddleboats.

Plan to stay: 6 hours.

Best way to avoid crowds: Come during the week, either early or late in the day.

Directions: Located 9 miles south of Harrison on scenic Highway 7 South. About a 45-minute drive from Branson, Missouri.

Nearby attractions: Country Time Jamboree, a country music show; Karts Plus, go-carts and miniature golf.

Kings Dominion in Doswell, Virginia, is just one of the many parks that offer top-notch Broadway-quality musical revues.

Fun Spot
Highway 62E
Eureka Springs, AR (501) 253–7548

"Non-stop Family Fun" is how this well-kept family entertainment center advertises itself, and how can anyone resist such a promise? With kiddie rides, adult bumper cars, batting cages, a video arcade, miniature golf, and go-carts, Fun Spot certainly has a lot to keep everyone busy.

Open daily from 10:00 A.M. until 11:00 P.M., Memorial Day to Labor Day. Free admission and attractions on a pay-as-you-go basis; a daily pay-one-price ticket is also available.

Magic Springs Family Theme Park
2001 Highway 70 East
Hot Springs, AR (501) 624–5411

Here is exactly the type of amusement park you'd expect to find in this part of America—hilly, shaded, with a lot of water and a nice mix of old and new rides and attractions.

The entrance plaza opens a half-hour before the park does and offers plenty of shops to keep you occupied. Fountains are near the entrance, and the park surrounds a large lake.

The 115-acre attraction has a "magic" theme and is divided into three sections: Milltown, Rivertown, and State Fair. There are 22 rides, including 6 for kids.

Food service: 3 sit-down buffet restaurants—Hilltop Chalet, Magicians Kitchen, and Springhouse—plus 4 walk-aways and several portables.

Entertainment: 6 shows, including a rainmaker, a puppet theater, and a magic show. In addition are shows that feature pop and country music.

Extras: Aqua Bikes and bumper boats, additional fee. Make sure you ride the Sky Hook ride—there aren't too many of these around. You'll climb into a cage, and a cable from a high tower will pull you up and down.

Special events: Gospel Fest, Memorial Day weekend; Soap Stars, late June; plus additional one-season-only activities and promotions.

Season: Late-April through September.

Operating hours: 10:30 A.M. to 6:00 P.M.

Admission policy: Pay-one-price, under $15. Free parking.

Top rides Spinaroo; Tilt-A-Whirl; Zephyr, flying swings; Big Wheel, a Ferris wheel; Magic Dragon, a swinging boat ride; Ozark Twister; Scrambler; bumper cars.

Plan to stay: 5 hours.

Best way to avoid crowds: Wednesday is the slowest day.

Directions: Take Exit 11 (Route 70) off I–30 and go west to Magic Springs Drive, just inside the Magic Springs city limits. Turn here and the park is less than ½ mile up the road. Located 45 miles west of Little Rock.

Nearby attractions: Mid-America Museum, a hands-on science museum; Ride the Ducks, tour rides of the area; Hot Springs National Park.

War Memorial Amusement Park
Jonesborough Drive
Little Rock, AR (501) 663–7083

Lying deep in War Memorial City Park, this good old-fashioned amusement park rests next to the Little Rock Zoo. The 15 acres are filled with stately trees and plenty of colorful landscaping.

Among the 17 rides in the park is a rare "Over the Jumps" carousel, the only one left of the four made by the Spillman Engineering Company during the early 1920s. The carousel runs hourly, on weekends only.

Food service: 2 concession stands, serving standard fast-food and snack items, and an ice-cream parlor.

Entertainment: There is no regularly scheduled in-park entertainment. The city park usually has something going on in its band shell.

Special events: Special celebrations and activities on the three major holidays during the summer.

Season: Easter through October.

Operating hours: 10:00 A.M. to 4:00 P.M. weekdays, and till 6:00 P.M. on weekends.

Admission policy: Free gate admission; rides on a pay-as-you-go basis. Pay-one-price also available, under $5. Free parking.

Top rides: Bumper cars; Tilt-A-Whirl; Scrambler; Star Jet.

Plan to stay: 2 hours.

Best way to avoid crowds: Usually not a problem here, but come early on weekends.

Directions: Take the Fair Park exit off I–630; then follow the signs to the park and the zoo.

Nearby attractions: Little Rock Zoo; War Memorial Stadium; golf courses and tennis courts.

California

Belmont Park's Giant Dipper
3190 Mission Boulevard
San Diego, CA (619) 488-1549

The Giant Dipper wooden roller coaster lives! Following fourteen years of legal battles and fund-raising efforts, this circa-1925 National Historic Landmark has been restored to its splendor and is open to the public.

Belmont Park, of which the coaster was once the major draw, was closed down in 1976. Now, as the only ride from that park still existing in its original location, the coaster is the focal point of an upscale shopping village. The owners have added a beautiful replica of an antique carousel to accompany the coaster classic.

Also on the grounds is a roller coaster museum, and The Plunge, Belmont Park's original indoor swimming pool, is still in operation.

Open daily during the peak summer months at 11:00 A.M. with closing at either 10:00 or 11:00 P.M. In winter, operations are cut back. Pay-as-you-play policy.

Castle Amusement Park
3500 Polk Street
Riverside, CA (714) 785–4140

Castle Park was founded by Bud Hurlbut in 1976 to showcase his large collection of rides. He previously had the rides concession at nearby Knott's Berry Farm, and when that enterprise decided to operate its own rides, Hurlbut built his own facility.

The 25 acres are divided into three sections and feature a large castle as the centerpiece. The castle itself is an arcade, offering more than 400 games, and to the right of the castle are 30 rides, including 12 for kids. Behind everything are four 18-hole championship miniature golf courses, widely regarded as four of the best such courses in the country.

Food service: Snack bar and an outdoor cafe that serves snack foods and sandwiches. Several locations throughout the park.

Entertainment: There is no entertainment scheduled.

Extras: Hurlbut has designed and built more than 50 "little trains" for parks throughout the world; 2 are set up here.

Season: Year-round.

Operating hours: Rides open at 6:00 P.M. during the week and at noon on weekends and close at 11:00 P.M. or midnight. Golf courses are open 10:00 A.M. to 10:00 P.M. daily. Rides are closed on Mondays during the summer and open only on weekends and holidays in the winter.

Admission policy: Free admission to the park. Pay-one-price ride ticket, as well as individual ride tickets, available. Parking charge when rides are open.

Top rides: The Log Ride, a flume ride; antique cars; a circa-1905 Dentzel carousel; Tornado, a compact steel coaster.

Plan to stay: 4 to 6 hours if you plan to play arcade games and/or golf.

Directions: Located at 3500 Polk Street, off Riverside Expressway between the La Sierra and Tyler Street exits.

Nearby attractions: Roller City 2001, a roller-skating rink.

Disneyland
1313 Harbor Boulevard
Anaheim, CA (714) 999–4445

A plaque at the entrance to Disneyland tells it all: HERE YOU LEAVE TODAY AND ENTER THE WORLD OF YESTERDAY, TOMORROW AND FANTASY. This creation of Walt Disney was the world's first ride park to offer major themes, and it set the standards for all the other theme parks.

TIM'S TRIVIA

The fantasy castle at California's Disneyland is Sleeping Beauty's Castle, whereas that at Florida's Walt Disney World is Cinderella's castle. Walt Disney wanted something bigger for his Florida park.

Divided into seven lands and Main Street U.S.A., the park is clean and friendly and has all the charm you'd expect to find at Disneyland. Most of the 38 rides can be ridden as a family, and many are long-time favorites that never grow old, no matter how often you ride them.

There's Disney magic in the air. There's also a whole cast of familiar characters walking around the park, including Mickey Mouse, Pluto, Donald Duck, Minnie Mouse, and Roger Rabbit. They'll hug you and give you an autograph, but you'll never hear them utter a word—they want to preserve that cartoon magic.

Food service: Restaurants abound; they include the Tahitian Terrace in Adventureland, serving Polynesian specialties, and the Hungry Bear Restaurant in Critter Country, offering the park's tastiest hamburgers and chicken. The Disney parks are the only amusement parks in the country that serve Orville Redenbacher popcorn, and it's delicious. In addition to the major restaurants, the park has 34 food eateries. A "Healthier Food Alternatives" menu at the back of the park's guidebook tells where you can find "healthy" food preferences.

Entertainment: Pick up a show schedule when you enter the park, and base your visit around the shows you want to see. There are several musical and character shows, along with the biggest in-park show Disney has ever produced, "One Man's Dream," a theatrical stage production of the dreams of Walt Disney. Though Disney characters can be found throughout the park and in various restaurants, the best way to see Mickey is to visit Town Square, his usual hangout.

Extras: The Haunted Mansion, a walk- and ride-through adventure, is absolutely the best haunted house in the world. The Disney Gallery, displaying more than thirty-five years of rare Disneyland art, is housed in the structure that was originally built as an apartment for Roy and Walt Disney. Both these attractions are free with admission. And, for great souvenirs, Disneyland has its own paper currency, featuring Mickey, Minnie, and Donald on $1, $5 and $10 bills.

Special events: Main Street Christmas parade, Thanksgiving through New Year's Day; Main Street Electrical parade, summer months.

Season: Year-round.

Operating hours: During peak summer hours, 9:00 A.M. to midnight or 1:00 A.M. During winter months, 10:00 A.M. to 6:00 or 10:00 P.M.

Admission policy: Pay-one-price, under $30. Two- and 3-day passes also available, at some saving. Parking charge.

Top rides: Splash Mountain, a log-flume ride with a *Song of the South* theme; Space Mountain, an indoor steel coaster with a space theme; Star Tours, a ride simulation through the galaxies; Dumbo the Flying Elephant, a landmark that you *have* to ride; Pirates of the Caribbean, an indoor boat ride with frisky pirates watching you from all angles; Jungle Cruise, a boat ride down a tropical river.

Plan to stay: Unless you're there during an extremely slow period, plan to stay at least 1½ days, or 2 days if you want to see everything.

Best way to avoid crowds: Come in the winter months during midmorning or midafternoon. Crowds surge when the park opens and right after lunch; they also tend to rush to the major rides first.

Directions: Take the Harbor Boulevard exit off I-5 (Santa Ana Freeway) and go south on Harbor. The park is right next to the interstate.

Nearby attractions: Disneyland Hotel, with restaurants, a water show, and shopping; Grand Hotel Dinner Theatre.

Escondido Family Fun Center
830 Dan Way
Escondido, CA (619) 741-1326

If you can find your way out of the challenging, ½-acre Giant Maze here, you might want to try one of the three 18-hole miniature golf courses—or the batting cages, go-carts, bumper boats, ball crawl, or pillow bounce. Or you might want to visit the Kid's County Fair attractions and ride the train, the merry-go-round, or one of the other kiddie rides.

Free admission and you pay as you play. Hours and days of operation vary; call first.

Funderland
in William Land Park
1465 Sutterville Road
Sacramento, CA (916) 456-0115

Thousands of families have enjoyed this cozy traditional park since its founding in 1948. It's located in a spacious city park, across the river from the Sacramento Zoo and adjacent to Fairytale Town, a storybook village.

Outside the gate is a large picnic area, and nearby is a pony-ride concession. A circa-1948 Allan Herschell carousel, a Tilt-A-Whirl, a Ferris wheel, and a small compact steel family roller coaster are among the 11 rides. A snack bar offers a full line of snack items, including popcorn, pink popcorn, ice cream, soft drinks, and candy.

Open daily from 11:00 A.M. to 6:00 P.M. during the summer and only on weekends from February through May and from Labor day through November. Free admission, with rides on a pay-as-you-go basis; pay-one-price available only on weekends.

Funderwoods
In Micke Grove County Park
11793 Micke Grove Road
Lodi, CA (209) 369–5437

Surrounded by picnic groves, this small traditional family park lies in the middle of a county-owned park, directly next to the Micke Grove Zoo.

A Tilt-A-Whirl, a Ferris wheel, and a small steel family roller coaster are among the 11 rides the park has to offer. A compact snack bar serves such fare as nachos, candy, ice cream, and popcorn, as well as a park specialty, pink popcorn.

Open daily from 11:00 A.M. to 6:00 P.M. during the summer and only on weekends from February through May and from September through November. Admission to the amusement park is free, with rides priced on a pay-as-you-go basis; pay-one-price available only on weekends. The county charges a parking fee for all who enter the county park.

Golf N' Stuff
10555 East Firestone Boulevard
Norwalk, CA (213) 868–9956

In addition to 4 beautifully landscaped miniature golf courses, this small family park has bumper cars, bumper boats, Model-T cars, Lil' Indy race cars, and 2 large arcades.

There is no admission charge; all activities are on a pay-as-you-go basis. Call for hours.

Great America
2401 Agnew Road
Santa Clara, CA (408) 988–1800

Beautifully landscaped and offering a great variety of rides, this 100-acre park rests in the middle of famed Silicon Valley. The park, founded in 1976, has a patriotic theme and features 31 rides, including 6 for kids.

The Carousel Plaza, just inside the front gate, is one of the most beautiful entrances to any park in the country. The double-decked Carousel

Columbia (listed in *Guinness* as the tallest one in the world) rests peacefully beside a small lake filled with ducks.

Such Hanna-Barbera characters as Yogi Bear and Huckleberry Hound can be seen throughout the park and at Fort Fun children's area, while those lovable Smurfs can be found in Smurf Woods.

The double-decked Carousel Columbia at Great America in Santa Clara, California, offers a beautiful backdrop to the park's entrance pavilion known as Carousel Plaza.

Food service: Throughout the park are more than 30 restaurants and snack facilities, serving everything from barbecued ribs and chicken to roast beef sandwiches to seafood and Oriental dinners. The Farmer's Market is a food-court area with 11 food stands.

TIM'S TRIVIA

Three major amusement parks opened during our nation's 1976 bicentennial: Libertyland, Memphis, Tennessee; Great America, Santa Clara, California; and Six Flags Great America, Gurnee, Illinois.

Entertainment: An ice-skating show, an IMAX film, the Kings of Komedy roving band, a puppet show featuring the Jetsons, a dolphin show, and 3 musical productions.

Extras: Redwood Amphitheater, providing concerts all summer long by big-name entertainers, extra charge in addition to park admission.

Special events: Spring Celebration, Christian music day, May; July 4 celebration, with Paul Revere & The Raiders, offering a vintage rock act each year; Joy Celebration, Christian music day, September.

Season: Mid-March through the first weekend of October.

Operating hours: Opens at 10:00 A.M. daily and closes at varying times during the season.

Admission policy: Pay-one-price, under $20. Parking charge.

Top rides: Demon, a steel double-looping corkscrew coaster; Rip Roaring Rapids, a raging-rapids ride; Grizzly, a wooden coaster; Skyhawk, a participatory flight ride; Rue Le Dodge, bumper cars; Whitewater Falls, a spill-water raft ride; a 1918 Philadelphia Toboggan Company carousel; Vortex, the West Coast's only stand-up roller coaster.

Plan to stay: 7 hours.

Best ways to avoid crowds: Arrive at opening hours on weekdays or Sunday morning.

Directions: Located 5 miles north of downtown San Jose. Take the Great America Parkway exit off Highway 101; then go east to the park.

Nearby attractions: Winchester Mystery House.

Happy Hollow Park and Zoo
1300 Senter Road
San Jose, CA (408) 295–8383

Almost hidden away in the city's Kelley Park, this small kiddie park and cozy animal zoo is open year-round. As you enter the facility, you'll cross a drawbridge through a castle; the zoo is to your right, the amusement area to your left.

The 5 rides include a train journey around the park, a kiddie carousel, Granny Bug roundabout, and a family roller coaster.

Free admission to the amusement area, with rides on a pay-as-you-go basis. Small gate admission to the zoo. Hours and days of operation vary; call first.

Hecker Pass: A Family Adventure
3050 Hecker Pass Highway
Gilroy, CA (408) 842-2121

The first phase of this $34 million park is set to open sometime in 1992. With a horticulture theme, that 25-acre section will have from 15 to 20 rides, several restaurants, a crafts area, an exposition center, a lake with a fountain and 3 waterfalls, and an excursion boat ride.

The section is to be filled with horticultural exhibits and garden displays, so that the owners say, "when you walk into the park, it will appear that you've entered an oak forest that has been there for years."

Knott's Berry Farm
8039 Beach Boulevard
Buena Park, CA (714) 827-1776

This is probably the only amusement park in the world that began as a chicken restaurant. Mrs. Knott's Chicken Dinner Restaurant was (and still is) a popular eatery, and during the 1940s the Knott family added a few attractions to keep people busy while they waited for a table.

Today the 150-acre park, divided into five areas with a theme, features 35 rides. Ghost Town is the original area, and the 6-acre Camp Snoopy, reminiscent of the California High Sierra, centers on Snoopy and all the Peanuts gang.

TIM'S TRIVIA

The oldest continuously operated amusement park in America is Lake Compounce Festival Park, in Bristol, Connecticut. It started out as a picnic and swimming park in 1846.

Food service: Mrs. Knott's Chicken Dinner Restaurant serves up the best fried chicken dinner at any amusement park in the country. Make sure you ask for a piece of the fabulous boysenberry pie. (Walter Knott is credited with developing the boysenberry.) The Ghost Town Grill and the Fireman's Brigade Barbecue are two of the additional 30 food outlets in the park.

Entertainment: 10 shows, including a computerized water show, a dolphin show, a 3-D movie theater, the Berry Stompin' Jazz Band, medicine-man shows, street gunfights, a Wild West stunt show, and various musical saloon-type shows.

Extras: Gold panning is available in Ghost Town for an extra charge, and a free museum dedicated to the Big Foot creature is set up across from the entrance to Big Foot Rapids.

Special events: The park becomes "Knott's Scary Farm" each Halloween season; Ghost Town Crafts Festival, Thanksgiving through Christmas.

Season: Year-round.

Operating hours: 10:00 A.M. to midnight or 1:00 A.M. during peak season and 10:00 A.M. to 6:00 P.M.. during winter months.

Admission policy: Pay-one-price, under $25; a saving of 40 percent can be had after 6:00 P.M. Parking charge.

Top rides: Kingdom of the Dinosaurs, an indoor ride through the days of the dinosaurs; Calico Log Ride, one of the first flume rides in the country; Big Foot Rapids, a raging-rapids ride; Boomerang, a three-loop steel coaster; Calico Mine Ride, a narrated ride through a gold mine; Montezooma's Revenge, a steel shuttle coaster; Stagecoach, involving a ride around the park in a vintage stagecoach during which your party is attacked by bad guys; a 1902 Dentzel carousel.

Plan to stay: 8 hours.

Best way to avoid crowds: Come during off-season or on a weekday morning during season.

Directions: Located 30 minutes south of downtown Los Angeles. Take the Beach Boulevard exit off I–5 and go 5 miles to Knott's.

Nearby attractions: Medieval Times Dinner and Tournament theater; Movieland Wax Museum.

Marine World/Africa USA
Marine World Parkway
Vallejo, CA (707) 644–4000

Myriad educational as well as entertaining displays, exhibits, and shows are at this 160-acre wildlife theme park. The well-kept family park comprises two sections: exotic animals and marine mammals.

You won't find mechanical rides here, but camel and elephant rides are available for an additional charge.

Food service: 5 major restaurants, including Captain Mobe's Sea Food and the Pizza Safari. Additional food and drink kiosks are located throughout the park. Food may be brought into the park.

Entertainment: 8 shows, among them a killer-whale show and various other animal presentations, dancing fountains, and a water-ski and boat show.

California

Season: Year-round.

Operating hours: 9:30 A.M. to 6:30 P.M.. Hours and days of operation are cut back during winter months.

Admission policy: Pay-one-price, under $20. Parking charge.

Plan to stay: 5 hours.

Best way to avoid crowds: Weekday afternoons during the summer, any day during off-season.

Directions: 30 miles northeast of San Francisco. Take the Highway 37 (Marine World Parkway) exit off I–80.

Nearby attractions: Napa Valley vineyards.

Marshal Scotty's
14011 Ridgehill Road
El Cajon, CA (619) 390–1700

A huge Conestoga wagon is about the first thing you'll see when you enter this 16-acre family park. It's used as an eating area for one of the park's restaurants and seats 21 people for a meal. Filled with oak and palm trees, this nice little 14-ride park has an "eclectic" theme: "If it had a theme it would probably be western," says Bill Lee, the owner. A great deal of Spanish influence is also visible.

Food service: 2 snack bars serve a variety of snack and fast-food items, including four kinds of hot dogs. Picnic lunches may be brought in; scattered throughout the park under the big oaks are more than 150 picnic tables.

Entertainment: A tabletop magician goes around to people sitting down and performs magic tricks. Regularly scheduled gunfights and train robberies also take place; the action has a posted schedule so that parents can avoid taking smaller children, who may be scared of gunfire, on that particular ride at the designated time.

Extras: 2 swimming pools, 1 for adults and 1 for children. An innertube water slide and go-carts are also available for an extra fee. Live pony rides, free with admission.

Special events: Easter Celebration, Easter Sunday; National Gunfighters Competition, mid-May; Ghost Train, a scary train ride, two days around Halloween.

Season: Year-round; during the winter months, weekends only.

Operating hours: 10:00 A.M. to 6:00 P.M.

Admission policy: Pay-one-price, under $10. Weekday pass available for slides and pools. Free parking.

Top rides: Little Dipper, a small steel kiddie coaster; San Antonio

Zumer, Octopus; a Ferris wheel; bumper cars; Marshal Scotty's Express, a train ride.

Plan to stay: 5 hours.

Best way to avoid crowds: Come during weekdays, midday.

Directions: Take the Lake Jennings Park Road exit off I-8; the park is down the road about 1 mile. Located 21 miles east of San Diego.

Nearby attractions: Lake Jennings, fishing and camping; Parkway Plaza, shopping and cinema.

Pixieland Park
In Willow Pass Park
2740 East Olivera Road
Concord, CA (415) 689-8841

You don't have to be a pixie to enjoy this inviting little family fun park nestled in the pleasant surroundings of a large community park. The gently rolling terrain and tree-lined walkways add to the attractiveness of this traditional park for the entire family.

A colorful family carousel, a children's Ferris wheel, and a train ride around a small pond are among the 7 rides. A small snack bar serves typical amusement park fare, and a great many picnic areas are available.

The rides are open daily from 11:00 A.M. to 6:00 P.M. during the summer and only on weekends from February through May and from September through November. There's no admission charge, and rides are on a pay-as-you-play basis. A pay-one-price ticket is available only on weekdays.

Santa Cruz Beach Boardwalk
400 Beach Street
Santa Cruz, CA (408) 423-5590

History lives on in the West Coast's only remaining major seaside amusement park. In fact, this park is so special that the entire facility is on the State Historic Landmark list and 2 of the rides are on the National Historic Landmark list. Visiting the park, especially at night, is nostalgic—the smells, lights, and music coming from the park's ballroom could easily be those from a long-gone decade. Lined up neatly along the mile-long boardwalk, the 27 rides, including 7 kiddie rides, present a colorful backdrop to the sandy beach.

Food service: 7 restaurants and 14 food outlets, serving everything from baked potatoes to fried chicken and pizza. Marini's famous (and tasty) saltwater taffy is still available along the boardwalk.

Entertainment: No regularly scheduled daily shows. Costumed characters—Popeye, Olive Oyl, and Brutus—stroll the boardwalk. Classic rock-and-roll bands play on the beach every Friday night from mid-July through August.

Extras: The Neptune's Kingdom entertainment center features a high-tech, double-decked indoor miniature golf course and a wide array of new and vintage arcade games. Sunday brunch in the glass-domed sun room of the historic Cocoanut Grove Grand Ballroom is a nice way to start the day.

Special events: Clam Chowder Cook-off and Festival, February; big-band dances, spring and fall; Soap Opera Festival, June; Brussel Sprout Festival, October.

Season: Year-round; during winter months, weekends only.

Operating hours: 11:00 A.M. to 6:00, 9:00, or 11:00 P.M., depending on season, crowds, and weather.

Admission policy: Free admission to boardwalk; rides on a per-ride basis. Pay-one-price also available. Prices are rolled back every Monday and Tuesday from late June through August for "1907 Nights." Parking charged in lots or at meters.

Top rides: Giant Dipper, a circa-1924 wooden coaster; a circa-1911 Looff carousel, one of the few that still give riders an opportunity to grab for the brass ring; Logger's Revenge, a log flume; Wave Jammer, a beach-theme spinning ride.

Plan to stay: 6 hours.

Best way to avoid crowds: Come midweek during the day.

Directions: Take Highway 17 or Highway 1 into Santa Cruz; then follow the numerous signs to the boardwalk.

Nearby attractions: Roaring Camp Railroad, a 10-mile train ride through the Redwood Forest; Monterey Bay Aquarium.

Santa Monica Pier
Santa Monica, CA (213) 458–8900

Marked for demolition in 1973, the pier has fought city hall, several major storms, and disrepair. Now in the middle of a major comeback, the pier is being restored in good taste, with many of the original elements, including signage, being retained.

Plans call for a major addition to the Fun Zone ride section of the pier in the next couple of years, but for now a beautiful, circa-1922 Philadelphia Toboggan Company carousel and 8 other rides offer plenty of old-time pier fun.

Admission to the pier is always free, and the rides are on a pay-as-you-go basis. The pier is located on the Pacific Ocean, at the end of Colorado Avenue at Ocean Avenue, near the junction of the Pacific Coast Highway and the Santa Monica Freeway. Hours and days of operation of rides vary; call first.

Santa's Village
Highway 18
Skyforest, CA (714) 337-2481

Tucked away among the tall firs and pine trees in the San Bernardino National Forest, this colorful, 15-acre fun park with an alpine theme continues to please entire families. "We're a magical blend of fun, forest and fantasy," says the owner. Santa is always here, along with his elves and reindeer. The buildings, all variations of log cabins, are quite interesting from an architectural standpoint.

TIM'S TRIVIA

Although the cost of liability insurance has forced most parks to prohibit carousel riders from grabbing for the brass ring, there are still several holdouts. Among them are Santa Cruz Beach Boardwalk, Santa Cruz, California; Knoebels Amusement Resort, Elysburg, Pennsylvania; and Dollywood, Pigeon Forge, Tennessee.

In addition to the 13 mechanical rides are rides on live burros and ponies, as well as a pumpkin-coach ride, drawn by two ponies.

Food service: Among the several eateries is the Pixie Pantry, serving fast foods and snacks. A barbecue restaurant opens on busier days. You'll also find a candy kitchen, an ice-cream parlor, and the Good Witch's Bakery, specializing in "good little gingerbread children."

Entertainment: 2 different puppet shows, and on occasion children's dance recitals are given in the park.

Extras: Alice's Mirror Maze, a petting zoo, and a 6-foot tall frozen North Pole, with an elf sitting on top.

Special events: Mountain Residents Week, mid-July.

Season: Open daily in summer months and in mid-November through mid-December. The rest of the year, weekends only. Closed March through May.

Operating hours: 10:00 A.M. to 5:00 P.M.

Admission policy: Pay-one-price, under $10.

Top rides: A circa-1922 Allan Herschell carousel; a Ferris wheel; antique cars; Bobsled, a small steel coaster; Bee-Ride, a monorail; a Christmas tree ride, in which kids ride in ornaments as they revolve around the tree.

Plan to stay: 3 hours.

Best way to avoid crowds: Come during the early part of the week. The largest crowds are here during November and December.

Directions: Take the Mountain Resorts Freeway (Highway 30) to the Waterman Avenue exit. Turn north on Waterman (Highway 18). The park is about 2 miles past the Lake Arrowhead turnoff. Located 20 miles from San Bernardino.

Nearby attractions: Lake Arrowhead Village, an entire resort/tourist town with an alpine theme; Ice Castle, ice skating.

Sea World of California
1720 South Shores Road
San Diego, CA (619) 226–3901

Marine studies and animal shows have not been the same since Sea World came onto the scene with its professional staff of animal experts. This is the original Sea World park, and it has the prettiest views of them all. Founded in 1964, the 150-acre park is located on Mission Bay.

The Sea World parks, although not true amusement parks, are educational gems. Best of all, you learn about marine life and marine conservation while you're having fun.

Food service: 2 cafeteria-style restaurants and 5 fast-food locations, including a sandwich shop and a bakery. Additional snack-food stands throughout park.

Entertainment: 8 shows, including the major Shamu the Killer Whale production. Other shows feature musical variety, magic, a computerized water event, whales and dolphins, and sea lions and otters, as well as various preshow entertainment offerings.

Extras: Secrets of Our Sea is a 90-minute guided tour of behind-the-scenes action, extra charge. Penguin Encounter, an Antarctic habitat, contains more than 300 penguins, and 4 aquariums hold a large collection of fresh and saltwater fish.

Special events: Summer Nights, a summer-long celebration of special shows, laser-light productions, and fireworks.

Season: Year-round.

Operating hours: 9:00 A.M. to 9:00 P.M. in summer and 9:00 A.M. to dusk in winter.

Admission policy: Pay-one-price, under $25. Free parking.

Top rides: The park has 2 mechanical rides, each costing extra to ride: Skytower, a 320-foot-tall rotating tower that provides fantastic views of the Mission Bay area; and Skyride, an enclosed gondola ride across Mis-

sion Bay and back. In addition, the Cap'n Kid's World is a 2-acre participatory play area.

Plan to stay: 7 hours.

Best way to avoid crowds: Come during off-season, or come midweek
during peak summer months. Because the killer whale show is extremely popular, get to Shamu Stadium early and plan the rest of your
stay around this show.

Directions: Take the Sea World Drive exit off I–5 and follow signs west
to the park.

Nearby attractions: San Diego Zoo.

Six Flags Magic Mountain
26101 Magic Mountain Parkway
Valencia, CA (805) 255–4111

Don't forget your sneakers if you're coming to this 111-acre park in the
Santa Clarita Valley—you'll be doing a great deal of walking. A fantastic
arsenal of thrill rides, plenty of exciting shows, and colorful landscaping
will dominate your attention here.

There are 42 rides, including 13 pint-size ones in the 6-acre Bugs
Bunny World. The major rides are almost hidden from one another by
the heavy woods and steep terrain throughout, whereas the kiddie rides
are located near the entrance on relatively flat land. Like the rest of the
Six Flags parks, the Looney Tunes cartoon characters are the official residents and can be found just about everywhere.

Food service: 16 eateries throughout the park, including the Four
Winds Restaurant on the top of Samurai Summit. Salads, sandwiches,
and a nightly dinner special are served here, along with a great view of
the park and the valley. The Baja Cantina serves Mexican specialties; the
Timbermill Restaurant, roast beef, chicken strips, and char-grilled burgers. Don't miss Wascal's, where "America's favorite fast food is served."

Entertainment: 10 shows, including a dolphin/sea lion presentation,
high divers, stunt shows, musical revues, and Looney Tunes costumed
character shows. During summer, a special show, plus fireworks, takes
place on Mystic Lake.

Extras: A shaded picnic area is located in the parking lot, in the "Syl-
vester" section. Psyclone Bay is a beach-themed shopping area adjacent
to the roller coaster of the same name. Six Flags Magic Mountain was
one of the three amusement parks featured in the movie *Rollercoaster,*
and was "Walley World" in the 1983 National Lampoon movie *Vacation.*

Special events: Toys for Tots, first two weeks of December; Christian
Music Festival, spring and fall; Father's Day Festival, Hispanic-themed
celebration.

California

Season: Year-round; during winter months, weekends only. The show schedule is cut back drastically during winter, with the dolphin/sea lion show the only one in operation.

Operating hours: 10:00 A.M. to 10:00 P.M. Most of the year, closing hours range from 6:00 P.M. to midnight.

Admission policy: Pay-one-price, under $25. Parking charge.

Top rides: Grand Carousel, a circa-1912 Philadelphia Toboggan Company carousel; Sandblaster, bumper cars; Log Jammer, a log flume; Viper, the world's largest looping coaster; Colossus, a large, double-tracked wooden coaster; Tidal Wave, a spill-water raft ride; Ninja, a suspended roller coaster; Psyclone, a wooden roller coaster, patterned after the Coney Island Cyclone.

Plan to stay: 8 hours.

Best way to avoid crowds: Get to the top of Samurai Summit either by walking or by taking a tram, monorail, or gondola ride. Then go up in the 38-story-tall Sky Tower. You'll be able to see every inch of the park and see the lay of the land and where the crowds are bottlenecked. Take along a map and plot your day around the show schedules. The crowds are fewer during the week and during off-season weekends.

Directions: Take the Magic Mountain Parkway exit off I–5 in Valencia. Go west a couple of minutes and you'll be at the park. Located 30 miles north of Hollywood.

Nearby attractions: Hart Park, a historical museum and country music walk of fame; Castaic Lake, swimming, boating, and fishing.

Tahoe Amusement Park
2401 Lake Tahoe Boulevard
South Lake Tahoe, CA (916) 541–1300

The soil beneath your feet around here isn't your basic dirt; it's decomposed granite. The 9 rides are set in a large, peaceful grove of tall pine trees, and even on a hot day it's pleasant in the park.

The park was founded in 1969. Its most popular rides are the Giant Slide, Tilt-A-Whirl, and Paratrooper. It also has a go-cart slick track.

Open Easter to mid-October. Hours vary; call first. Admission is free, with rides on a pay-as-you-go basis.

Universal Studios Hollywood
100 Universal City Plaza
Universal City, CA (818) 508–9600

Action is one thing you'll get plenty of here. You'll go face to face with King Kong, see the seas part, watch Jaws attack a fisherman, be stranded

25

King Kong becomes more than a movie when you visit either of the Universal Studios—Hollywood or Florida.

in a subway during an earthquake, and be caught in the middle of a flash flood—and all this can be experienced during your first 45 minutes in the park.

The working studio here has been in operation since 1925; the public tour segment opened in 1964. Once primarily a tram tour through the back lots, the facility has become more visitor friendly and now allows visitors to proceed at their own pace, rather than being kept prisoner in the tram for 2 hours.

You'll enter at the top of the hill in the Entertainment Center, where you'll find a multitude of live action shows, active movie sets,and fine restaurants and shops. To visit the new Studio Plaza in the lower lot, adjacent to the sound stages, follow the signs to the Starway Escalator and ride it down a 200-foot vertical drop. There you'll find more shops, attractions, and the boarding area for the action-packed tram ride.

Food service: Wonderful food is everywhere. From the fifties-style Mel's Diner to Winston's Grill, offering ribs and chicken, a great variety of food is available. The Moulin Rouge features herb chicken and honey-baked ham sandwiches. And Alpha Inn, a British pub, serves up a full line of beers and ales and vinegar chips.

Entertainment: Numerous live action shows include Riot Act, an action comedy stunt show; Star Trek, a 3-D participatory attraction; An American Tail, a musical stage production based on the movie; the Back to the Future special-effects stage; the Miami Vice special-effects stunt show; and the Animal Actors Stage, an animal presentation.

Extras: The Lucy Tribute is an exhibition and museum honoring the late Lucille Ball. You'll see a large collection of memorabilia, a composite film of her career, and much more; don't miss it. Fievel's Playland, a participatory play area based on the movie *An American Tail,* lets the little ones experience life from a mouse-eye perspective, slide down a 15-foot banana peel, and find their way out of an 11-foot-tall hunk of Swiss cheese.

Special events: President's Weekend Celebration, February; Easter Celebration, Easter Sunday weekend; Soap Opera Festival, May; Tele Novella, a Hispanic festival, November.

Season: Year-round.

Operating hours: Open daily, except Thanksgiving and Christmas. Peak-season hours: 7:00 A.M. to 5:00 P.M. Restaurants and shops stay open longer. Hours are shortened during off-season months.

Admission policy: Pay-one-price, under $25. Parking charge.

Top rides: The 45-minute tram ride is action packed, and will take you through the top attractions, including Earthquake—The Big One, Jaws, King Kong, the flash flood, and the collapsing bridge. The tram is the only way those attractions can be experienced. E.T.—The Ride is located in Studio Plaza.

Plan to stay: 8 hours.

Best way to avoid crowds: Come early in the day during the week and during nonholiday times.

Directions: Take the Universal Center or Lankershim Boulevard exit off the Hollywood Freeway (Highway 101). The studio is located between Hollywood and the San Fernando Valley.

Nearby attractions: Hollywood Bowl amphitheater; Griffith Park Zoo and Planetarium; NBC Burbank Studios.

Colorado

Elitch Gardens
4620 West 38th Avenue
Denver, CO (303) 455–4771

For years, people came here just to see the colorful gardens and enjoy the immaculate landscaping. Founded in 1890 as a public garden, apple orchard, and zoo, the park has kept close to its origins, paying careful attention to the upkeep of the grounds.

From palm trees to a cactus garden to flowering carousel animals, lushness abounds in this Rocky Mountain park.

27

With 26 rides, including 8 for kids, the park is looking for a new home so it can expand and continue the Elitch tradition. Plans call for it to begin its 1993 season in a new Denver location.

Food service: 6 sit-down restaurants, among them the Palace, serving barbecue fare and salads, and Wheels Restaurant, offering sandwiches and soft drinks. During busy periods, as many as 12 more food and beverage outlets open in the park.

Entertainment: 5 shows: 3 musical revues, a flea circus, and high divers. Live bands are booked nearly every weekend during the season, plus a great many school musical groups are asked to perform.

Extras: The park's theater building houses the oldest continuously operated summer theater in the country, celebrating its hundredth year in 1991. Some of the biggest names in American theater spent their summers working here. Miniature golf course, extra charge.

Special events: June is Kid's Month, with each of the four weeks highlighting something different: safety, animals, sports, costumed characters; August is Festival Month, with a different festival each week.

Season: Mid-April through Labor Day.

Operating hours: 10:00 A.M. to 11:00 P.M.

Admission policy: Small admission fee which includes all entertainment, with rides on a pay-as-you-go basis. Pay-one-price also available, under $15. Free parking.

Top rides: Twister and Wildcat, two wooden roller coasters; a circa-1926 Philadelphia Toboggan Company carousel; Sidewinder, a steel shuttle-loop coaster; Splinter, a log flume; a sky ride; a dark ride.

Plan to stay: 4 hours.

Best way to avoid crowds: Less crowded during the week between opening and 5:00 P.M.

TIM'S TRIVIA

Cecil B. DeMille, Douglas Fairbanks, and Tyrone Power are but three of the top-name actors who have spent summers at the Elitch Gardens summer theater in Denver, Colorado. The Elitch Theatre is the oldest continuously operated summer theater in the country.

Directions: Take the Sheridan Boulevard exit south off I–70. Go 10 blocks to 38th Avenue and turn left; the park is on your right.

Nearby attractions: Water-World, a water park; Larimer Square, a reconstruction of old-time Denver that features shopping and restaurants; The Tivoli, an old brewery turned into a shopping and eating attraction.

Fun Junction
2878 North Avenue
Grand Junction, CO (303) 243-1522

There's much to do here in beautiful western Colorado, and visiting this small but nice amusement park is a popular summertime outing for many local families. There are 18 rides, including bumper cars; a Ferris wheel; Wild Mouse, a compact steel coaster; flying scooters; and a kiddie roller coaster. Also here are paddleboats, go-carts, bumper boats, miniature golf, castle-bounce, puppet shows, and a large games arcade. Open daily at 6:30 P.M. and on weekends at 1:00 P.M.; the season starts in May and runs through September. Call for admission prices.

Funtastic Nathan's
Indoors at the Cinderella City Mall
701 West Hampden Avenue
Englewood, CO (303) 761-8701

Physical activity is the name of the game here. In addition to the ball crawls, net and rope climbs, and a giant slide, there are 6 mechanical kiddie rides. Plus you'll find a giant rocking chair, a giant horse, and a giant teddy bear to climb on. And a little-tyke activity room amuses those under 3.

Admission is pay-one-price, under $10, with adults paying a third of what the child pays. Tuesday and Wednesday are half-price days. Food service consists of a nostalgic candy shop and a snack-food menu that includes peanut butter and jelly sandwiches. Hours are basically the same as the mall's.

Lakeside Park
4601 Sheridan Boulevard
Denver, CO (303) 477-1621

Nostalgia buffs will love this intriguing park, founded in 1908. Everywhere you look, there is Art Deco architecture and neon lighting. Where neon doesn't light something, thousands of light bulbs do, and this place is a delight at night.

Through the years, the owner has been successful in blending contemporary rides and attractions while preserving as much of the classic elements of the park as possible. There are 40 rides, including 15 for kids set off in their own kiddieland.

Food service: Eatway Inn is the park's main restaurant. In addition, there are 9 other eateries.

Entertainment: There is no regularly scheduled in-park entertainment.

Extras: Paddleboats, included in the pay-one-price admission.

Special events: Nickel Day, July 4 and Labor Day Weekend—all rides are 5 cents.

Season: May through Labor Day.

Operating hours: Kiddie Playland, 1:00 to 10:00 P.M.; major rides, 6:00 to 11:00 P.M.. All rides open at noon on weekends, with closing times depending on crowds and weather.

Admission policy: General admission, with rides and attractions on a pay-as-you-play basis. Pay-one-price also available, under $10. Free parking.

Top rides: Cyclone, a wooden roller coaster; Wild Chipmunk, a compact steel coaster; Dragon, a kiddie roller coaster; Steam Train, a trip around the lake in the train that ran at the 1904 World's Fair; a circa-1908 Parker carousel.

Plan to stay: 5 hours.

Best way to avoid crowds: Mondays are the slowest days.

Directions: Take the Sheridan Boulevard exit off I–70 and go south for 2 blocks. The park is on the right.

Nearby attractions: The park is located near Elitch Gardens; see that listing for nearby attractions.

Lollipop Park
7195 North Sheridan
Westminster, CO (303) 427–1887

The family is celebrated here, with every Thursday, Friday, and Saturday night being "Family Fun Nights." For a reduced rate, a family of four receives an unlimited ride pass, a pizza and soft drinks.

Inside its own storefront in a shopping center, the park has 6 mechanical kiddie rides, a snack-food service, an air bounce, and a ball crawl.

Admission is pay-one-price, under $10, with adults paying a third of what the child pays. Call for hours.

Santa's Workshop
Highway 24
North Pole, CO (719) 684–9432

If you didn't do so before, you'll believe in the big bearded guy after visiting this park—his magic is everywhere.

Located on 27 acres at the foot of Pike's Peak, the park has 22 rides, including 16 for children. The park's layout is unusual: It's located on a hillside and has five distinct levels of activities. In the middle of the Alpine theme park is a duck pond, and next to that is the North Pole, a tall pole that stays frozen all year and provides a great place to cool down on a hot summer's day.

Food service: 3 restaurants, serving fast-food items, plus ice cream and funnel cakes.

Entertainment: 2 different magic shows daily. A live Nativity scene is enacted each morning; costumed characters and elves are available for picture-taking opportunities each afternoon.

Extras: A petting zoo, complete with reindeer, is included

TIM'S TRIVIA

The father of the raging rapids river ride is Bill Crandall. He got the idea in 1978 while watching kayak races down a manmade river in Munich, Germany. Ride manufacturer Intamin engineered and built the first one, Thunder River, based on Crandall's design. It's still in use at AstroWorld, Houston, Texas.

in the gate admission. And, of course, Santa and Mrs. Claus are here every day to meet people.

Special events: Fun Week, a sponsored children's party, mid-June.

Season: Mid-May through Christmas.

Operating hours: 9:00 A.M. to 6:00 P.M.

Admission policy: Pay-one-price, under $10. Free parking.

Top rides: Peppermint Slide, a giant slide inside a tall stack of candy canes, with Santa on top; a circa-1920 Herschell-Spillman carousel, with reindeer and horses; Christmas Tree Ride, enabling kids to ride ornaments; antique cars; Candy Cane Coaster, a small steel kiddie roller coaster.

Plan to stay: 3 hours.

Best ways to avoid crowds: Come either on fall weekends or midday during peak season.

Directions: Take Exit 141 off I-25 and go west on Highway 24. Located 10 miles west of Colorado Springs.

Nearby attractions: Pike's Peak Toll Road; Cog Railroad; Pixieland, miniature golf.

Time Out On The Court
Indoors at Thornton Town Center
I-25 and 104th Street
Thornton, CO (303) 252-9178

In the center of the mall adjacent to the food court, this fun center has 6 kiddie rides and an 18-hole miniature golf course, "Around the World in 18 Holes." Located 15 minutes north of downtown Denver, the facility also offers an arcade containing games of skill and video games.

There is no admission fee; rides, games and attractions are on a pay-as-you-go basis. Open during mall hours.

Connecticut

Lake Compounce Festival Park
822 Lake Avenue
Bristol, CT (203) 582–6333

After all these years, the place is more beautiful than ever. Known as the oldest continuously operated amusement park in the country, Lake Compounce Festival Park has 20 rides, including 8 for kids.

Surrounded by wooded hills, the 70-acre complex has a 28-acre lake and is nicely landscaped throughout. In 1988, the state's largest amphitheater was built within the park and has since hosted some of the biggest names in the entertainment industry. The facility opened in 1846 as a picnic and swimming park.

Food service: 12 food outlets, including, Lakeside Dog House, specializing in Hebrew National hot dogs; Crocodile Cafe, offering lakeside dining and a menu of gourmet burgers, beer, and wine; Sweet Shoppe, serving Ben & Jerry's ice cream, gourmet popcorn, and yogurt.

Entertainment: Roving performers, costumed characters, musical productions, and ethnic weekend entertainment.

Extras: Top-name concerts in amphitheater, extra charge; paddleboats included in admission.

Special events: Street Rod show, May; July 4 Celebration, a music festival and fireworks; Festa Italiana, mid-July; Polkabration, two weekends of polka music and dancing, late July; Memory Weekend, the park's anniversary celebration, late August.

Season: May through first week of October.

Operating hours: Opens at 11:00 A.M. daily; closes at 10:00 P.M. during the week and 11:00 P.M. on weekends.

Admission policy: Pay-one-price, under $15. Sunset saving after 4:00 P.M. Free parking.

Top rides: The Wildcat, a circa-1927 wooden roller coaster, completely rebuilt in 1986; a one-of-a-kind carousel, assembled in 1911 from older carousel pieces dating to 1896 and restored in 1986; Gillette Train, offering a ride around the lake in the antique train that actor William Gillette had built for his estate in 1928 (has been in the park since 1944); Zoomflume, a log flume; Traffic Jam, bumper cars.

Plan to stay: 2 hours.

Best way to avoid crowds: Midweek is the slowest period.

Directions: Take exit 31 off I-84 and go north on Route 229 for about 3 miles. Entrance to the park is on the left.

Nearby attractions: New England Carousel Museum; Clock Museum; Lock Museum of America.

Quassy Amusement Park
Route 64 at Lake Quassapaug
Middlebury, CT (203) 758-9690

If you're looking for a quaint, traditional family amusement park, you've found it here. This 22-acre lakefront complex features 26 rides, including 15 for children, and a large arcade for video and other games.

Quassy is known as a picnic park; for more than eighty years, the locals have been coming here with family and friends for the entertainment and the nice sandy beach.

Food service: 5 outlets, including a sit-down restaurant and the Hot Dog Express.

Entertainment: Costumed characters, magic and comedy, strolling musicians, and Sam the Tramp, a clown.

Extras: Swimming beach, miniature golf, and boat rides, extra charge. Free petting zoo.

Special events: Fireworks, July 4.

Season: Late-April through Labor Day.

Operating hours: Rides open at 10:00 A.M. or noon and close at 9:00 P.M.

Admission policy: Free admission, with rides and attractions on a pay-as-you-play basis. Pay-one-price also available, under $10 for all day, and under $5 after 5:00 P.M. Every Friday night from 5:00 to 10:00 P.M., all rides, hot dogs, colas, snow cones, and cotton candy are 25-cents each. Parking charge.

Top rides: Train ride around park; reproduction of antique carousel; Monster Mouse, a compact steel roller coaster; Flying Bobs; bumper cars.

Plan to stay: 2 hours.

Best way to avoid crowds: The crowds are lightest during midweek.

Directions: Take Exit 16 (Route 64) off I-84. Go west about 4 miles; the park is on the right.

Nearby attractions: Whittemore Glen State Park; Mattatuck Historical Society Museum; Post College.

Delaware

Funland
6 Delaware Avenue
Rehoboth Beach, DE (302) 227–2785

This little boardwalk park is one of the least expensive amusement parks in the United States. It's amazing what you get for your money here. What's more, Funland has friendly folks running the place, a nice selection of family rides, and a splendid view of the Atlantic Ocean.

You won't have to walk much, either. With 18 rides on 1¼ acres, the park keeps everything pretty close to everything else. Among the notable rides is the great suspended, 2-story Haunted Mansion, one of the best dark rides in the country. Other rides include Sea Dragon, Paratrooper, bumper cars, and a carousel.

The park itself has no food service, but as is true of most other East Coast boardwalk parks, a bevy of additional attractions and food outlets can be found within a few blocks. The arcade opens daily at 10:00 A.M., and the rides open at 1:00 P.M.; the Haunted Mansion opens at 6:30 P.M. Closing time varies, depending on crowds and the weather.

Open from mid-May through September. Admission is free, with rides and attractions on a pay-as-you-play basis.

Florida

Busch Gardens, The Dark Continent
3000 Busch Boulevard
Tampa, FL (813) 971–8282

Here's your chance to visit Africa during your Florida vacation. When you walk through the front gates, you'll feel like you're entering turn-of-the-century Africa. Complete with areas representing Morocco, the Serengeti Plain, and other regions, the park combines its tropical landscape with Florida's humid climate to create a realistic effect.

Along with its 23 rides, the 300-acre park also features a zoological garden that ranks among the top ones in the country. And, some of the Budweiser Clydesdales call the park their home.

Food service: The Crown Colony House is a full-service restaurant with Victorian ambience; it overlooks the animal-filled Serengeti Plains. Das Festhaus is an authentic German beer house, complete with big mugs of beer and a German oompah band. Additional food outlets appear throughout the park. *Warning:* If you're walking around while eating, beware of sea gulls. They'll dive and take the food out of your hand with no warning.

Entertainment: Several musical shows, including a nostalgia rock-and-roll revue, country and gospel concerts, an ice show, productions featuring dolphins and other animals, and a children's theater in which live performers enact classic myths. You'll also find a bevy of snake charmers, jugglers, and acrobats.

Extras: Included in park admission is a monorail, skyride, and steam-train ride through the 60-acre Serengeti Plains, where more than 500 large African animals live. There's also a petting zoo. The park is located next to an Anheuser-Busch brewery, where free, self-guided tours and free samples are available.

Season: Year-round.

Operating hours: 9:30 A.M. to 6:00 P.M.

Admission policy: Pay-one-price, under $25. Parking charge.

Top rides: Tanganyiki Tidal Wave, a spill-water raft ride; Congo River Rapids, a raging-rapids ride; Scorpion, a steel looping coaster; Stanley Falls, a log flume.

Plan to stay: 8 hours.

Best way to avoid crowds: Come during the fall when the crowds are most scarce, or midafternoon during the peak season.

Directions: Located at the corner of Busch Boulevard and 40th Street, 8 miles northeast of downtown Tampa. Take Exit 33 (Busch Boulevard) off I–75 and go east 2 miles to the park. Or take Exit 54 (Fowler Avenue) off I–75, go west 2 miles,and follow the signs.

Nearby attractions: Adventure Island, a water park; Alessi Farmers Market; Salvador Dali Museum; Ybor City, a historic Latin community.

Cypress Gardens
State Road 540
Winter Haven, FL (800) 237–4826

Historically speaking, this may be the most significant theme park in the country, next to Disneyland. Nestled along the banks of Lake Eloise, the 233-acre botanical garden and show park is steeped in history and tradition. The facility's gardens, water-ski shows, and lovely Southern Belles have been a draw since 1936. Of all Florida's attractions, this one has the most colorful, mature, and lush surroundings. If you're looking for beauty and solitude after visiting the other attractions in central Florida, stop here to regain your sanity.

Food service: The Crossroads Restaurant is a full-service, air-conditioned eatery with a varied Southern-style menu. In addition, Village

Fare, the Landing, and Frank-N-Brew offer sit-down dinners. Other restaurants and portable snack stands are located throughout the park. The cookies from the bakery are scrumptious.

Entertainment: The major show here, besides the constant show of color in the gardens, is the water-ski production—some of the best skiers in the world have worked here.

Extras: Cypress Junction is the site of an elaborate model railroad, containing 1,200 feet of track, and Hug Haven is the name of the baby-animal nursery; both are free with park admission. Narrated tours of Lake Eloise on a pontoon boat are available for an extra charge. And the beautiful young ladies you see standing around in those charming dresses are the world-famous Southern Belles.

Special events: Gospel Sing-out, end of October; Mustang Car Show, end of October; Chrysanthemum Festival, mid-November.

Season: Year-round.

Operating hours: 9:00 A.M. to 6:00 P.M. every day of the year.

Admission policy: Pay-one-price, under $20. Free parking.

Top rides: Carousel Cove feature 7 kiddie rides and a Grand Carousel that the entire family can ride. The Island in the Sky is a rotating platform that is raised by a counterbalance to a height of 153 feet.

Plan to stay: 6 hours.

Best way to avoid the crowds: Come during the park's off-season: July and August. Otherwise, come around noon on any day.

Directions: Located about 45 minutes south of Walt Disney World, a few miles off Route 27 on State Road 540, near Winter Haven.

Nearby attractions: American Water Ski Museum; Spook Hill, a mystery hill; Bok Tower, botanical gardens and carillon.

Fun 'N Wheels
3711 West Vine Street
Kissimmee, FL (407) 870-2222

Unlike many family fun centers, this one actually does cater to the entire family. Everywhere you look, you'll see parents enjoying the activities with their children. Those activities include kiddie rides, miniature golf, a water slide, bumper boats, a kiddie play area, and 4 go-cart tracks.

There is no charge to get in, and rides are on a pay-as-you-go basis. A pay-one-price is also available, under $10. Call for hours.

Fun 'N Wheels
6739 Sand Lake Road
Orlando, FL (407) 351-5651

Although laid out a bit differently, this fun center is similar to its sister park in Kissimmee. In addition to the activities already listed, this park has a Ferris wheel and a few more games and rides. Admission fees are also the same as in Kissimmee; call for hours.

Lion Country Safari
Southern Boulevard West (State Route 80)
West Palm Beach, FL (407) 793-1084

In addition to having what is considered the nation's first drive-through cageless zoo, this complex also houses the Safari World Amusement Park, which features paddleboats, a boat ride on the *Safari Queen,* a petting zoo, miniature golf, a dinosaur and reptile nature walk, and a carousel.

A pay-one-price admission includes all activities at both facilities, under $15. Call for hours.

Lowry Amusement Park
7520 North Boulevard
Tampa, FL (813) 931- 4389

Picturesque, moss-laden trees abound in this 16-ride amusement park, located within the city's Lowry Park. As you enter, you'll walk past colorful statues from various Grimm Brothers' fairy tales. Once in the amusement area of the park, you'll find games, a food concession, and the rides, including a Ferris wheel, bumper cars, a carousel, and antique cars.

The park is open daily, year-round. It opens at 10:00 A.M. every day and closes at 6:00 P.M. Sunday through Thursday and 10:00 P.M. on Friday and Saturday. There is no admission fee; rides and attractions are on a pay-as-you-go basis.

In Lowry Park itself are a zoo, a children's safety village, and an amphitheater.

Miami Metrozoo
12400 South West 152nd Street
Miami, FL (305) 251-0403

This large facility not only has a great selection of animals and zoo-related activities on its 290 acres but also has kiddie rides, elephant rides, a fantastic monorail ride, a petting zoo, boat rides, paddleboats, and a participatory children's play area. The amphitheater regularly books top-notch entertainment. Admission is pay-one-price, under $10. Call for hours.

Miracle Strip Amusement Park
12000 West Highway 98A
Panama City, FL (904) 234–5810

Across the street from the beautiful white-sand beaches of the Gulf of Mexico, this park is a traditional, well-maintained, family-oriented attraction offering a good mix of rides, games, and excitement.

Along with its 27 rides, the park offers a wide selection of things to do. Three of the rides are inside unique structures and feature music, light shows, and air-conditioning. Though the park itself has no theme, many of the individual rides do. One such ride is Dante's Inferno, housed in a giant, devil-shaped building that you enter by walking across the devil's tongue. Another ride is set inside a huge igloo.

Make sure you're in the park after dark—its colorful lights, including neon lining all the ticket booths, are spectacular. Many of the original buildings, dating to 1963, when the park was constructed, are still in use today.

Food service: 1 sit-down buffet and 13 outlets throughout the park, offering a full lineup of fast-food and snack items. Don't miss the soft ice cream that's served in homemade waffle bowls.

Entertainment: At various times throughout the season, the park schedules regular daily entertainment. A dance is set for every Friday night and features a band and a disk jockey. The park also works with local radio stations and holds several live band concerts and other activities during the season.

Extras: A large midway games area plus arcade is a popular stopping place. The Old House is an excellent walk-through haunted house, and the Road Runner consists of go-carts in a turnpike setting. Both are free with pay-one-price admission.

Special events: High School band festival, three weekends during May.

Season: Mid-March through Labor Day.

Operating hours: Open every night until 11:30 P.M. Opens at 5:00 P.M. on weekdays, 1:00 P.M. on Saturdays and 3:00 P.M. on Sundays.

Admission policy: General admission plus rides. Pay-one-price also available, under $15. Free parking.

Top rides: A log flume; Starliner, a wooden roller coaster; Haunted Castle, a dark ride; The Dungeon, an enclosed Tilt-A-Whirl; a Ferris wheel that offers a great view of the park.

Plan to stay: 3½ hours.

Best ways to avoid crowds: Avoid Saturdays. Best times to visit are weekday nights or anytime during the last two weeks in August, when the resort community begins to thin out.

Directions: Take Route 231 south from I-10. Turn right on Highway 98 and go 10 miles. The park is on the right.

Nearby attractions: Top 'O The Strip, an observation tower; Shipwreck Island, a water park; and Shipwreck Golf, miniature golf. Panama City is a resort town with plenty of other beach attractions nearby.

Old Town
5770 West Irlo Bronson Highway
Kissimmee, FL (407) 396-4888

Take a walk back in history when you enter Old Town, a recreation of a Florida community at the turn of the century. Shops, restaurants, the world-famous Little Darlin's Rock 'n' Roll Palace, an amusement area, and the Super Stars Hall of Fame are all elements of this nostalgic attraction, situated just 2½ miles from Disney World. Rides include a Ferris wheel and a 1909 Mangels-Looff antique carousel.

Admission is free, with activities on a pay-as-you-play basis. Call for specific hours that the rides are in operation.

Raceway Park
1218 Miracle
Ft. Walton Beach, FL (904) 243-4386

Though this family fun center specializes in go-cart rides, it has a great deal more to offer. In addition to its "raceway" activities, it has kiddie rides, a clown bounce, bumper boats, power wheels and a large arcade. Call for hours and admission prices.

Sea World of Florida
7007 Sea World Drive
Orlando, FL (407) 351-3600

Shamu and baby makes two. This marine park has gone down in history books as the facility where the first killer whale was born and thrived in captivity. Since then, two other Sea World facilities have done the same.

Similar to the other Sea World parks in Ohio, Texas, and California, this 135-acre park features a variety of marine animals in themed productions and exhibits.

Food service: 6 restaurants and numerous food, drink, and snack kiosks. The major eatery is Al E. Gators Key West Eatery, serving cuisine inspired by the Florida Keys and Caribbean islands; others include The Spinnaker Cafe (for burgers and fries), Chicken 'n Biscuits and Pizza 'n Pasta.

Entertainment: 7 major shows and 23 educational exhibits. Shows include a water-ski exhibition and the major trademark show of all Sea Worlds, the Shamu Killer Whale show.

Extras: The Penguin Encounter lets you see a variety of penguins in an environment you'll find nowhere else except at the other Sea Worlds and the Antarctic.

Special events: Night Magic, a summer-long, nightly celebration that includes a special killer-whale show, laser-light shows, and a luau dinner show.

Season: Year-round.

Operating hours: 9:00 A.M. to 7:00 P.M. Extended hours during the peak summer season and on holidays.

Admission policy: Pay-one-price, under $30. Nominal parking fee.

Top rides: The park has only one ride: a 400-foot-tall sky tower that rises over the lake in the center of the park, extra charge. Also offered is a 2½-acre participatory play area for the kids; it has a nautical theme.

Plan to stay: 8 hours.

Best way to avoid crowds: Come during off-season, in late afternoon; few of the locals visit the park from May through Labor Day or on holidays. During the season, come early and take in the major shows first; then wander through the exhibits at your own pace.

Directions: Located at the intersection of I–4 and the Bee Line Expressway, 10 minutes from downtown Orlando.

Nearby attractions: Wet 'N Wild, a water park; Water Mania, a water park; Mystery Fun House, a family fun center; Gatorland, a zoo and wildlife center; Congo River Golf & Exploration Company, a miniature golf course and family fun center with a safari theme; Medieval Times Dinner & Tournament theater; Larzland, a family fun center.

Universal Studios Florida
1000 Universal Studios Plaza
Orlando, FL (407) 363–8000

Here's your chance to come face to face with King Kong and feel the bite of Jaws. The newest of the major-studio theme parks, Universal is also the most sophisticated in its rides and attractions. Opened in 1990, the 444-acre park is a working film studio with everything having been built for use in the filmmaking process.

You can walk among the movie sets, whose facades range from the streets of New York City to the architecture and lagoons of Amity Harbor to the San Francisco wharf area. Although new, these streets and buildings look like they've been there for years. The rides and attractions are located in various theme areas of the facility. All but one are located indoors, with most of the waiting lines for the attractions being shaded or in air-conditioned areas. The rides are all original and are state-of-the-art computer driven operations. The park's slogan—"You'll ride the movies"—is accurate, as each ride puts the guest into a familiar movie setting. Meanwhile, the shows and attractions put you in the movies by making the audience part of the presentation.

All things considered, this operation is the most advanced and sophisticated amusement park in the world.

Food service: 15 locations, plus the world's largest Hard Rock Cafe, built in the shape of a guitar. All restaurants have a movie theme and serve marvelous food. A good, moderately priced, fun-filled restaurant is Mel's Drive-In, a fifties-style diner, patterned after the one in the movie *American Graffiti*. Finnegan's Pub, on the streets of New York City, serves up some authentic Irish food and brew, while out on Hollywood Boulevard, a replica of the famous Schwab's Pharmacy concocts terrific malteds. *Note:* To make sure you can eat when and where you want, stop by the restaurant and make reservations as soon as you get to the park.

Entertainment: 7 live and interactive shows: Phantom of the Opera Horror Make-Up Show; Screen Test; Alfred Hitchcock—The Art of Making Movies; Murder She Wrote, a postproduction offering; Ghostbusters, an action show; Animal Actors Stage; and a live stunt show on the lagoon. Costumed characters include Woody Woodpecker and George Jetson. Walkabout celebrity look-alikes include Mae West and Charlie Chaplin.

Extras: The studio is home to the Nickelodeon kid's network; tours and auditions for kids to get onto one of the network's shows take place several times daily. The Boneyard is a storage area for filmdom's most memorable props. Production and VIP tours are also available.

Season: Year-round.

Operating hours: 9:00 A.M. to 10:00 P.M.

Admission policy: Pay-one-price, under $35. Parking charge.

Top rides: 6 rides: Kongfrontation, a tram ride in which you'll get attacked by King Kong while you smell his banana breath; E.T. Adventure, enabling you to take E.T. back to the Green Planet on a flying bicycle; Earthquake—The Big One, letting you experience an earthquake while riding a subway car; FUNtastic World of Hanna-Barbera, a ride simulator taking you on a space mission to rescue Elroy Jetson; Jaws, in which you're attacked by a huge shark while cruising the lagoon on a pontoon boat; Back to the Future, where you ride with Doc Brown to another time.

Plan to stay: 1 long day or 2 slower-paced days.

Best way to avoid crowds: Most shows and attractions have preshows that help cut the anticipated waits. Don't be fooled by the short lines you see outside: Most of the lines here are inside air-conditioned buildings. Midmornings are least crowded.

Directions: Main entrance is ½ mile north of I-4, off Exit 30B (Kirkman Road/Highway 435). Another entrance is off Turkey Lane Road: Take Exit 29 (Sand Lake) off I-4 and turn right onto Turkey Lane Road within ½ mile of the interstate.

Nearby attractions: Mystery Fun House, miniature golf, a fun house, and an arcade; Wet 'n Wild, a water park.

Walt Disney World Resort
Routes 4 and 192
Lake Buena Vista, FL (407) 824-4321

The "Wonderful World of Disney" has never looked, sounded, or tasted better than it does today. Constantly adding rides, shows, and attractions, this place always has something new and magical going on. Covering 43 square miles, Walt Disney World is much more than an amusement park—it's the world's largest and most whimsical family resort complex. And the image of Mickey Mouse is everywhere: From the water tower (known as the Earful Tower) to the topiary to the bars of soap in the rest rooms, the mighty mouse makes his presence known.

There's something special about a company whose executives wear Mickey Mouse watches and ties. If there's a heaven on earth, no doubt this is it.

Located 20 miles southwest of Orlando, the resort has three separate theme parks that welcome more than 30 million guests a year: the Magic Kingdom, Epcot Center, and the Disney–MGM Studio Theme Park. In addition, the complex has myriad smaller attractions.

Keeping in mind that entire volumes have been published about the complex, I have presented the basics and a few highlights about each of the three parks. That information is followed by general data pertaining to all the parks.

The Magic Kingdom

Carved out of the swamp in 1971, this park is the one most people associate with Walt Disney World. With 45 rides and attractions, the Magic Kingdom holds the hallmark Disney rides and is the top choice if you're looking for activities the whole family will enjoy. The 100-acre site is divided into seven lands: Liberty Square, Frontierland, Adventureland,

Florida

Main Street USA, Fantasyland, Tomorrowland, and the newest area, Mickey's Starland.

Shows and attractions: Stake your claim along Main Street in plenty of time to have a front-row view of the daily parade that starts near the front gate and winds through Frontierland; a special electrical parade is presented in summers and during holiday periods. Another must-see is the Country Bear Jamboree, offering animatronics at its best. Check the daily schedule for times and additional Disney-quality shows.

TIM'S TRIVIA

Employees in the Magic Kingdom at Walt Disney World, near Orlando, Florida, walk to their workstations via a series of underground tunnels. That's why you never see a person wearing a Tomorrowland uniform, for example, in Adventureland. Supplies are delivered to each area in the same manner.

Rides: A few of the landmark rides you must experience are Pirates of the Caribbean, a boat ride through a pirate's world; Haunted Mansion, the best of its kind worldwide; Big Thunder Mountain Railroad, a mine train roller coaster; Jungle Cruise, a ride on a boat that gets attacked by (animatronic) alligators and snakes; Space Mountain, an indoor roller coaster with a space theme; and Dumbo, the flying elephant.

Epcot Center

The 260-acre Experimental Prototype Community of Tomorrow (EPCOT) represents a lifelong dream of Walt Disney that became a reality in 1982. It's divided into two sections: the World Showcase, focusing on the culture, food, and products of eleven foreign nations, and Future World, highlighting man's past and future relationship with communication, the environment, energy, and transportation.

Shows and Rides: It's hard to categorize the attractions at Epcot. In the World Showcase, each of the eleven countries offers a variety of attractions, rides, food, and shopping experiences within its own pavilion. Norway, for example, features a fine restaurant, a large shopping area, a film depicting the nation's history, and a magnificent Viking boat ride, called the Maelstrom, taking visitors through Nordic times. Other countries present similar experiences.

In Future World, attractions are much the same, except that the pavilions are sponsored by large corporations rather than countries and center on specific themes, such as communications, energy, and health. Spaceship Earth, the large sphere that has become an Epcot landmark, houses a fantastic dark ride that provides a look at our planet. A boat ride through The Land pavilion highlights experimental farming techniques; a restaurant in that pavilion also serves some of the best food in

Epcot. And the Wonders of Life exhibit is the best the park has to offer. It combines shows, food, interactive educational exhibits, and a simulated ride through the body, called Body Wars.

Epcot closes each night with a magnificent show on the lagoon. Called IllumiNations, it's a laser, fireworks, fountain, and musical extravaganza.

Disney–MGM Studios Theme Park

The newest of the three parks, this one opened in 1988 and contains an operating movie production studio along with the rest of the attractions.

EPCOT, at Walt Disney World in Orlando, stands for the Experimental Prototype Community of Tomorrow, but to many of the 33,000 employees at the massive complex, EPCOT merely stands for Every Paycheck Comes on Thursday.

Here's where you'll find the newest Disney characters, the Muppets. Make sure you stop by the Prime Time Cafe, a fifties-style diner where you'll eat at chrome and Formica tables you may well remember from your childhood days. At most tables is a TV set showing reruns of the classics. You're the guest of "Mom" here, and if you misbehave or don't eat your veggies, you may well be ridiculed by the personnel. Prime Time is a show and a great place to eat all wrapped up in one. Try their peanut butter and jelly milk shakes—there's nothing in this world better!

The indoor Sci-Fi Drive-In Diner has booths shaped like classic cars, all pointing to a drive-in screen where movies are shown. Servers, on roller skates, deliver food and beverages.

Plans call for this theme park to double in size by 1995, and so new elements are being premiered several times a year.

Shows and attractions: Most of the shows have a Hollywood or movie production theme. Dick Tracy is featured in a live musical whodunit, and the Muppets star in two different musical presentations. The Indiana Jones Epic Stunt Presentation is one of the best stunt thrillers in production anywhere, and the Magic of Disney Animation studio and tour present a fascinating lesson in the art form that started it all for Walt Disney.

Several other movie-related shows are offered; many more are on the drawing boards. Check the daily show schedule for up-to-date information.

Rides: Don't miss Star Tours, the celebrated simulated journey through space. Although the Body Wars ride in Epcot uses the same technology, the journey in Star Tours is quite different. The Great Movie Ride is a live-narration journey through the history of film; here you'll see good guys beat the gangsters both on the screen and in your car. And the Backstage Studio Tour tram ride takes you past several very familiar houses on the back lot and through Catastrophe Canyon where you'll experience floods, fires, and explosions, all within a couple of minutes.

Thunder Express, the mine-train roller coaster at Dollywood in Pigeon Forge, Tennessee, takes riders on a high-speed twisting and turning ride.

Viable information for all Disney attractions:

Food service: In total, the complex has more than 150 locations where food can be purchased, ranging from counter service to buffeterias to full-menu, table-service restaurants. Beer, wine, and spirits are available at all table-service restaurants except those in the Magic Kingdom. If you have kids with you, try to catch one of the character meals. There are 6 different breakfast and 2 lunch locations where Disney characters, including Mickey and Minnie, walk around and visit diners at their tables—a nice way to give your kids a little one-on-one time with their favorite character.

Reservations are needed for the character meals, as well as for the 4 nightly dinner shows. Most of the other larger restaurants also require lunch or dinner reservations. If you're staying at one of the Disney hotels, you can call an in-park number. If you're staying off-property, find the guest relations building as you enter any of the parks; its staff can make them for you.

Extras: Within the Walt Disney World complex are 5 other notable Disney attractions: Pleasure Island, a 6-acre, 6-nightclub theme park for adults; Typhoon Lagoon, a water park with the world's largest inland surfing lagoon; River Country, a water-themed playground with swimming, slides, and other activities; Discovery Island, a zoological park containing more than 90 animal species; and Village Marketplace, a shopping area whose 19 shops offer the latest in goods ranging from European designs to Mickey Mouse socks.

Plan to stay: A family of four will want to spend at least a day in each of the theme parks. During the peak summer and holiday seasons, even more time is needed to see everything.

Season: Everything is open every day of every year.

Operating hours: During the peak season, the gates open at the three parks no later than 8:00 A.M. and close anywhere from 9:00 to 11:00 P.M.

Admission policy: Pay-one-price, under $35. Four and 5-day passports are available at a good saving and are honored at all three parks. The passports have no expiration date and don't have to be used on consecutive days; thus, you can use them anytime you choose. Parking charge.

Best way to avoid crowds: Sundays, Thursdays, and Fridays are usually the least crowded days. In general, January, May, October, and November are the least busy times.

The best way to get around is to obtain a map and plan your visit. Arrive early, take a break during the heat of the midafternoon sun, and then come back and stay until the park closes.

Expect lines for everything; be grateful for a short wait, but don't be surprised by a long one.

Georgia

American Adventures
250 North Cobb Parkway
Marietta, GA (404) 424–9283

To encourage family interaction and enjoyment, parents get to ride free with their children at this unique family entertainment center. With a turn-of-the-century ambience, the park offers Victorian-style rides and architecture and a nostalgic setting.

The 7 family rides include a balloon ride, a buffalo-themed roller coaster, and a train. Hidden Harbor is a state-of-the-art, 18-hole miniature golf course providing animated characters, music, and audio presentations; an animatronic character talks you through the last hole. Indoors, Main Street is a 9-hole miniature golf course with a "Main Street USA" theme. Also inside is an antique carousel, a large penny arcade, and Professor Plinker's participatory play area. The adjacent White Water water park is run by the same owners.

Year-round, the park opens at 11:00 A.M. daily and closes at 11:00 P.M. during the week and midnight on weekends. There's no admission fee; you pay as you play.

Lake Winnepesaukah
Lakeview Drive
Rossville, GA (404) 866–5681

Established in 1925 on 110 acres, this is one of the Southeast's most beautiful traditional parks. With 33 rides, including 14 rides for kids, the park is built around three sides of a lake, just 4 miles from the Tennessee border, near Chattanooga.

It offers plenty of old-time charm and a great deal of lakeside shade and benches for relaxing.

Food service: Several food outlets serving sandwiches and chicken and barbecue plates, as well as hot dogs, hamburgers, and popcorn.

Entertainment: Top-name entertainers perform every Sunday afternoon in Jukebox Junction, no additional charge.

Extras: Miniature golf and paddleboats are available for an additional charge.

Season: Mid-April through September.

Operating hours: Opens at 10:00 A.M. on Thursday and Saturday and noon on Friday and Sunday. Closed Monday (except holiday Mondays), Tuesday, and Wednesday.

Admission policy: Small gate admission charged, with rides and attractions on a pay-as-you-go basis. Pay-one-price also available, under $10. Admission includes access to the park and to all entertainment. Free parking.

Top rides: The Cannon Ball, a wooden roller coaster; Himalaya; Pirate Ship, a swinging ride; Boat Shoot, a circa-1926, tunnel-of-love type of spill-water attraction; Matterhorn; an aerial ride taking you over the lake and back; a circa-1916 Philadelphia Toboggan Company carousel in superb shape.

Plan to stay: 4 hours.

Best way to avoid crowds: Be there when the park opens and get to the far side of park, where the coaster is located. Enjoy that side of the park first, and then the area near the exit. Because there is only one path from one side of the lake to another, getting around through the crowds can be time-consuming.

Directions: Take the Route 41 exit off I-75. Take Ringold Road 2 miles to McBrien Road, turn left, and the park is about 2 miles at the end of McBrien Road on Lakeview Drive.

Nearby attractions: Rock City; Ruby Falls; The World's Steepest Incline Railway; Adventure Park, a hang-gliding and water park.

Six Flags Over Georgia
I-20 and Six Flags Parkway
Atlanta, GA (404) 739-3400

All the Six Flags parks are known for their wide selection of rides, games, and attractions, but this one, founded in 1967, has also earned a reputation as one of the prettiest. Its 331 hilly acres have matured nicely and offer guests lots of shade and landscaping beauty to enjoy.

The park is especially pretty at night, when colorful neon and various other lighting packages illuminate the rides. There are 31 rides, with 9 of them being for kids and located in Bugs Bunny Land. Other areas with specific themes are the Confederate, Cotton States, Georgia, Lick Skillet, and Modern sections.

Food service: 20 food and drink locations throughout the park, serving everything from complete, sit-down meals to the usual fast-food items like pizza, hamburgers, and funnel cakes. An additional 40 mobile carts are utilized when necessary.

Entertainment: 7 shows, including an oldies musical revue, a magic and music show, a Cinema-180, High Divers, and a Looney Tunes character show for the kids.

Extras: The Monster Plantation is an excellent boat trip through a flooded antebellum mansion, where some unbelievable monsters come out to greet you. The Southern Star Amphitheater features top name entertainers throughout the summer, with some concerts requiring an additional fee.

Special events: Fright Nights, Halloween activities, weekends in late October; Holiday in the Park, Christmas and holiday activities, Thanksgiving through December; Christian Music Festival, June.

Season: Mid-March through October. Reopens after Thanksgiving until the beginning of January.

Operating hours: 10:00 A.M. to 10:00 P.M.

Admission policy: Pay-one-price, under $25. Second-day ticket for use anytime during the season also available for an additional $2. Parking charge.

Top rides: Great American Scream Machine, a wooden roller coaster; Georgia Cyclone, a wooden roller coaster built to resemble New York's classic Coney Island Cyclone; Thunder River, a raging-rapids ride; The Great Gasp, a 20-story-tall parachute drop; Mind Bender, a triple-loop roller coaster; Ragin' Rivers, a series of 4 wet/dry rides, including 2 speed slides and 2 tube slides.

Plan to stay: 8 hours.

Best way to avoid crowds: Come early in the week, and see everything in one area the first time you visit it. Doubling back at a park this size is very time-consuming.

Directions: 12 miles west of Atlanta on I-20. Take Exit 7B (I-20 West) off Outerbelt I-285 and go about 2 miles to Exit 13. The park is 1 block south on Six Flags Road.

Nearby attractions: White Water, a water park; Stone Mountain Memorial State Park, a Confederate memorial cut into the side of a mountain; Underground Atlanta, stores, restaurants, and nightclubs; Cable News Network (CNN) studios and offices (hourly tours); The World of Coca-Cola museum.

Tybee Island Amusement Park
16th Street and Butler Avenue
Tybee Island, GA (912) 786–8806

Just 50 yards from the beach, this park is a must-see if you're in the area. It's a small, family-owned and -operated facility in the center of the business district. The locals have supported this park since its opening in 1965 and are very proud of it. A small roller coaster and a Ferris wheel are the most popular of the 13 rides.

Open daily during the summer, the park has free admission, with rides on a pay-as-you-go basis.

Hawaii

Fun Factory
Indoors, Kahului Shopping Center
Puunene and Kamehameha Avenues
Kahului, Maui, HI (808) 871–6673

As the largest tenant in the shopping center, Fun Factory has its own outside entrance and its own hours. This family fun center features 2 kiddie rides and a large participatory play area, in addition to a wide variety of video games, games of skill, and an area devoted strictly to sports games. If you're looking for a games center where you can save tickets for the big prize you've always wanted, this is the place—it has one of the largest prize-redemption operations in the state. Food offerings range from hamburgers and hot dogs to pizza and popcorn.

The park is open daily until 11:00 P.M. or later. Free admission; pay-as-you-go.

Waimea Falls Park
59–864 Kamehameha Highway
Haleiwa, Oahu, HI (808) 638–8511

Traditional Hawaiian customs are the centerpiece of this beautiful show park. A huge waterfall and lush botanic gardens are the natural wonders here, and the owners have added just enough modern conveniences to make this a site you'll talk about for years.

If you want to see everything this facility has to offer, wear comfortable shoes, as you'll be doing a lot of walking. Tram tours are available if you don't want to walk.

There are four separate shows repeated several times each day. These include cliff diving, ancient Hawaiian hula dancing, Hawaiian games, and wildlife shows.

The Proud Peacock serves up traditional Island grub as well as a full menu of continental items.

The park is open daily 10:00 A.M. to 5:30 P.M. 365 days a year. Admission is by pay-one-price. If you're looking for Hawaiian-made items, make sure to stop by Charley's Country Store. It offers one of the best selection of Island-made crafts that you'll find anywhere.

Idaho

Julia Davis Fun Depot
Julia Davis Park
Boise, ID (208) 343–1141

In the middle of Boise, in the middle of Julia Davis Park, lies the Fun Depot, an 8-acre amusement park that has a train theme. Surrounded by huge trees, the buildings resemble a train depot and are painted in a green-and-red scheme.

As the only amusement park in Boise, the Fun Depot is popular with families. It has 11 rides, including 6 for kids.

Food service: 2 concession stands, selling fast-food and snack items.

Entertainment: No regularly scheduled in-park entertainment. A local TV station sponsors monthly kids' days at the park and brings along entertainment for that day.

Extras: Paddleboats and miniature golf, extra cost.

Season: April through October.

Operating hours: Noon to 10:00 P.M.

Admission policy: Free admission; rides are on a pay-as-you-go basis. Every Monday is 25-cents day, with all rides going for a quarter each.

Top rides: Bumper cars; Mad Mouse, a compact steel roller coaster; Tilt-A-Whirl; a carousel.

Plan to stay: 1½ hours.

Directions: Take River Road off Capital and follow it to Julia Davis Park. Once in the park, follow the signs to the ride area.

Nearby attractions: Boise Zoo; Wild Waters, a water park.

Silverwood Theme Park
North 26225 Highway 95
Athol, ID (208) 772–0515

Although there are quite a few parks that you can visit by boat, this may very well be the only amusement park in the country that you can visit by flying your own plane to it. Originally solely an airstrip, the facility now has 15 rides and some beautiful turn-of-the century (reproduced) architecture.

Visitors enter the park through an old mining town and work their way back to the ride area known as the Country Carnival.

Food service: 2 restaurants: Lindy's (as in Lindbergh), a full-service, fine-dining eatery, and Country Barbecue, specializing in sandwiches.

51

An ice-cream parlor and various other food outlets provide a full array of snack items and beverages. Make sure you try the baby back ribs and the onion ring loaf at Lindy's.

Entertainment: Daily air shows, old-time movies, honky-tonk piano sing-alongs, jugglers, and a magic show. The Monarch Mountain Boys stroll the park and play some great music.

Extras: Biplane and glider rides are available (about $60), and an airplane museum is open to the public. There's also an RV Park.

The corkscrew roller coaster, moved here from Knott's Berry Farm in California, is the first such coaster ever built.

Silverwood Theme Park, in Athol, Idaho, was an airstrip before being converted to an amusement park. Now biplane and glider rides are available from that airstrip for about $60 apiece.

Season: May through September.

Operating hours: 11:00 A.M. to 8:00 P.M.

Admission policy: Pay-one-price, under $15. Free parking.

Top rides: The Gravity Defying Corkscrew, the state's only corkscrew roller coaster; Wet & Wild, a log flume; a Ferris wheel; bumper boats; antique cars; a narrow-gauge steam train, taking you out into the wilderness, where you'll be robbed.

Plan to stay: 6 hours.

Best way to avoid crowds: Come during the week and avoid the holidays.

Directions: 15 miles north of I–90 and Coeur d'Alene, on Highway 95. Located 40 miles northeast of Spokane, Washington.

Nearby attractions: Silver Mountain's World's Longest Gondola ride; plus plenty of fishing, boating, swimming, and para-sailing on the area's seventy lakes.

Illinois

Blackberry Historical Farm
591 Barnes Road
Aurora, IL (708) 892–1550

You'll take a step back into time when you enter the front gates of this 55-acre complex, whose theme is Midwest village life during 1840 to

1910. Numerous costumed guides and other old-time touches make this an educational as well as entertaining place to visit.

There are 4 rides, including a train and a carousel; in addition, there are pony and wagon rides, as well as a free petting zoo. Folk music is scheduled most Sundays.

Pay-one-price, under $10. Open May to mid-October, 10:00 A.M. to 4:30 P.M.

The Loch Ness Monster at Busch Gardens, The Old Country, in Williamsburg, Virginia, takes riders up thirteen stories before plunging them down 114 feet and then whipping them through two interlocking loops.

Kiddieland
8400 West North Avenue
Melrose Park, IL (708) 343–8000

A colorful neon sign, with two neon kids hanging from it greets visitors to this 17-acre park in suburban Chicago. Though founded in 1929 as a kiddie park, the facility has grown beyond that scope and now bills itself as a family park.

As you enter the park, you'll pass a beautifully restored, circa-1925 Philadelphia Toboggan Company carousel on your left and, to your right, a wonderful little German carousel. The park offers 22 rides, including 12 for kids, along with a delightful play area called Volcano Playcenter.

Food service: 3 food stands, each serving a full line of fast-food and snack items. Food and drink may be brought into the park.

Entertainment: No regular scheduled in-park entertainment. Outside performers, including magicians, are occasionally brought in for special events.

Extras: A large forest preserve, located across the street, offers picnic areas and barbecue pits.

Special events: Large fireworks display every July 4.

Season: April through October.

Operating hours: Noon to 10:00 P.M.

Admission policy: Small gate fee, plus rides on a pay-as-you-go-basis. Pay-one-price also available, under $10. Free parking.

Top rides: Little Dipper, a small wooden roller coaster; antique cars; bumper cars; Galleon, a swinging pirate ship; Tilt-A-Whirl; Tractors, a unique, motorized-tractor ride for kids.

Plan to stay: 3 hours.

Best way to avoid crowds: Avoid visiting in the early afternoon. The area's day-camp groups come at noon and stay until around 3:00 P.M. Between then and 7:00 P.M. is generally the slowest time, after 7:00 P.M., a discounted rate brings out the crowds again.

Directions: Located between the Eisenhower and Kennedy expressways, 15 miles from downtown Chicago. Take I–294 to the Eisenhower Expressway and go east to First Avenue. Go north on First until you reach the park, at the corner of North and First avenues.

Nearby attractions: North Avenue Skating, miniature golf and roller skating; Maywood Park, horse racing.

Knight's Action Park
1700 Recreation Drive
Springfield, IL (217) 546–8881

The name Action Park aptly describes this 56-acre participatory amusement park. Everywhere you look, there's activity going on—for example, bumper boats, paddleboats, baseball cages, go-carts, flume water slides, a pair of 18-hole miniature golf courses, and a golf driving range. And Herbie's Place, a special kiddieland, is filled with rides and all sorts of activities for the kids.

Admission is free, with rides and activities on a pay-as-you-go basis. Call for hours.

Rockome Gardens
Route 133
Arcola, IL (217) 268–4106

Just about every weekend here, a special event takes place, usually emphasizing crafts and our national heritage. A wealth of shows and exhibitions—from Indian Pow Wows, to auto shows, quilt shows, and antique toy shows—ensures that there's almost always something different going on.

Located in the heart of Illinois Amish country, the 14-acre park has 5 rides and walk-through attractions, including a train ride and a haunted cave. Food is amply available as are quality Amish goods to be purchased. Of special note is the Bottle House, made from 7,000 7-Up bottles.

Pay-one-price, under $10. Open May through October.

Six Flags Great America
I-95 and Route 132
Gurnee, IL (708) 249–1776

TIM'S TRIVIA

What's in a name? When Cedar Point, Sandusky, Ohio, built the world's largest and fastest roller coaster in 1989, the park wanted a powerful name. It came up with Magnum XL200—Magnum for powerful, XL for extra large, and 200 for its height.

American patriotism is the theme at this park, built in 1976 during America's bicentennial. The park is divided into five areas, each representing a different era in the nation's growth: Orleans Place, Yankee Harbor, Yukon Territory, Hometown Square, and County Fair. Rides, games, and food in each section have been designed with a corresponding theme.

Included in the 38 rides, the park's double-decked carousel is listed in the *Guinness Book of World Records* as one of the two tallest carousels in the world; the other carousel is at the Great America park in Santa Clara,

California. Although both parks were built in 1976 by the Marriott Corporation as exact duplicates, both have subsequently been sold to other concerns and have expanded in completely different ways.

The Looney Tunes characters are the official mascots of this, as well as the other, Six Flags parks and make their home in the children's play area, Bugs Bunny Land.

Food service: 5 major sit-down restaurants and numerous snack and fast-food facilities. The Hometown Boarding House is known for its old-fashioned fried chicken meals; the Klondike Cafe, for its barbecued chicken, beef, and ribs.

Entertainment: 6 productions, including an ice show, a Looney Tunes character show, a song-and-dance revue, an IMAX film, and a saloon musical comedy show.

Special events: JoyFest, contemporary Christian celebrations, every May and August.

Season: The end of April through the first week of October.

Operating hours: 10:00 A.M. to 9:00 or 10:00 P.M.

Admission policy: Pay-one-price, under $25. Second-day ticket available for $3 extra. Parking charge.

Top rides: A circa-1920–22 Dentzel carousel; Iron Wolf, a looping, stand-up roller coaster; American Eagle, a wooden roller coaster; Roaring Rapids, a raging-rapids ride; Shockwave, a multi-element steel coaster; Logger's Run, a log flume.

Plan to stay: 8 hours.

Best way to avoid crowds: Come midmorning or midafternoon on Friday, Wednesday, or Thursday.

Directions: Located between Chicago and Milwaukee on I–94 at Route 132 East (Grand Avenue).

Nearby attractions: Holiday Park, a ski area; Fort Sheridan; Great Lakes Naval Training Center; Illinois Beach State Park.

Three Worlds of Santa's Village
Routes 25 & 72
Dundee, IL (708) 426–6751

Santa Claus shows up to work here every day the park is open. He can be found in an (air-conditioned) alpine house, sitting next to a roaring fire.

The 55-acre, heavily wooded park has three distinct areas, of which Santa's Village, with its Christmas decorations and lollipop architecture, is the oldest and most picturesque. The other two areas are Old Mac-Donald's Farm, containing a large petting zoo, and Coney Island, in which most of the park's 28 family-oriented rides are located.

Food service: 12 food outlets, including 4 sit-down restaurants: Alpine Room, Pixie Pantry, Hofbrau House, and Mother Hubbard's Ice Cream Parlor. Food may be brought into the park.

Entertainment: The Evergreen Theatre features 2 different live musical productions each day.

Extras: Public ice skating, October through March, in the Polar Dome Ice Arena, extra charge.

Season: Mid-May through September.

Operating hours: 10:00 A.M. to 6:00 P.M. or dusk.

Admission policy: Pay-one-price, under $10. Free parking.

Top rides: The park has several rides built specifically for its theme. One is the Christ-

TIM'S TRIVIA

Talk about recycling! Through the years, the owners of Knoebels Amusement Park Resort in Elysburg, Pennsylvania, have purchased used rides and equipment from other parks and have carefully reconditioned and rebuilt them and put them back into use. Today the history of more than thirty parks, many now defunct, lives on at Knoebels.

mas Tree, a kiddie ride that revolves, with the guest riding in ornaments. Another is Fire Trucks, a full-size antique fire engine pulling tramlike cars into a neighborhood where a house is on fire; the kids have water hoses and put the fire out while squirting at it from their seats. Additional rides of note include a horse-powered carousel and the Snowball, a Cuddle-up ride with a winter theme.

Plan to stay: 5 hours.

Best way to avoid crowds: Visit on weekdays and after Labor Day.

Directions: Located 45 minutes from downtown Chicago among the tall timbers of the Fox River Valley area. Take the Route 25 exit off I–90 at Elgin; go north 2 miles to the intersection of Routes 25 and 72.

Nearby attractions: The park owns Racing Rapids, a large water park adjacent to Santa's Village. A combination ticket can be purchased for both parks at a substantial saving.

Indiana

Adventureland
Highway 13
North Webster, IN (219) 834–2554

In a resort area that boasts 101 lakes, one can only imagine how many people come directly from the beaches or their boats to this park in order to experience additional fun and adventure. Founded as a miniature golf course in 1966, the 12-acre park has added attractions regularly. It now offers 13 rides, plus bumper boats, bank-shot basketball, trampolines, 3 arcade buildings, batting cages, a go-cart track, and a pair of 18-hole miniature golf courses.

TIM'S TRIVIA

There are three Adventurelands in the United States: in East Farmingdale, New York; in Des Moines, Iowa; in North Webster, Indiana.

Food service: 1 major snack bar in the middle of the park, offering a bevy of snack and fast-food items. Food may be brought into the park. Peaceful, shaded picnic areas line a channel that goes out to Lake Webster.

Entertainment: Clowns and other entertainers are occasionally booked in. Every Saturday morning, an event called Candy Rain is especially popular with kids: From high atop a ride, members of the park management throw out candy to the kids gathered below.

Season: May through September.

Operating hours: Noon to 11:00 P.M.

Admission policy: Free gate, with rides and attractions on a pay-as-you-go basis. Pay-one-price also available from 6:00 to 11:00 P.M., under $7 (but does not include miniature golf or go-carts). Free parking.

Top rides: Roll-O-Plane; Rock-O-Plane; Octopus; Tilt-A-Whirl; bumper boats.

Plan to stay: 3 hours.

Best way to avoid crowds: Come during the afternoon, when most of the others are enjoying the lakes. Big business here is after dark.

Directions: Take Highway 13 north out of Webster. The park is located 8 miles north of Highway 30, on your right.

Nearby attractions: *The Dixie,* paddle-wheel excursions on Lake Webster; plus numerous public beaches, boat rentals, and other activities within the area.

Enchanted Forest Amusement Park
150 East U.S. Highway 20
Chesterton, IN (219) 926–2161

A group of wooden *Wizard of Oz* figures greet you as you enter this 19-acre park, not too far from Lake Michigan. But don't let those fool you—you're not entering the land of Oz. What you are entering is a land full of great family rides and entertainment. There are 25 rides, including 8 for children.

Indiana

Food service: 3 restaurants—Forest Inn, Golden Fawn, and Pirates Cove—plus additional outlets throughout the park. Make sure you try the elephant ears; they're famous in this part of the country. Picnic tables are scattered throughout, and food may be brought into the park.

Entertainment: No shows are scheduled on a daily basis, but special events are held all season, usually every weekend.

Extras: Large arcade of games of skill and video games.

Special events: Rock and Roll weekend, late August.

Season: Late-May through Labor Day.

Operating hours: Opens Tuesday through Sunday at 11:00 A.M.; closes weekdays at 5:00 P.M. and weekends at 7:00 P.M. Closed Mondays.

Admission policy: Pay-one-price, under $10. Free parking.

Top rides: Mad Mouse, a compact steel roller coaster; a 1½-mile train ride through the park; Swiss Toboggan; a Ferris wheel; a carousel.

Plan to stay: 5 hours.

Best way to avoid crowds: Weekdays are less crowded. Come midday after the morning rush.

Directions: Take Exit 26B (Highway 20) off I–94. Go west ¼ mile; the park is at the intersection of Highways 20 and 49.

Nearby attractions: Indiana Dunes State Park; plus myriad other outdoors activities in the Lake Michigan area.

Fun Spot Amusement Park
County Road 200W
Angola, IN (219) 833–2972

A big happy clown sign welcomes you to this family fun park. Although a relatively new park, this 50-acre facility has much to offer and, according to the owner, is only going to get bigger and better in the years to come.

With an eye to history, the owner is building a traditional family park here, one distinguished by quality, color, and traditional values. In creating the landscaping, special care is being taken to add color and texture to the existing rides and buildings.

The park offers 18 rides, including a special children's area in which 4 of the smaller rides are under a covered pavilion.

Food service: 3 concession stands: Pit Stop, Barrel and Bun, and Pizza in the Park. Hot dogs, hamburgers and pizza, along with other fast-food and snack items, are on the menus. Picnics may brought into the park; grills are provided, or you can bring your own.

Entertainment: No regularly scheduled in-park entertainment; however, family shows are booked in at various times throughout the season.

Extras: Go-carts, miniature golf, and batting cages, all at extra charge. A big neon sign points out the arcade, a facility the owner says is the largest air-conditioned arcade in the state.

Special events: 3 major fireworks shows each year: Memorial Day, July 4, and Labor Day.

Season: May through September.

Operating hours: Opens daily at noon; closes at 10:00 P.M. Sunday through Thursday, and at 11:00 P.M. on Fridays and Saturdays.

Admission policy: Small gate admission, with rides on a pay-as-you-go basis. Pay-one-price also available, under $10. Free parking.

Top rides: The Bullet; Roll-O-Plane; Zyklon, a compact steel roller coaster; Tilt-A-Whirl; a Ferris wheel; Afterburner, a steel shuttle-loop roller coaster.

Plan to stay: 4 hours.

Best way to avoid crowds: Come during the week. Lines are usually long only on holidays.

Directions: Take Exit 150 off I-69, and follow County Road 220W ¾ mile to the park. Located 40 miles north of Ft. Wayne.

Nearby attractions: Auburn Cord Duesenberg Museum; Pokagon State Park, swimming, horseback riding, and hiking.

Holiday World
Routes 162 and 145
Santa Claus, IN (812) 937-4401

Opened in 1946 as Santa Claus Land, this park has evolved into a unique salute to some of the biggest holidays of the year. The three sections of the 50-acre park—Christmas, Halloween, and Fourth of July—are loaded with rides, attractions, architecture, and eateries representative of those holidays.

TIM'S TRIVIA

Santa Claus' lap is available all summer long at five parks: Holiday World, Santa Claus, Indiana; Santa's Land, Cherokee, North Carolina; Three Worlds of Santa's Village, Dundee, Illinois; Santa's Village, Skyforest, California; and Santa's Workshop, North Pole, Colorado.

Nine of the 21 rides are kiddie rides, located in a children's area called Rudolph's Reindeer Ranch; each of the rides is named after one of Santa's reindeer.

Food service: A complete turkey or chicken Christmas dinner is served daily at the Christmas Room restaurant, along with other entrees, including the Santa burger. Thirteen other food outlets serve foods ranging from tacos to fried chicken dinners to chocolate-covered waffles.

Entertainment: 4 major shows, including high divers and musical revues. Costumed characters roam the park.

Extras: A petting zoo, a wax museum, an antique toy collection, and an opportunity to meet Santa Claus, all for no additional charge. The Santa Claus Post Office, located just outside the gates of the park, is a wonderful place from which to send your postcards or Christmas cards, stamped with a unique postmark.

Special events: Halloween celebration, October weekends; Santafest, November and December weekends.

Season: April through December.

Operating hours: 10:00 A.M. to 7:00 or 10:00 P.M.

Admission policy: Pay-one-price, under $15. Free parking.

Top rides: Raging Rapids, a raging-rapids ride with a western theme; Frightful Falls, a log flume; Banshee, a 360-degree pendulum ride in which riders stay upright; Firecracker, a compact steel roller coaster.

Plan to stay: 5 hours.

Best way to avoid crowds: Because the front section, Santa Land, is usually less crowded, start your day in the other areas and then work your way back to the front. Less crowded times are midweek and fall and spring weekends.

Directions: Located in the southwestern part of the state about 5 miles off I-64. Take the U.S. 231 or Indiana 162 exits off the interstate and head south to the park entrance, where the two roads meet.

Nearby attractions: Young Abe Lincoln Musical Outdoor Drama.

Indiana Beach
306 Indiana Beach Drive
Monticello, IN (219) 583–4141

A traditional lakeside resort complex, Indiana Beach features a 32-ride amusement park, a motel, cottages, and campgrounds. The park, situated next to the 1,400-acre Lake Shafer, has been run by the same family since its founding in 1926.

The rides and attractions are along the ½-mile boardwalk that runs beside the lake. A large Ferris wheel is located at the end of the boardwalk on a point out in the lake; at night, the lights from the wheel can be seen for miles. A water park and a great swimming pool, with a sand beach, are also a part of this resort.

Food service: 4 sit-down restaurants, including the Skyroom, which serves a full menu of continental and American cuisine. Additional fast-food and snack outlets appear throughout the park and resort area.

Entertainment: Daily water-ski show and dancing nightly to live bands in the Roof Garden Lounge.

Extras: Miniature golf, antique autos, Dr. Frankenstein's Castle (a great spooky walk-through), boat tag, and pedal boats, all at extra charge. Water park and beach, extra charge.

Special events: Fireworks, July 4 and the Sunday before Labor Day; Anniversary Sunday, closest Sunday to June 18, when all rides are 25 cents each.

Season: May through mid-September.

Operating hours: Rides are open 11:00 A.M. to 11:00 P.M. daily. The beach opens at 9:00 A.M.; the water park, at 10:00 A.M.

Admission policy: General admission, plus rides, water park, and beach on a pay-as-you-go basis. A 7-hour, pay-one-price ticket also available, under $10. Free parking.

Top rides: *Shafer Queen,* a paddle-wheel excursion on Lake Shafer; The Tiger, a compact steel roller coaster; Flume, a log flume; Falling Star, a 360-degree looping ride in which the rider always stays upright; Gondola Wheel, a Ferris wheel with gondola cars.

Plan to stay: 8 hours if you use the water park.

Best way to avoid crowds: Come midweek or anytime in early June or late August.

Directions: Take Route 24 to the 6th Street exit in Monticello. Go north through town to the lake; the park is on your right. Located 95 miles northwest of Indianapolis and 120 miles from Chicago.

Nearby attractions: Canoe and raft rentals for use on Lake Shafer; Battleground of Tippecanoe.

Indianapolis Zoo
1200 West Washington
Indianapolis, IN (317) 630–2001

In addition to the fun and excitement the zoo itself provides, this facility has a beautifully restored, 1910 Parker carousel and 3 other rides, plus camel, pony, and elephant rides. It's located on 64-acres, a few blocks from downtown.

The zoo and rides are open every day of the year, weather permitting, with peak season hours of 9:00 A.M. to 6:00 P.M. Pay-one-price, under $10. Parking charge.

Old Indiana Fun Park
Route 47
Thorntown, IN (317) 436-2401

Upon entering Old Indiana, you'll find it hard to believe the park is such a youngster. Founded in 1985, it's wooded, well maintained, and beautifully landscaped and offers a fine selection of rides and attractions. Half the 26 rides are for children, and the park is geared mainly to young families with kids in the 4 to 14 age-group.

Food service: 1 large sit-down restaurant, serving an array of foods; additional concessions throughout. Food and beverages may be brought into the park.

Entertainment: More than 20 live performances daily, including musicals. The park is home to Larry Battson's Amazing World of Animals.

Extras: Miniature golf and a narrated horseback ride/nature trip, extra charge.

Special events: The park started out as a month-long Renaissance Festival that is still held each September. Additionally, the Festival of the Turning Leaves is held during late September.

Season: Mid-May through September.

Operating hours: 10:30 A.M. to 7:30 P.M. Park closed nonholiday Mondays and Tuesdays.

Inside the Abominable Sno' Man at Miracle Strip Amusement Park in Panama City, Florida, you'll find a wonderfully scary Scrambler ride.

Admission policy: Pay-one-price, under $10. Free parking.

Top rides: Parachute, a family parachute drop; a log flume; Montagne Russe Wildcat, a compact steel coaster; and a Ferris wheel.

Plan to stay: 4 hours.

Best way to avoid crowds: Midweek— be there when the rides open.

Directions: Located on Indiana State Route 47, about 35 miles northwest of Indianapolis. Take Exit 146 (Route 47) west off I–65 to the park.

Nearby attractions: Museum of Transportation and Communication; Conner Prairie Pioneer Settlement.

Redbrush Park
Highway 258
Seymour, IN (812) 497–2420

All kinds of outdoor offerings are available at this 750-acre family resort, among them 12 lakes, miles of walking and horseback trails, swimming, and an amusement area. The 9 rides include bumper boats, a skyride, and water slides; paddleboats, miniature golf, go-carts, a petting zoo, and an outdoor roller skating rink are here, too.

The lodge's restaurant is known widely for its country fried chicken and papaw bread.

Open May through mid-September. Water park and rides are open 11:00 A.M. to 6:00 P.M. Pay-one-price, under $10.

River Fair Family Fun Park
Indoors at the River Falls Mall
I–65 and Route 131
Clarksville, IN (812) 284–6255

Turn-of-the-century southern Indiana is the theme here, and there's plenty for all to do in that nostalgic atmosphere. In addition to the 6 kiddie rides, there's an 18-hole miniature golf course, remote-control boats and Indy cars. Hooper and Hanna Belle Hound are the costumed character mascots, with one being around most weekdays, and both being present on weekends.

A grand carousel is the park's centerpiece; a train ride takes you under a waterfall, around the golf course, and through a tunnel; and the River Belle Fun Boat is a custom-created participatory play area for the kids.

For the hungry, there's a 10-merchant food court adjacent to the park. Free admission, with rides and attractions on a pay-as-you-play basis. Pay-one-price tickets also available, under $5. Open during mall hours.

Sauzer's Kiddieland
Routes 30 and 41
Schererville, IN (219) 865-8160

Don't let the name of this neat little park fool you. It's much more than a kiddieland and has lots of rides and fun for the entire family. The 40-acre park is a favorite local site for corporate and family picnics, as well as for birthday parties.

The terrain is flat, the trees are plentiful and mature, and a nice relaxed feeling surrounds the entire operation. Adjacent to a small lake, the park contains 18 family and kiddie rides all grouped together, with steel shelters covering the small rides.

Food service: 1 major concession stand, serving sandwiches, snacks, and beverages. Food may not be brought in; however, there's a small picnic area outside the park.

Entertainment: There is no regularly scheduled in-park entertainment.

Extras: A fishing pond—pay a fee and catch up to five catfish that you can take home with you.

Season: May through September.

Operating hours: 11:00 A.M. to 5:00 P.M. Closed Mondays.

Admission policy: Free general admission with a minimum purchase of ride tickets. Pay-one-price also available, under $10. Free parking.

Top rides: A Ferris wheel; bumper cars; Tilt-A-Whirl; Round-up; an old, restored carousel housed in a geodesic dome.

Plan to stay: 2½ hours.

Best way to avoid crowds: Come during the week.

Directions: Take the Indianapolis Boulevard exit off I-80/94 and head south. The road turns into U.S. Highway 41. Five miles south of the interstate Highway 30 crosses 41; turn left and the park is on your left.

Nearby attractions: Holiday Star Theatre; Celebration Station, go-carts and miniature golf.

Iowa

Adventureland
I-80 & Highway 65
Des Moines, IA (515) 266-2121

As you walk into the park and under the railroad tracks, you'll be looking at historical Iowa. Every building along Main Street is a replica of an actual building from somewhere in the state at the turn of the century. Add to that nostalgic feeling the 15,000 flowering plants, the majestic trees, and the large expanses of well-groomed grass areas and you've got yourself the most visited amusement park in the state.

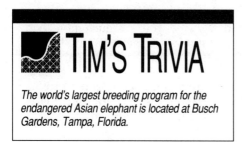

TIM'S TRIVIA

The world's largest breeding program for the endangered Asian elephant is located at Busch Gardens, Tampa, Florida.

Adventureland has 27 rides in five areas: Farm, Alpine, Old Frontier, River City, and Dragon Island.

Food service: 17 food outlets, including the 4 in the food court; the Rathskeller, serving German foods and pizza; and the Iowa Cafe, an air-conditioned, sit-down, full-meal restaurant sponsored by the Iowa Pork Association.

Entertainment: 5 shows: an animated presentation; a magic show; a water attraction in Aqua Theatre; a nostalgic musical revue; and a major musical presentation at the Show Palace Theatre.

Extras: A nice picnic area lies next to the parking lot, outside the gate. A hotel and RV camping facilities are also on the property. Don't miss the distorted mirror maze, located at the exit of the Dragon roller coaster in the back of the park; as people get off the coaster, they look at the mirrors and are dismayed to see what the Dragon did to them.

Season: May through September.

Operating hours: 10:00 A.M. to 10:00 P.M.

Admission policy: Pay-one-price, under $15. Parking charge.

Top rides: The Dragon, a steel two-loop roller coaster; Lady Luck, a roulette wheel–themed Trabant, a spinning platform ride; Tornado, a circa-1979 wooden roller coaster; Silly Silo, a rotor inside a silo; The Super Screamer, a steel compact coaster; Raging River, a raging-rapids ride.

Plan to stay: 6½ hours.

Best way to avoid crowds: Tuesday is the least crowded day. Once you leave the Main Street area, go through the park in a clockwise fashion.

Directions: Take Exit 142A (Highway 65) off I–80, east of Des Moines. The park is at that intersection.

Nearby attractions: WhiteWater University, a water park; Prairie Meadows, a horse-racing track; Manufacturers Outlet Mall.

Arnolds Park
Highway 71 and Lake Street
Arnolds Park, IA (712) 332-7781

The good-time feelings of yesteryear will be with you once you enter this lakeside resort amusement park. Before you do anything, stop by the big wishing well, at the base of the tall flagpole, right inside the park, and throw in a few coins—your visit here will be nothing short of first-class fun.

Located on the shores of Lake Okoboji, the park has 24 rides, including 12 for kids that are set off in their own kiddieland. If you wish, come by boat, there's plenty of dockside parking available.

The park, which has been completely restored, is especially beautiful at night, with all its lights and sounds. It also has one of the most interesting parking-lot entrances around. To enter, you drive under a sign mounted on the side of a section of reconstructed roller coaster, complete with two coaster trains climbing the hill. The sign proclaims that you're entering AN IOWA CLASSIC.

Food service: In addition to the 6 fast-food and snack locations in the park, are a McDonald's franchise and a Godfather's Pizza. The two share a seating area and offer you the opportunity to enjoy a beer with your Big Mac.

Entertainment: A country hoedown and a patriotic song-and-dance revue are the only regularly scheduled shows, although jugglers, fiddlers and other street performers walk the park often.

Extras: Go-carts, paddleboats, and kayaks are available for extra charge. The Tipsy House and the House of Mirrors are unusual walk-through attractions that shouldn't be missed; both are included in the admission fee.

Special events: July 4 fireworks; monthly car shows; a fishing jamboree, during summer months; a monthly concert series.

Season: Mid-May through early September.

Operating hours: Opens at 11:00 A.M. daily; closes at 10:00 P.M. on weekdays and at midnight on Fridays and Saturdays.

Admission policy: Pay-one-price, under $10. Free car and boat parking.

Top rides: The Big Coaster, a circa-1927 wooden roller coaster, completely rebuilt in 1989; the Great Lakes Himalaya; a Ferris wheel, providing a splendid view of the lake; bumper cars.

Plan to stay: 5 hours.

Best way to avoid crowds: This is a compact park, involving not too much walking, but during peak times, the midways can get crowded.

Early June, before the resort cabins fill up, is a good time to visit; during the season, Wednesdays are usually less crowded.

Directions: Take the Jackson Mountain exit off I–90 and go south on Route 71 to the park.

Nearby attractions: *Queen II,* a lake excursion boat.

Kansas

Joyland
2801 South Hillside
Wichita, KS (316) 684–0179

If you're looking for a well-run traditional park in this neck of the woods, you've found it here. A family-owned and -operated park, Joyland finds that most of its business is local, including various company and industrial picnics.

The park has lots of shade, colorful landscaping, and 22 rides, including 8 for kids.

Food service: 3 fast-food stands. Food may be brought into the park.

Entertainment: No regularly scheduled shows. A local radio station produces several shows a year as promotional events at the park.

Extras: Roller skating and go-carts, extra charges.

Special events: Easter Egg Hunt, April.

Season: April through mid-October

Operating hours: 2:00 to 10:00 P.M. on weekends and holidays and 6:30 to 10:00 P.M. on weekdays.

Admission policy: General admission charge, with rides on a pay-as-you-go basis. Pay-one-price "Ride-a-Rama" ticket also available, under $10. Free parking.

Top rides: Roller Coaster, a wooden coaster; Log Jam, a flume ride; Wacky Shack, a dark ride.

Plan to stay: 4 hours.

Best way to avoid crowds: Come during the week.

Directions: Take Exit K15 off the Kansas Turnpike; go east on Route 15 to Thirty-first Street. Then go east to Hillside Avenue and north 5 blocks to the park.

Nearby attractions: Cowtown Museum; Omnisphere Planetarium; Sedgewick County Zoo; Sports World, miniature golf and go-carts.

Theel Kiddieland
915 Spruce
Leavenworth, KS (913) 682–4351

Theel Manufacturing Company, a builder of amusement rides, set up this little park of 9 rides in 1951 as a display showcase for its own products and found that the neighborhood loved it. Since then, it has become a traditional place to take the kids. In addition to the mechanical rides, there are Shetland pony rides. And a miniature train takes riders under "the world's largest Dinosaur Rex" for added thrill. Call for hours and days of operation and admission prices.

Kentucky

Beech Bend Amusement Park
End of Riverview Drive
Bowling Green, KY (502) 781–7634

This could be the biggest little park in the country. Founded in 1888, the park flourished in the early part of the 1900s. But when it was dismantled and sold in the early 1980s, most people thought they'd heard the last of Beech Bend. Not so.

The park is making a comeback and now has about a dozen rides, mostly for the kids. It also has a miniature golf course, a great swimming pool, and dozens of picnic shelters. The nostalgic feeling of the park is strong, with many of the original buildings still standing among the hundreds of big trees. Also on the property are a Figure-8 car-racing track and a drag strip.

A small general admission fee is charged, and activities are on a pay-as-you-go basis. Hours vary; call first. The park is located 2 miles off Highway 31 West on Riverview Drive, in the deep woods.

Guntown Mountain
I–65 and Highway 70
Cave City, KY (502) 773–3530

The Old West comes alive at the top of a mountain here in middle Kentucky. The 10 rides are at the base of the mountain and the entertainment and the western town are at the top, via a chair lift. If the ride to the top looks too scary, a bus will transport you.

Food service: Several food outlets, selling traditional fast-food and snack items.

Entertainment: 20 performances daily in Western Town, including gunfights, cancan dancing, magic shows, and stunt shows.

Extras: Onyx Cave lies beneath the property; guided tours are given hourly. Admission to the traditional old haunted house is included in the all-day pass, as is a thrilling water slide that shoots down the side of the mountain.

TIM'S TRIVIA

Two American amusement parks have cave tours as part of their offerings. Guntown Mountain, in Cave City, Kentucky, has Onyx Cave, and Silver Dollar City, in Branson, Missouri, has Marvel Cave.

Season: May through mid-October.

Operating hours: Daily, 10:00 A.M. to 9:00 P.M.

Admission policy: General admission, plus rides, or a pay-one-price ticket, under $10. Free parking.

Top rides: Tilt-A-Whirl; a train that takes you on a scenic ride around the mountain, with a stop at a petting zoo deep in the woods; Kiddie Whip, a classic kiddie ride.

Plan to stay: 3 hours for rides and shows, 4 hours if you go on the cave tour.

Directions: Located within view of I-65. Take Exit 53 (Highway 70), west to the entrance.

Nearby attractions: Mammoth Cave National Park; Horse Cave; Hillbilly Hound, miniature golf; Mammoth Cave Wax Museum.

Kentucky Action Park
Highway 70
Cave City, KY (502) 773–2636

Here is a small park that uses the rugged terrain of the area to its advantage. Here you can ride a chair lift to the top of the mountain and come speeding back down on an alpine slide. There are also bumper boats, a water slide, go-carts, and a riding stable.

Ice cream and snacks are available. Admission is pay-as-you-play. Hours and days of operation vary; call first. Located 1 mile from Interstate-65.

Kentucky Kingdom Amusement Park
Kentucky State Fairgrounds
Louisville, KY (502) 366–2231

This local amusement park is well kept, clean and colorful. It reopened in 1990 with 20 rides, including 2 world-class roller coasters. Nestled in the corner of the fairgrounds, the park becomes a part of the carnival midway during the state fair in August.

As you enter, look to your right and you'll see a unique carousel. It's called the Concert Carousel, and instead of riding animals, you ride oversize orchestra instruments, including tubas and drums. King Louie's Playground is the kiddieland here, and the kids will love the costumed mascot, King Louie.

Food service: A Papa John's Pizza franchise operates a 250-seat, sitdown restaurant. Additional outlets include A Sundae Kind of Love, for ice cream; DogGone Good, for hot dogs; Incredible Eatables, for assorted foods and snacks; and the Hamburger Construction Company.

Entertainment: Most of the regularly scheduled, daily entertainment is planned for kids and includes a marionette show and a circus participatory show. In addition, a rock-and-roll dance takes place every Friday night in the amphitheater.

Extras: The Fontaine Ferry Museum takes the visitor back to the days of Louisville's premier amusement park, Fontaine Ferry. Free with admission.

Season: Memorial Day weekend through September.

Operating hours: Open daily 11:00 A.M. to 10:00 or 11:00 P.M.

Admission policy: Pay-one-price, under $10. Rates will change during the state fair. Because the parking lot is shared with the buildings on the fairgrounds, a parking fee is charged at times.

Top rides: Vampire, a steel boomerang roller coaster; Starchaser, an indoor roller coaster; Squid, a four-slide, wet/dry water ride; Thunder Run, a wooden roller coaster.

Plan to stay: 4 hours.

Best way to avoid crowds: Come early during the week. The park is laid out in a circular pattern, with plenty of space between rides. Crowds are not usually a problem.

Directions: Take the Watterson Expressway (I–264) exit off I–65, south of downtown Louisville. Follow the signs to the fairgrounds.

Nearby attractions: *Belle of Louisville,* paddle-wheel rides on the Ohio River; Humana Building, an example of award-winning architecture; Kentucky Center for the Arts; birthplace of Abraham Lincoln.

Tombstone Junction
Highway 90
Parkers Lake, KY (606) 376–5087

Out in the middle of the rugged Big South Fork National River and Recreation Area lies Cumberland Falls State Park. One mile down the highway from that site lies a reproduction of a post–Civil War town, known as Tombstone Junction.

Entertainment here includes gunfights, magic and ventriloquist shows, and rides on an authentic steam locomotive, Ol' #77. There are also a handful of adult and kiddie rides and concerts by top-name country entertainers.

Admission is pay-one-price for all activities, except rides, under $5. Hours vary; call first.

Louisiana

Carousel Gardens
City Park, #1 Dreyfous
New Orleans, LA (504) 483-9385

Tucked away in a shaded corner of the huge City Park lies this small family amusement park, mostly hidden by the large oak trees. Restored in 1985, the park looks like a turn-of-the-century facility, complete with brick sidewalks. It has 8 rides, including a 1910 Carmel/Looff antique carousel that's housed in a vintage, beautifully renovated carousel building. A 20-minute train ride takes you out of the amusement park and around the large City Park and across several of its bayous.

Adjacent to the amusement park is Storyland, a storybook park with puppet shows, roving entertainers, and costumed characters.

Gate admission fee, plus rides on a pay-as-you-go basis. Hours vary; call first.

Fun Fair Park
8475 Florida Boulevard
Baton Rouge, LA (504) 924-6266

At one time, this cozy park was surrounded by woods. Now it's across the street from one of the city's major malls and surrounded by commercial developments.

The 7 kiddie rides, covered by a large pavilion, form the centerpiece of a booming birthday party business. The 8 other rides are located on the other side of the 6-acre park.

Food service: 1 large concession stand, providing fast-food and snack items, as well as the catering for birthday parties.

Entertainment: No regularly scheduled daily shows, but various forms of entertainment are brought into the park several times each season.

Extras: Midway offering games of skill.

Season: Mid-March through mid-October for all rides. The kiddie rides are also open during winter.

Operating hours: Major rides open at 6:00 P.M. on weekdays and 1:00 P.M. on weekends. Kiddie rides open at 10:00 A.M. on weekdays and 1:00 P.M. on weekends. All rides close at 10:00 P.M. nightly.

Admission policy: Free gate, with a pay-as-you-play policy. Pay-one-price also available, under $10. Free parking.

Top rides: Galaxy, a compact steel roller coaster; bumper cars; Paratrooper; Spider.

Plan to stay: 2 hours.

Best way to avoid crowds: Come during the week.

Directions: Take the Airline Highway exit off I–12. Follow the highway north until you cross the Florida Boulevard overpass. Make the first exit to your left and you'll see the park.

Nearby attractions: Blue Bayou, a water park; Cortana Mall, shopping, eating, and movie theaters; Baton Rouge Zoo; Putt-Putt, miniature golf.

Hamel's Park
3232 East 70th Street
Shreveport, LA (318) 869–3566

If you appreciate large oak and elm trees in the amusement parks you frequent, you'll love this 30-acre family facility. Located across the parkway from the Red River, the 17 rides are built into the environment, thereby offering a great deal of green and open spaces throughout. The well-maintained park has a nice selection of rides for the entire family, with 6 of the kiddie rides being located inside a 12,000-square-foot building.

Food service: 4 major eateries, serving various fast foods, and 4 smaller stands, serving snacks and drinks. And how long has it been since you've eaten a genuine meat pie? The popular and tasty Natchitoches Meat Pies are served here.

Entertainment: Happy Hamel, the big, smiling-dog mascot of the park, is always here, as is a clown who does magic acts. Additional acts are booked in for special events.

Extras: The go-cart track here may be one of the best at any amusement park in the country. The carts run down between tall, landscaped levees, not only making the track interesting to run but also keeping the noise away from the rest of the park.

Special events: Italian Festival, late March; JuneTeenth, black cultural celebration, Father's Day; Country Music Festival, late June; Labor Day Outing, a labor-union event sponsored by the local newspaper.

Season: Mid-March through mid-October.

Operating hours: Open 6:00 to 10:00 P.M. Wednesday through Friday,

Molly and Carrie O'Brien, the author's daughters, made great sacrifices to help their father research this book. They're shown here researching the Grand Carousel at River Fair Family Fun Park in Clarksville, Indiana.

Maine

1:00 to 10:00 P.M. Saturday, and 1:00 to 7:00 P.M. Sunday. Closed Monday and Tuesday.

Admission policy: Small gate fee, with rides on a pay-as-you-go basis. Pay-one-price also available, under $10. Special pay-one-price promotions offered during the week. Free parking.

Top rides: A Ferris wheel; bumper cars; a train ride around park and through a tunnel; a log flume; Thunderail, a Zyklon compact steel roller coaster.

Plan to stay: 3 hours.

Best way to avoid crowds: Come during the week or in early June or late August, when the crowds are smallest. Even on weekends, though, unless there is a major promotion going on, the lines here are rarely long.

Directions: Located in the southeast corner of the city on the north side of the 70th Street Bridge. Take the Market Street exit off I–20; then take Highway 1 South to 70th Street (Route 511) and turn left. Go 2 miles to the park.

Nearby attractions: National Rose Society Gardens; Louisiana State Exhibit Museum; Watertown, a water park; Eighth Air Force Museum; Louisiana Downs, a racetrack.

Maine

Funtown USA
774 Portland Road
Saco, ME (207) 284–5139

Myriad attractions will keep you busy in this small, nicely maintained family park that has been around since 1967. Plenty of shaded picnic areas are well spaced among the 11 adult and family rides and 9 kiddie rides.

Don't be confused when you first see this park. There's a water park built directly next door and although the two look like they are one facility, they aren't. Make sure you go through the correct gates.

Food service: 3 restaurants—serving Mexican food, seafood, and hamburgers—plus several snack bars. On a hot day, make sure you try one of the exotic, nonalcoholic frozen drinks. Food may be brought into the park.

Entertainment: Magic and ventriloquist shows.

Extras: A large game arcade.

Special events: The park's three major sponsors—Pringles Potato Chips, McDonald's, and Pepsi-Cola—all have special promotions with the park each summer.

Season: May through mid-September.

Operating hours: 10:30 A.M. to 11:00 P.M.

Admission policy: Free gate, with rides and attractions on a pay-as-you-go basis. Pay-one-price also available, under $15. Free parking.

Top rides: Thunderfalls, a log flume; Astrosphere, an indoor Scrambler with a light show and music; Flying Trapeze, flying swings.

Plan to stay: 4 hours.

Best way to avoid crowds: The slowest days of the week are Monday, Tuesday, and Friday.

Directions: Take I–95 to Exit 5, which is a spur of the interstate. Take that to Exit 2B (Highway 1) and go north about 1 mile.

Nearby attractions: Cascades, a water park and miniature golf; Aqua Boggan, a water park.

Palace Playland
Old Orchard Street
Old Orchard Beach, ME (207) 934–2001

The present owners have built a top-notch, well-maintained amusement park here, following a disastrous fire in 1972 that destroyed much of the original oceanfront park. Colorful flags, plenty of flower boxes, and a boardwalk separating the beach from the ride area makes this a nice, relaxing place to visit. Besides the 28 rides and a three-flume water slide, the park has a large arcade building that houses more than 200 video games and games of skill.

Food service: A large, beachfront restaurant-bar provides sit-down service with a full menu, including clams and lobster dinners; 10 additional eateries offer a full line of traditional snacks and fast-food items.

Entertainment: Acts and costumed characters are occasionally booked in for special events. Fireworks every Friday night.

Extras: The park has 2 noteworthy walk-throughs, the haunted house and the fun house.

Season: Late-May through mid-September.

Operating hours: 11:00 A.M. to 11:00 P.M.

Admission policy: Free admission, with rides and attractions on a pay-as-you-go basis. Pay-one-price also available, under $15. Special pay-one-price discount ticket offered after 7:00 P.M. Paid parking on the street and at various city lots.

Top rides: A Ferris wheel; a circa-1910 Philadelphia Toboggan Company carousel, in beautiful condition; Pirate, a swinging pirate ship; Matterhorn.

Plan to stay: 5 hours.

Best way to avoid crowds: The park is least crowded on Mondays. September weekends are also a good time to visit—just enough crowds and just enough sun to make the outing fun.

Directions: Take Route 112 off I–95 east to Route 1. At the Route 5 intersection, go north to Old Orchard. The park is located on the beach at the dead end of Old Orchard Street.

Nearby attractions: Pirates Cove and Schooners, each offering miniature golf; Cascades, a water park; plus beach and other oceanfront tourist attractions.

York's Wild Kingdom Zoo and Amusement Park
Route 1
York Beach, ME (800) 456–4911

You'll find a wild time here. From wild and hairy animals to wild and scary rides, this 100-acre complex contains not only the state's largest zoo but also a great little ride area. There are 15 rides, including 9 just for the little members of the family.

Food service: 3 sit-down eateries and 2 smaller fast-food and snack outlets. The french fries and onion rings are some of the best in this part of the country.

Entertainment: Animal shows, a walk-about clown and juggler, and the Fort Wild Kingdom bank robbery show.

Extras: Miniature golf, paddleboats, go-carts, and live animal rides, all for an extra fee.

Season: Rides, Memorial Day through Labor Day. Zoo, May through Columbus Day.

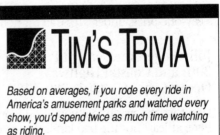

TIM'S TRIVIA

Based on averages, if you rode every ride in America's amusement parks and watched every show, you'd spend twice as much time watching as riding.

Operating hours: Rides: Noon to 10:00 P.M. Zoo: 10:00 A.M. to 5:00 P.M.

Admission policy: Admission to the rides part of the park is free, with a pay-one-price ticket available. Zoo admission extra. Combination ride and zoo tickets also available.

Top rides: Jaguar, a Himalaya; a merry-go-round; go-carts; bumper cars.

Plan to stay: 2 to 3 hours to visit the zoo and ride the rides.

Best way to avoid crowds: Come on weekdays during July and August.
Directions: Take the York exit off I–95; go east on Exit Road to Route 1 and proceed 2½ miles north.

Maryland

The Baltimore Zoo
Druid Park Lake Drive
Baltimore, MD (301) 396–7102

This wonderful zoo is the third oldest in the country, but its brand-new children's zoo is state of the art. In addition to the animals and exhibits here, you'll find 3 kiddie and family rides, including an antique carousel.

Admission to the zoo is pay-one-price, under $5, and includes the rides. Hours of rides vary; call first.

Frontier Town Western Park
Route 611
Ocean City, MD (301) 289–7877

The Old West comes back to life here each summer when the sounds of the train whistle and gunfire fills the air. Besides the train, stagecoach, and horseback rides are pony rides, paddleboat rides on the lake, and a lot of action throughout the park. Live shows include gunfights, a can-can musical show, an Indian show, and a rodeo.

Pay-one-price, under $10. Call for hours and days of operation.

Jolly Roger Amusement Park
30th and Coastal Highway
Ocean City, MD (301) 289–3477

Don't let the name fool you—you won't find too many pirates around here, at least not the bad kind. What you *will* find is a 38-acre park providing 36 rides and a whole lot of other things to keep you and your family busy. The park is divided into three areas: the ride section, including a 29-ride kiddieland; Splash Mountain, a water park; and Speed World, featuring gas-powered cars and boats.

Note: The facility is quite flat and offers little shade; be sure to dress appropriately. And the walkways between the rides are crushed stone; thus, if you're with someone in a wheelchair, or are using a stroller for your small child, you'll want to plan accordingly.

Food service: The Dough Roller Restaurant is a walk-up with patio seating. There are also 3 fast-food and snack locations, plus an ice-cream parlor in the parking lot next door.

Entertainment: A magic show and 5 animal shows, featuring birds, sea lions, monkeys, elephants, and dogs.

Extras: 2 miniature golf courses: Jungle Golf and Treasure Hunt, extra charge. Bumper boats and speedboats, extra charge. Free petting zoo.

Season: The ride section and water park are open Memorial Day through Labor Day; other facilities, open Easter through Labor Day.

Operating hours: Noon to midnight.

Admission policy: General admission, plus rides and attractions on a pay-as-you-go basis. Pay-one-price also available, under $15. Use of water park is extra, by the hour, half-day or full day. In-park go-carts are included in pay-one-price, but Speed World activities cost extra. Free parking.

Top rides: Time Twister, a steel corkscrew roller coaster; Water Flume, a log flume; Tilt-A-Whirl; bumper cars; Swing Ride, a wave swinger.

Plan to stay: 8 hours.

Best way to avoid crowds: The least busy days are Friday and Saturday.

Directions: Follow Route 50 across the bridge into Ocean City. When the highway ends, take Philadelphia Avenue north (it becomes the Coastal Highway) to 30th Street; the park is on the left.

Nearby attractions: Many beach activities, including sailing, fishing, waterskiing, and beachcombing.

Ocean Pier Rides
401 South Boardwalk
Ocean City, MD (301) 289–3031

Talk about a multipurpose pier! As you walk off the boardwalk onto this pier, you'll pass the games and rides, then you'll come to the Riptide Water Park. The area at the very end is used as a fishing pier.

Located in the heart of the old town section of the city, the park started out as a ballroom-dancing pavilion in the early 1900s; the rides were added in the 1930s. Currently there are 6 major rides and a participatory play unit for children.

Food service: The park itself has no food service, but on the boardwalk next to the pier are 3 of the best food stands on the East Coast: Thrasher's Fries, which has been here since 1929 and always has lines of people waiting for the tender morsels; Bull on the Beach, serving up the biggest roast beef sandwich you'll ever see; and the Alaska Stand, featuring a variety of foods and excellent ice cream.

Extras: Morbid Manor is a walk-through haunted house. There's also a walk-through fun house.

Season: Easter through the third week of September.

Operating hours: Rides open at 1:00 P.M., with closing times depending on crowds and weather. The water park is open from 10:00 A.M. to 10:00 P.M.

Admission policy: The rides and water park are priced separately. Admission to the ride park is free, with rides and attractions on a pay-as-you-go basis. Admission to the water park is by the hour, half-day, or full day. Meter parking on street.

Top rides: Hurricane, a Himalaya with pictures of Ocean City storms of the past; Giant Wheel, a Ferris wheel; 1001 Nights, a 360-degree platform ride.

Plan to stay: 4 hours.

Best way to avoid crowds: Tuesdays and Wednesdays are the slowest days.

Directions: Follow Route 50 across the bridge into Ocean City. When Route 50 ends, turn right onto Philadelphia Avenue and go to Wicomico Street. Turn left; go 2 blocks to the boardwalk.

Nearby attractions: As with most tourist/beach areas, the boardwalk area has plenty of attractions. And some 30 miniature golf courses are within 15 minutes of the pier.

Trimper's Rides and Amusements
South 1st Street and Boardwalk
Ocean City, MD (301) 289–8617

The first thing you'll see here is the big steel roller coaster soaring high above the other area attractions. With 37 rides, this park, founded in 1892 and still owned by the same family, has more rides than any other park in the state.

The park is spread out over a 3-block area on the land side of the boardwalk, and its 15 kiddie rides are all indoors.

Food service: 3 walk-up fast food and snack stands on the boardwalk. A Burger King is located across the boardwalk from the park.

Extras: Miniature golf, tank tag, gallery guns, extra charge. Also offered are an unusual mirror maze and an interesting walk-through called Pirates Cove, both included in pay-one-price admission. Be sure to look over the display (near the carousel) of old photos of the park.

Season: Indoor rides run on weekends from February through Easter. The entire park is open Easter Sunday through October.

Operating hours: Opens at 1:00 P.M. on weekdays and at noon on weekends; closes at midnight every night.

Admission policy: Free admission, with rides and attractions on a pay-as-you-go basis. Pay-one-price also available, under $10. Parking at meters and paid lots nearby.

Top rides: Tidal Wave, a steel boomerang roller coaster; tank tag; a circa-1902 Herschell-Spillman carousel; Zipper; Double Sky Wheel. The Haunted House, which you ride through sitting in minicoffins made of wood, is located along the boardwalk, away from the park proper.

Plan to stay: 3 hours.

Best way to avoid crowds: Mondays and Tuesdays are the slowest days.

Directions: Follow Route 50 across the bridge into Ocean City. The highway ends at Philadelphia Avenue; turn right and go 5 blocks to Division Street. Then turn left and go 2 blocks to the boardwalk.

Nearby attractions: Lifeguard Museum; Trimper's Shopping Village, plus the rest of the fun to be had at an oceanside resort town.

Wild World
13710 Central Avenue
Largo, MD (301) 249–1500

A nice mix of activities spread out over 68 wooded, rolling acres can be found here. Originally operated by the naturalist Jim Fowler and called the Wildlife Preserve, the park now has 7 adult rides; 8 kiddie rides in Kiddie City; 14 water rides, including a multiactivity area called Paradise Island; and a wave pool.

Food service: 5 sit-down restaurants and 5 additional walk-away snack stands.

Entertainment: 4 different shows, including a marionette show for the kids, a surfing show featuring beach music, and a song, dance, and magic presentation. Big Tooth, the shark mascot, can be seen in a game-show contest at Big Tooth's Aquarium.

Extras: Golf City, miniature golf, extra charge.

TIM'S TRIVIA

Wild World, in Largo, Maryland, is a real sweetheart of an amusement park. Three couples have gotten married on its Wild One wooden roller coaster; one couple got married in its wave pool; and one couple tied the knot on Paradise Island, the park's water-slide area.

Special events: Christian Youth Day, Memorial Day weekend; Gospel Day, early June; Fireworks, July 4; costumed character shows, late in season. Additional special events are held just about every weekend.

Season: Mid-May through Labor Day.

Operating hours: Opens at 10:00 A.M. daily; closes at 9:00 P.M. during the week and 10:00 P.M. on weekends.

Admission policy: Pay-one-price, under $15. Special after–5:00 P.M. rate. Parking charge.

Top rides: Wild One, a wooden roller coaster; Rafter's Run, tube slides; Rainbow Zoom Flume; Wild Wave, a wave pool; a train ride; a carousel.

Plan to stay: 6 hours.

Best way to avoid crowds: Monday is the slowest day. Most people enjoy the water rides during midday and then ride the mechanical rides at night. To avoid lines, do the opposite.

Directions: Take Exit 15A off I–95; follow the signs to the park. Located 15 minutes from Washington, D.C., and 30 minutes from Baltimore.

Nearby attractions: Goddard Space Center; in Baltimore, Maryland Science Center and for shopping and restaurants, Harbor Place, where you'll also find a 1912 Herschell-Spillman carousel, on Light Street.

Massachusetts

Edaville Railroad
Route 58
South Carver, MA (508) 866–4526

This crafts village and family fun park is smack-dab in the middle of cranberry country. In fact, the park's 5½-mile train ride was once the working railroad for the world's largest cranberry plantation.

Entertainment includes jugglers, clowns, Dixieland bands, and marionette shows. In addition to the train ride are adult and kiddie rides, including antique fire engines, a circa-1912 antique Dutch carousel, paddleboats, paddle-wheel excursion boat rides on Cranberry Lake, and a petting zoo.

Open from May through January. Admission is by a pay-one-price ticket, under $15.

Pirates Fun Park
Route 1A
Salisbury Beach, MA (508) 465–3731

A short distance from the oceanside boardwalk, this busy little park is the hub of the entertainment area of the town. It's a popular spot not only with tourists but with locals as well.

Along with its 22 rides, including 6 for kids, the park offers a variety of water rides, midway games, and an arcade. Two food outlets provide traditional amusement park "fun" food. The Pirate's Den is a nice ride-through haunted house, and the Island Adventure is a walk-through fun house.

Admission is pay-as-you-go; pay-one-price is also available. Hours vary; call first.

Riverside Park
Route 159
Agawam, MA (413) 786–9300

What a wonderful traditional family park this is! With more than 100 rides, games, and attractions, it's New England's largest amusement park. Founded in 1940, the park rests on 170 acres and its landscaping is mature and colorful.

Two kiddielands contain 15 rides, while the arsenal of 25 major rides includes 3 roller coasters and a giant wheel that provides a view of the park and the Connecticut River.

Food service: 16 food and drink locations, including Fannie's Fabulous Fries, curly and spicy fries; International Dome Food Court, a large selection of international foods; Fast Eddie's, hamburgers, hot dogs, Belgian waffles, and grinders; and Chicken Fancy, broasted chicken, fantail shrimp, and fried clams.

Entertainment: Captain Rivi, the park's "ambassador of happiness," and his costumed animal friends meet and greet visitors daily. In addition, there are regularly scheduled variety, magic, and puppet shows daily. On some Friday evenings during the year, live concerts are held, some by top-name entertainers. Every Saturday at 6:00 P.M., NASCAR races take place in the park's speedway. Admission to races is separate, but a combination ticket for the race and the park is available.

Extras: Petting zoo, included in admission. Miniature golf, additional charge.

Season: April through Labor Day.

Operating hours: 11:00 A.M. to 10:00 P.M. Closing times vary during the season, depending on crowds and weather.

Admission policy: Pay-one-price, under $20. Parking charge.

Top rides: Riverside Cyclone, a wooden roller coaster; Black Widow, a steel shuttle-loop coaster; Thunderbolt, a circa-1941 wooden roller coaster; Colossus, a 150-foot tall Ferris wheel; Red River Rapids, a log flume; Wild River Falls, a series of 3 water-action wet/dry rides; Swiss Sky Ride; a circa-1909 Mangels-Illions carousel with original band organ; a monorail.

Plan to stay: 6 hours.

Best way to avoid crowds: Mondays, Tuesdays, and Thursdays are the slowest days.

Directions: Take Exit 4 off the Massachusetts Turnpike and follow Route 5 south 5.8 miles to Route 57 (Agawam–Southwick). Follow Route 57 to Route 159 South (Main Street) and go south 3 miles.

Nearby attractions: Basketball Hall of Fame; Indian Motorcycle Museum and Hall of Fame; Springfield Science Museum; Old Storrowton Village Museum, restored buildings; Connecticut Valley Historical Museum.

Whalom Park
Route 13
Whalom District
Fitchburg, MA (508) 342–3707

The picturesque drive to the park gets you ready for the beauty you'll see once you enter the front gates. This century-old lakeside amusement facility bills itself as the "cleanest, greenest amusement park in New England."

The heavily wooded park has picnic areas situated throughout, and much of the architecture reflects its past heritage as a trolley park at the turn of the century. There are 22 adult and 13 kiddie rides.

Food service: Several food stands throughout the park, offering such items as pizza, hamburgers, baked potatoes, salads, hand-dipped ice cream, and fried dough. Food and beverages may be brought into the park.

Entertainment: Musical variety shows, puppet and marionette shows, costumed characters, marching bands, circus acts, and strolling performers.

Extras: Swimming in Lake Whalom, with bathhouses for changing, no additional charge. Miniature golf, paddleboats, and aqua cycles, extra charge.

Special events: Park birthday party, every August 18; Fireworks Party, July 3; Kid's Fest, Labor Day weekend.

Massachusetts

Season: April through Labor Day weekend.

Operating hours: Closed Mondays. Open noon to 9:00 or 10:00 P.M. all other days during peak summer season.

On a hot day you can't beat a nice, wet, rapids ride, such as Big Foot Rapids, at Knott's Berry Farm in Buena Park, California. (© 1991 Knott's Berry Farm)

Admission policy: General admission, plus rides and attractions, or pay-one-price, under $15.

Top rides: Flyer Comet, a wooden coaster; Tumble Bug, an old favorite (only a few left in operation); Turnpike, antique cars; Giant Slide; a circa-1909/10 Looff carousel.

Plan to stay: 5 hours.

Best way to avoid crowds: Come early in the season anytime or during the season midweek.

Directions: Located on Route 13, 3 miles off Route 2, in Lunenburg.

Nearby attractions: Fitchburg Art Museum; Mt. Wachusett State Park.

Michigan

Bear's Lair Family Fun Park
5600 Highway 12
Tipton, MI (517) 431–2217

This is a great little 6-acre family fun park located among the rolling landscape of the Irish Hills area, 50 miles west of Detroit. It offers plenty of picnic tables and barbecue pits, and if you forget your lunch fixin's you can buy them at the party store right on the grounds.

There are 9 rides total, with 3 just for the little ones. And, there are water slides, miniature golf, go-carts, a video arcade, a snack bar, and a swimming pool.

Admission is pay-as-you-go. Hours vary; call first.

Boblo Island
Middle of Detroit River
(Access from Detroit and Canada)
(313) 843–8800

This may be the only amusement park in the world where you can't go home when you want to: You have to wait for the boat.

The park is on a 272-acre island in the lower Detroit River, near Lake Erie. An island of entertainment, it has no interference from the noises of the real world and is a true haven. The midway, containing 30 rides and an additional 35 shows and attractions, takes up a small portion of the island. The rest is a heavily wooded forest with walking paths and picnic groves.

Food service: The Island House restaurant, offering fine dining with table service; the International Pavilion, a large food court featuring various international and American foods; and snack stands throughout.

Entertainment: A water-ski show takes place along the shores of the river. Additionally, Mark Wilson, a renowned magician, has created an illusion show for the park. A clown band roams the midway.

Extras: Rent a bicycle and explore the island on paved paths, play miniature golf, or roller-skate in an outdoor rink, all at additional cost.

Special events: Oktoberfest, October; cheerleading contests, September; overnight camping for scouts on the first and last day of the season.

Season: Mid-May through September.

Operating hours: First boat leaves at 9:30 A.M.; last boat returns at 10:30 P.M.

Admission policy: Pay-one-price, under $20. Includes round-trip boat transportation. Parking charge at docks.

Top rides: Sky Streak, a steel roller coaster; The Nightmare, an enclosed compact steel roller coaster; The Screamer, a multielement coaster; Sky Tower, a rotating tower that provides visitors with a view of up to 20 miles; a train that takes riders on a 2-mile tour of the island past a historic lighthouse.

Plan to stay: 6 hours.

Best way to avoid crowds: Go early in the season on a weekday morning.

Directions: The boat leaves from two U.S. docks, Detroit and Gibraltar. From Detroit, take I–75 to the Clark Avenue exit (47A) and go south 2 blocks toward the river to the Boblo Dock; the boat trip to the park takes 90 minutes from here. From Gibraltar, take I–75 to the Gibraltar exit (29A), turn east on Middle Gibraltar Road, go about 2½ miles to North Gibraltar Road, turn left, and go ½ mile to the dock; the boat trip to the park takes 45 minutes from here.

Nearby attractions: Henry Ford Museum and Greenfield Village in Greenfield; Greektown and Trapper's Alley in downtown Detroit.

Dutch Village
12350 James Street
Holland, MI (616) 396–1475

 **TIM'S TRIVIA**

A scale at Dutch Village, in Holland, Michigan, gives you your weight and then presents you with a certificate that proves you're not a witch or a warlock, unless, of course, you are.

Here's a reproduction of what a quaint Dutch burg would look like if you found it in the Netherlands. The park offers 20 acres of canals, Dutch architecture, and gardens, as well as 5 rides, including a circa-1924 Herschell Spillman carousel, a Dutch swing ride, and a giant wooden-shoe slide. Also on hand are plenty of authentic crafts and foods, plus dancers and other entertainers. In operation, too, is an authentic witch's scale from the Museum of the Netherlands: It weighs you and presents you with a certificate that proves you aren't a witch or warlock—unless, of course, you are.

Pay-one-price, under $5. Open from the end of April through September, 9:00 A.M. to 6:00 P.M.

Interlochen Fun Country
9320 U.S. 31 South
Interlochen, MI (616) 276–6360

This is a great place for a small family fun park. The well-shaded facility features 9 rides, including a carousel, bumper boats, go-carts, and water slides. It also offers a 1-mile train ride on an authentic twenty-four-gauge railroad, taking you through scenic woods. Available as well are a miniature golf course and a games arcade.

The park is open Memorial Day through Labor Day, 11:00 A.M. to 8:00 P.M. daily. General admission charge, plus rides; a pay-one-price ticket is also available.

Michigan's Adventure Amusement Park
4750 Whitehall Road
Muskegon, MI (616) 766–3377

Ride the state's only wooden roller coaster, and then take a short stroll along a well-landscaped path to the state's largest water park. There's a great deal to do here in Michigan's largest wet/dry park. That's a lot of superlatives, but this 80-acre park, just 6 miles from Lake Michigan, fills the bill on all accounts. With 20 mechanical rides, including 5 for the kids, the park added WildWater Adventure, a water park, in 1990 and doubled its size. The park is surrounded by trees and offers ample shade and resting areas for sitting and watching, if you so choose.

Food service: 6 food and drink outlets, serving a full line of fast-food and snack items. Numerous picnic tables available.

Entertainment: Several musical revues and strolling entertainers.

Season: May through Labor Day.

Operating hours: 11:00 A.M. to 6:00, 7:00, or 8:00 P.M.

Admission policy: Pay-one-price, under $15. Parking charge.

Top rides: Wolverine Wildcat, a wooden roller coaster; Corkscrew, a steel corkscrew coaster; a log flume; Falling Star, a 360-degree platform ride that keeps riders upright at all times; Sea Dragon, a swinging pirate ship; antique cars; a 90-foot-tall, gondola-type Ferris wheel; Grand Carousel.

Plan to stay: 7 hours.

Best way to avoid crowds: June is the slowest month of the season. During July and August, come early during the week.

Directions: Take the Russell Street exit off Route 31 and go north to Riley Thompson Road. Go west on Riley Thompson for about 2 miles; the park is on the right at Whitehall Road.

Nearby attractions: Duck Lake and Muskegon state parks, swimming, hiking, and picnicking; Manistee National Forest, lakes, hiking, and biking trails.

Minnesota.

Como Park Amusement Park
Hamlin and Midway Parkway in Como Park
St. Paul, MN (612) 484–6565

You have to be looking for this wonderful little park to find it. Nestled in city-owned Como Park next to the zoo, the facility displays no signs, no fences, nothing fancy. You'll know you're there when you see the rides and a lone ticket booth.

With 15 rides, including 10 for kids, this is the perfect place for a family to visit for an hour or two and let the kids play. Expect to see new rides and attractions each time you visit. The owners, the O'Neil family, enjoy changing things around quite often.

Open daily from Palm Sunday through Labor Day, 10:30 A.M. to 8:00 P.M. There is no admission charge; you pay as you play.

Family Funways
2100 North Frontage Road
Burnsville, MN (612) 894–9782

When they built this park in 1980, the owners wanted to make sure they offered something for everyone. And they were successful: With a large kiddieland of 20 rides and about a dozen additional family rides, the park has a nice mix of attractions for the entire family.

Here you'll find a miniature golf course, go-cart tracks, bumper boats, batting cages, a haunted mine-shaft elevator ride, a petting zoo, games, and a small video arcade. The park is filled with individual animatronic scenes that are activated by token. Among other activities, you can watch a cowboy getting a shave, a surgeon during a very bloody operation, or the goings-on at an early blacksmith shop.

Admission is free, and attractions are on a pay-as-you-go basis. Hours vary; call first.

Knott's Camp Snoopy
Indoors, Mall of America
8100 24th Avenue
Bloomington, MN (612) 851-3500

Under a glass roof in what some are saying will be the largest shopping mall in the United States, this state-of-the-art, 7-acre theme park is set to open in 1992.

This wonderland is expected to provide all the elements of an outdoor theme park, from rides and shows to food and merchandise. The 16 rides, including kiddie, family, and thrill rides, will be built into a landscape of waterfalls, mountains, and jungle-type foliage.

The 500-seat Snoopy Theatre will be the site of daily live shows, and an adjacent miniature golf course will start on the third floor and end on the main floor.

The Peanuts cartoon gang, including Snoopy and Charlie Brown, will be here as costumed characters. The park is being developed by California's Knott's Berry Farm, thus its name.

Valleyfair!
1 Valleyfair Drive
Shakopee, MN (612) 445-7600

If you appreciate great neon artistry, the fun starts here before you even leave the highway. The park's unique and colorful neon sign is one of the best in the country. The sign depicts three moving rides—a Ferris wheel, a roller coaster, and a carousel—in neon.

Inside the gates, turn-of-the-century architecture, eye-catching gardens and a wealth of hanging plants dominate the 68 acres of landscape. There's much to keep you busy, or if you choose, you can find a nice shady spot, grab yourself a cold drink, and watch the world—and the roller coasters—go by.

Three roller coasters and 12 kiddie rides are among the park's 30 rides.

Food service: 8 major eateries and several food stands—among them the Red Garter Saloon and Restaurant, the Old Time Caboose Beer Garden, Fryar Tuck's French Fries, and the Palatable Palace. They have a wonderful way of serving caramel apples here. They slice the apples, put them in a bowl, and pour hot caramel over them . . . delicious and easy to eat!

Entertainment: 6 major shows, including an IMAX theater, hot-dog ski jumpers, and various musical shows featuring rock-and-roll, big band music of the 1930s and 1940s, jazz, pop, and country.

Extras: Liquid Lightning, a water park with several slides, lockers, and a bathhouse; unlike most water parks, this one has heated water. This area requires a separate admission. Next to the front gate is a Grand Prix–style go-cart track.

Special events: Ice Cream Social, Memorial Day weekend; Fireworks, July 4; a three-day corn feast over Labor Day weekend.

Season: May through September.

Operating hours: Opens at 10:00 A.M. and closes at either 10:00 P.M. or midnight.

Admission policy: Pay-one-price, under $20. Special starlight admission after 5:00 P.M. every day saves $5. Parking charge.

Top rides: Thunder Canyon, a raging-rapids ride; a circa-1915, Philadelphia Toboggan Company carousel; a log flume; Excalibur, a large steel roller coaster; a gondola-style Ferris wheel from which you can see the Minnesota River Valley; Corkscrew, a steel corkscrew coaster; High Roller, a wooden roller coaster.

Plan to stay: 7½ hours.

Best way to avoid crowds: Come on weekdays, early in the day. The park is laid out in a circular pattern, and by sticking to the pattern, you'll have very little need to double back.

Directions: Located southwest of Minneapolis on Highway 101, 9 miles west of the intersection of Highways 13 and 35 West.

Nearby attractions: Minnesota Zoo; Canterbury Downs, horse racing; Murphy's Landing, a re-created, nineteenth-century village; Minnesota Harvard Apple Orchard, serving old-time apple dishes and music to match.

Mississippi

Fun Time USA
Highway 90 and Cowan Road
Gulfport, MS (601) 896–7315

Located on the beach, halfway between Gulfport and Biloxi, this small, clean park offers miniature golf, go-carts, a large arcade with video games, and Skee-ball. It also has 11 rides, including bumper boats, Tilt-A-Whirl, a small steel roller coaster, and 8 kiddie rides.

Admission is free, with rides on a pay-as-you-go basis. The park is open daily until midnight.

Magic Golf/Biloxi Beach Amusement Park
1785 Beach Boulevard
Biloxi, MS (601) 374-4338

The Gulf of Mexico provides a great backdrop for this family park with a fairyland theme. The beachside park has 13 rides, "magical" miniature golf, go-carts, and a games arcade. The Ferris wheel; Dragon, a roller coaster; and bumper cars are the most popular rides. A small kiddieland features 6 rides for the wee ones.

There is no charge to get in and everything is on a pay-as-you-play basis. Hours vary; call first.

Missouri

Fun Spot
West Highway 76
Branson, MO (417) 334-5979

This busy family park along the strip in Branson has 12 rides, including 6 for children; a miniature golf course; and go-carts.

Among the adult rides, the Ferris wheel, bumper cars, and the Scrambler are the most popular. The little ones especially like the kiddie bumper cars, the kiddie raceway, and the kiddie go-carts. Batting cages, arcade games, and Skee-ball are also available.

There is no admission charge; all rides and games are on a pay-as-you-play basis. Hours vary; call first.

Silver Dollar City
Off Highway 76
Branson, MO (417) 338-2611

Far from the glitter, glitz, and country music sounds of nearby Branson, this turn-of-the-century theme park started out as a place that offered tours of Marvel Cave and has grown to be an oasis for frontier craftspeople. The park's resident crafts colony now numbers more than 100, with 40 demonstrating their talents at any one time among the hilly, well-shaded acreage.

Among the quaint architecture, you'll find 13 rides, including 6 for kids.

Food service: 9 sit-down restaurants, including The Mill and The Mine, where you'll find everything from steak and shrimp to fried chicken. This may be the best overall food park in the country next to Disney and Universal Studios. Most of the food is made in the park and served fresh and tasty.

Entertainment: More than a dozen different shows are performed daily, including a country hoedown, an evening musical presentation, and various other shows featuring Cajun and southern gospel music.

Extras: A 55-minute guided tour of Marvel Cave is free with admission to the park.

TIM'S TRIVIA

The Riverview Carousel, now located at Six Flags Over Georgia in Atlanta, was built in 1908 for Riverview Park in Chicago. While there, it was ridden by Al Capone, William Randolph Hearst, and President Warren G. Harding, among others.

Special Events: Flower and Garden Show, April; Olde Country Folk Festival, featuring European performers, May; National Quilt Festival, late August; National Crafts Festival, September and October; Ozark Mountain Christmas, November through mid-December.

Season: Mid-April through mid-December.

Operating hours: 9:30 A.M. to 6:00 or 7:00 P.M. during peak season.

Admission policy: Pay-one-price, under $20. Free parking.

Top rides: Great Shoot-out, a ride-through shooting gallery; Lost River of the Ozarks, a raging-rapids ride; Great American Plunge, a log flume; Frisco, a steam train.

Plan to stay: 7 hours.

Best way to avoid crowds: The park is laid out in a circle; pick up a map and follow the circle without doubling back or crossing over. Weekdays, as well as spring and fall weekends, entail fewer people.

Directions: Located off Highway 76, 9 miles west of Branson, 40 miles south of Springfield.

Nearby attractions: White Water, a water park; 26 music theaters in nearby Branson; Table Rock Lake, a recreation area.

Six Flags Mid-America
Six Flags Outer Road
Eureka, MO (314) 938–4800

Nicely landscaped and full of action, this 200-acre park is a member of the Six Flags family and has many of the same accouterments, including the Looney Tunes characters and a children's area built around the cartoon bunch.

Spread out among the trees and the theming of the six areas are 28 rides. In each area, the rides, architecture and activities all carry out the theme of the area—the United States, France, Illinois, Missouri, Spain, or England.

You enter the park through the Missouri section, which has a turn-of-the-century theme and includes the magnificent Palace Music Hall, where the major musical productions are held.

TIM'S TRIVIA

The Screamin' Eagle wooden roller coaster at Six Flags Mid-America, Eureka, Missouri, was painted with Sears Weatherbeater paint and featured in Sears's 1990 commercials.

Food service: 6 restaurants, including the full-service D.J.'s Diner; the Stockyards, creating tasty barbecue platters; and Wascals's, serving a noteworthy hamburger and fries platter. Portable carts and small stands are also located throughout. The information guide handed to you when you enter the park has information on special "meal deals" and which restaurants serve them.

Entertainment: 9 shows, including a dolphin presentation, high divers, ragtime song and dance, nostalgia musical shows, and an ice show.

Extras: Food may not be brought into the park; however, adjacent to the parking lot is a fantastic picnic area, just for guests. It has plenty of shaded tables, a nice lake in the middle (with lots of hungry ducks), and bathrooms.

Special events: 3 Joy Celebration, Christian music weekends, mid-April, late June, and late September; Country Fair, weekends in September; Fright Nights, weekends in late October.

Season: April through October.

Operating hours: Opens at 10:00 A.M. every day and closes at 9:00 P.M. on weeknights, midnight on Fridays, and 11:00 P.M. on Saturdays and Sundays.

Admission policy: Pay-one-price, under $20. Special sponsored promotions run throughout the summer, letting you enter after 5:00 P.M. for half-price. Second-day admission available for under $5 additional. Parking charge.

Top rides: Screamin' Eagle, a wooden roller coaster; Colossus, a giant Ferris wheel; Ninja, a corkscrew, looping steel roller coaster; Grand Ole Carousel, a circa-1915 Philadelphia Toboggan Company carousel.

Plan to stay: 8 hours.

Best way to avoid crowds: The least busy days are Tuesdays, Wednesdays, and Thursdays. Otherwise, come early, get a map, plan the shows you want to see, and try to avoid doubling back.

Directions: Take the Allenton exit off I–44, 30 minutes southwest of St. Louis. The park is located there on the service road.

Nearby attractions: Meramec Caverns, where Jesse James hung out; St. Louis Zoo; St. Louis Arch; plus riverfront activities and restaurants along the Mississippi River in St. Louis.

Worlds of Fun
4545 Worlds of Fun Avenue
Kansas City, MO (816) 454–4545

Jules Verne's *Around the World in Eighty Days* is the theme of this 170-acre park, with each of its five areas representing different parts of the world—the Orient, Scandinavia, Europe, Africa, and America.

All food, rides, games, and architecture in each area reflect its theme. The park has 35 rides, including 14 for kids and Pandamonium, a kids' play area. After crossing the gangplank and entering the park, you'll find that the rides and attractions are laid out in a big circle, making the park easy to get around in. You'll never be too far from anything.

Food service: Inn of the Four Winds—a large, sit-down restaurant providing an all-you-can-eat buffet—plus 25 other eateries offering everything from breakfast entrees to burritos.

Entertainment: 7 shows, including a dolphin show, a Broadway musical extravaganza, puppet and costumed-character shows, and a country hoedown.

The Screamin' Eagle roller coaster at Six Flags Mid-America in Eureka, Missouri, thrills riders at 62-miles-per-hour.

Extras: The Forum Amphitheatre presents top-name entertainment throughout the season, extra charge. Shaded picnic areas located outside the park, adjacent to the parking lot.

Special events: Christian Music Festival, spring; Big Thrill, a re-creation of the sock-hop days, fall; Oktoberfest, October.

Season: April through October.

Operating hours: 10:00 A.M. to 9:00 or 10:00 P.M.

Admission policy: Pay-one-price, under $20; in after 3:00 P.M., next day free. Second-day ticket available for $6 extra. Parking charge.

Top rides: Timber Wolf, a wooden roller coaster; Orient Express, a looping steel coaster; Fury of the Nile, a raging-rapids ride; Python Plunge, a wet/dry water slide using one-person boats; Viking Voyager, a log flume.

Plan to stay: 9 hours.

Best way to avoid crowds: Come on weekdays during the peak season or on Sundays in spring and fall. Go to the farthest distance from the gate and work toward the front.

Directions: Located on I–435 at Exit 54, just north of the Missouri River.

Nearby attractions: Oceans of Fun, a tropical water park, directly adjacent to Worlds of Fun.

Nebraska

Peony Park
Cass at 81st Street
Omaha, NE (402) 391–6253

America at the turn of the century is the theme of this pretty, 40-acre park, close to the center of the city. As you enter the park, you'll be face to face with a unique water clock and waterwheel. Brick walks take you past shops and eateries, and at night the quaint streetlights add a nice glow to the park.

With 20 rides, including 7 just for kids, the park is a popular playground for the entire region.

Food service: 3 food outlets, including the Little Chef, for grilled hamburgers, and the Well's Blue Bunny, an ice-cream parlor. Food may be brought into the park, and picnic tables are available throughout and in the picnic pavilion.

Entertainment: Daily shows change on a weekly basis. One week you might find a juggling troupe; the next, a mime.

Extras: A ¼-mile sand-beach swimming pool with 4 water slides.

Special events: The park hosts the Muscular Dystrophy telethon over Labor Day weekend and features special entertainment. Also held over Labor Day is a three-day Italian festival.

Season: Mid-May through September.

Operating hours: During the week, noon to 8:00 P.M.; on weekends, 11:00 A.M. to 9:00 P.M.

Admission policy: General admission, with rides and attractions on a pay-as-you-go basis. Pay-one-price also available for slides, pool, and rides, under $15. Free parking.

Top rides: Galaxy, a compact steel roller coaster; Flying Bobs and Trabant, both spinning thrill rides; bumper cars.

Plan to stay: 4 hours.

Best way to avoid crowds: There's seldom a wait of more than 5 minutes for any ride during the week.

Directions: Take the Dodge Street exit off I–80 and go east to 81st Street. Turn left; the park is 1 block down.

Nearby attractions: Omaha Zoo; Kart Ranch, go-carts and miniature golf; Fun Plex, go-carts and an arcade; Putt-Putt, miniature golf.

Nevada

MGM Grand Movie Theme Park
3805 Las Vegas Boulevard
Las Vegas, NV (702) 739–1500

When the MGM Grand Hotel reopens in 1992, it not only will have been totally renovated, but also it will have an adult-oriented movie theme park in its backyard. The hotel will also have the same movieland theme.

A combination of movie-oriented rides, shows, and participatory attractions will be the backbone of the $250 million facility.

Playland Park
In Idlewild City Park
1900 Cowon Drive
Reno, NV (702) 329–6008

Billing itself as the "biggest little playground in the world," this neat little amusement area is located next to the Truckee River in Idlewild Park, about a mile from downtown Reno.

It has 7 rides that almost everyone in the family can enjoy together, including a Tilt-A-Whirl, a train rides, tea cups, and a small steel roller coaster. A public swimming pool is also located in the city park. Adjacent to the rides is a large playground operated by the Reno Arch Lions Club.
Playland is open daily from mid-May through October 11:00 A.M. to 6:00 P.M. and on weekends during the rest of the year, weather permitting.
Admission is free, with rides on a pay-as-you-play basis.

Riviera Amusement Pavilion
2901 Las Vegas Boulevard South
Las Vegas, NV (702) 734–5110

This 20-ride indoor amusement facility is set for a 1992 opening. Attached to the Riviera Hotel and Casino, the large structure will also house a food court and a games-of-skill midway.
One highlight of the park will be a 90-foot-high Ferris wheel that will provide a view of the Las Vegas skyline through the glass atrium.

New Hampshire

Canobie Lake Park
North Policy Street
Salem, NH (603) 893–3506

The screams and the clickety-click from the big old wooden roller coaster greet you as you enter this wonderful old traditional park. The coaster runs out into the parking lot and past the main entrance, providing a great preview of things to come.
Unlike most traditional parks, this one has almost all the original buildings, dating back to 1902, still standing and in use. The tranquil lakeside setting forms the backdrop for 40 rides, including 12 for kids. The Old Canobie Village area of the park has a turn-of-the-century theme and offers a rustic look at early New Hampshire.
The big stone fountain was in operation when the park opened, as was the carousel building, just inside the main entrance. The picnic pavilions are almost always packed with local parties and company picnics—a sure sign of a popular park.
Food service: 4 sit-down restaurants and 6 walk-away fast-food and snack locations. The Portofino serves grinders, pizza, and Italian food, with seating overlooking the lake. The International Food Plaza is a food court offering cuisine from 5 countries, and the Wharf Restaurant features a full menu, including chicken and fish.

Entertainment: 5 shows feature Broadway and country music, a children's presentation, a magic show, and the Canobie Critters, a group of costumed characters.

Extras: A swimming pool and a 20-minute excursion on the lake aboard the 150-passenger *Canobie Queen* paddle-wheel boat, both included in park admission.

Special events: Corvette Show, May; Hot Rod Show, July; Fireworks, every Saturday night during July and August.

Season: Mid-April through Labor Day.

Operating hours: Noon to 10:00 P.M.

Admission policy: Pay-one-price, under $15. Discount of $5 after 6:00 P.M. Free parking.

Top rides: Yankee Cannonball, a wooden roller coaster; Policy Pond Sawmill, a log flume; Haunted Mine, a dark ride; Psycho-Drome, an indoor Scrambler with lights and sound effects; Canobie Corkscrew, a steel corkscrew coaster; Canobie Express, a steam train; a 90-foot-tall, gondola-style Ferris wheel with a computerized, nighttime light show; a 1906 Looff/Dentzel antique carousel, with some horses dating back to the 1880s.

Plan to stay: 7 hours.

Best way to avoid crowds: Come early in the day or late afternoon during the week. The weekends are quite busy with commercial picnics and party groups.

Directions: Take the Salem exit (Exit 2) off Route 93 and turn left at the light. Follow Policy Street down about ½ mile to the park. Located 35 minutes from Boston.

Nearby attractions: Rockingham Race Track, daily horse racing; Robert Frost Homestead; America's Stonehenge.

Story Land
Route 16
Glen, NH (603) 383–4293

Fairy tales do come true, and it could happen to you if you visit this magical, child-size world where well-known tales come to life. The heavily wooded, beautiful grounds appeal as much to adults as the activities do to children.

There are 15 family rides.

Food service: Several eateries with a storybook theme, including a sit-down restaurant with line service. Picnics may be brought into the park.

Entertainment: Two shows: a live musical and an animated character show called Farm Follies.

Season: Father's Day through Columbus Day.

Operating hours: 9:00 A.M. to 6:00 P.M.

Admission policy: Pay-one price, under $15. Free parking.

Top rides: Dr. Geyser's Remarkable Raft Ride, a tamed-down version of the raging-rapids ride; a walrus-shaped kiddie coaster; *Story Land Queen,* a boat ride on the lake in a large swan; Pirate Ship, a participatory ride on the lake wherein the 30 passengers all row the boat; Pumpkin Coach Ride, taking the rider up to Cinderella's Castle; Voyage to the Moon, a dark ride in a bullet-shaped rocket ship with a Jules Verne theme.

Plan to stay: 6 hours. A park official says that the "park usually outlasts the kids."

Best way to avoid crowds: The park is least busy on weekends, due to the travel patterns of this part of New England.

Directions: Located in the White Mountain National Forest area, 6 miles north of North Conway, on Route 16, just north of the intersection of Routes 16 and 302.

New Jersey

The following six parks are grouped together because they all share one big attraction—the Atlantic Ocean. They are located on the boardwalk, along with many other attractions, restaurants, and activities. They are not theme parks, and most have no entertainment within the park itself. They are good old-fashioned seafront amusement parks. Go to each one and enjoy!

Casino Pier
Boardwalk at Grant Avenue
Seaside Heights, NJ (201) 793-6488

If only the old-time fisherman could see this pier now. Though Casino Pier was used as a fishing pier until 1933, the old salts left quickly when the rides moved in. The pier has the best selection of rides and attractions in Seaside Heights, with a total of 31 rides, including 10 just for the tykes.

Don't miss the wonderful, circa-1910 Dentzel/Looff carousel, called the Dr. Floyd Moreland Carousel; some of its hand-carved animals date back to the 1890s. Other rides include the Nightmare Manor, a ride-through haunted house; the Wizard's Cavern, a steel roller coaster; Colorado River, a log flume; and the Poltergeist, an indoor Scrambler.

Make sure you eat at Meatball City or play a round of miniature golf on the rooftop course. Waterworks, a water park owned by the same people, is located across the street and has 27 attractions.

Free admission, with rides and attractions on a pay-as-you-go basis (no pay-one-price available). Open from mid-April through September. Opens during the summer months at 1:00 P.M. and closes at various times.

Fun City Amusement Park
Boardwalk at 32nd Street
Sea Isle City, NJ (609) 263-3862

A good array of rides can be found at this block-long seaside park, which is open daily from 6:30 to 11:00 P.M. There are 19 rides, including 11 kiddies. Among the highlights are a beautiful 1949 Allan Herschell carousel in mint condition, a Tilt-A-Whirl, Flying Bobs, and Big Valley, a music ride.

The park is open Memorial Day through Labor Day and has free admission, with rides on a pay-as-you-go basis.

Fun Town Pier
Boardwalk at Porter Avenue
Seaside Heights, NJ (201) 830-9262

What a unique log-flume ride they have here! It's quite an experience to be riding a water ride high above the park and to look out onto the Atlantic Ocean and see a seaworthy freighter chugging by not much faster than you're going.

In addition to the flume ride, this park features 23 other rides, including 13 for children. Here you'll find the popular tank-tag ride/game, a looping roller coaster called the Roller Coast Loop, and the Giant Wheel, a ride that also provides a great view of the oceanfront. And where else can you touch a live shark for only six tickets?

Opening for limited operation on Easter Sunday, the park remains in operation until the third week of September. Closing times vary, depending on weather and season, but rides crank up daily at noon. Admission is free, with rides and attractions on a pay-as-you-go basis (no pay-one-price is available).

Jenkinson's Pavilion
3 Broadway
Point Pleasant Beach, NJ (201) 892-0844

Stretched out along a mile-long boardwalk, this facility has 50 rides and a wide selection of just about anything you'd ever want while on a boardwalk, including 2 miniature golf courses, batting cages, and gift and souvenir shops.

There are more than 50 walk-up eateries, including the Pavilion Restaurant, seating up to 1,500; a candy shop; a bar; and a nightclub. Live musical entertainment occurs nightly, with a free concert on the beach every Wednesday night, and fireworks take place every Thursday. Events are scheduled year-round at the pavilion.

Among the more popular rides are the Himalaya; Galleon, a swinging pirate ship; Spider; and a Ferris wheel.

The park is open April through October, and the games arcade is open every day of the year. There's no admission charge, with all rides and attractions on a pay-as-you-go basis.

Playland
1020 Boardwalk at 10th Street
Ocean City, NJ (609) 399–4757

Partly indoors, partly outdoors, this boardwalk entertainment complex has 17 rides, including 11 for kids. The carousel and arcade games are inside, while the larger rides are behind a large, circa-1940 expo building.

Rides include a merry-go-round; Dragon, a roller coaster; Tilt-A-Whirl; a Ferris wheel; and a train ride.

Free admission, with rides and attractions on a pay-as-you-go basis. The arcade opens at 10:00 A.M., the rides at 1:00 P.M., and everything closes at 10:30 P.M.

Wonderland Pier
Boardwalk at 6th Street
Ocean City, NJ (609) 399–7082

This is one of the nicest seafront parks on the East Coast. Family operated, the park offers a clean, well-supervised entertainment area, with 32 rides, including 7 for kids. Two costumed characters, Wonder and Landy, walk the park daily.

Part of the complex is indoors, so don't let the bad weather keep you away from the boardwalk. The circa-1925 Philadelphia Toboggan Company carousel, in beautiful condition, is the focal point of the rest of the rides, which include a monorail; a giant Ferris wheel; the Zugspitze, a Himalaya ride; City Jet, a compact steel roller coaster; and the Raiders, a kid's participatory play unit.

The season runs from Memorial Day through mid-September and is open from noon to midnight daily. Admission is free, with rides and attractions on a pay-as-you-go basis (no pay-one-price available). The same family also owns Gillian's WaterWonderland, a water park, 1 block south on the boardwalk.

■ ■ ■

Action Park
Route 94
McAfee, NJ (201) 827-2000

If you're a passive type of park-goer who likes things done for you, you're out of luck here—this is a unique, "self-operated" park in which you do the work . . . and you have the fun.

As part of the 200-acre Great Gorge Ski Area, the park is located in a lovely mountainside setting with abundant trees and landscaping. There are three distinct areas: Water World, Alpine Center, and Motor World.

Bring your bathing suit—park officials say theirs is the world's largest water park.

Food service: 9 stands, including Alpine Center, a sit-down, cafeteria-style diner.

Entertainment: Daily entertainment includes a rock-and-roll show, jugglers, roving mimes, and a magic show called the Famed Illusion Maker.

Extras: Miniature golf and Grand Prix raceway, extra charge.

Special events: Polka Festival, Memorial Day; Irish Festival, first week in August; German Festival, last week in August.

Season: Memorial Day through early September.

Operating hours: 10:00 A.M. to 9:00 P.M.

Admission policy: Pay-one-price, under $25. Free parking.

Top rides: Aerodium, in which a DC-3 jet engine provides enough up-lift for people to float midair; Transmobile, a people mover resembling a sideway monorail; Colorado River, a raging-rapids ride; Roaring Springs, an 8-acre water-activity area with spas; speedboats; auto races; a chair lift; Tidal Wave, a wave pool.

Plan to stay: 8 hours.

Best way to avoid crowds: Tuesdays are the slowest; weekends are packed!

Directions: Take the Route 23 exit off I–80 and go north to Route 94. Go north on Route 94 for 2 miles. The park spans both sides of the highway. Located between McAfee and Vernon.

Nearby attractions: Franklin Mineral Museum; Space Farms Zoo and Museum; plus other activities at Great Gorge, including tennis, golf, spas, restaurants, and overnight lodging.

Bowcraft Amusement Park
Route 22
Scotch Plains, NJ (201) 233–0675

This well-kept, little park is located in the foothills of the Watchung Mountain and caters to young families with kids from 3 through the midteen years. With 18 rides that the entire family can enjoy together, as well as plenty of games and other activities, the park offers something for everyone.

Food service: 3 walk-up locations, serving fast-food items like hot dogs, and hamburgers. Another eatery features ice cream and snacks. Food may be brought into the park.

Entertainment: Costumed characters are occasionally in the park. There is no regularly scheduled in-park entertainment.

Extras: 18-hole miniature golf course and a 150-game arcade.

Season: Palm Sunday through Thanksgiving. The arcade is open year-round.

Operating hours: 10:00 A.M. to 10:00 P.M.

Admission policy: Free admission, with rides and attractions on a pay-as-you-play basis (no pay-one-price available). Free parking.

Top rides: Bumper cars; Ferris wheel; Tilt-A-Whirl; a train ride around the park; Elephant Tower, a pink pachyderm kiddie ride.

Plan to stay: 2 hours.

Best way to avoid crowds: Come during the week, any time of day.

Directions: Take Exit 140 (Route 22) off the Garden State Parkway and go west 7 miles to the park. Located 15 miles from Newark.

Nearby attractions: Drake House Museum; Washington Rock State Park; Wallace House and Old Dutch Parsonage.

Captain Good Times
Whitman Plaza Shopping Center
Route 42 and Whitman Drive
Turnersville, NJ (609) 227–5437

Located indoors in its own storefront, this family entertainment center has 6 kiddie rides and a large participatory play area. Regularly scheduled live entertainment and an animatronic musical revue are featured. Food service consists of an ice-cream parlor and a deli.

Admission is free, with rides on a pay-as-you-go basis, or a pay-one-price ticket is available, under $10. Hours vary; call first.

Casino Pier, see page 100.

Central Pier
1400 Boardwalk
Atlantic City, NJ (609) 348-4201

An ornate entrance area welcomes visitors to this last remaining amusement pier along the world's oldest boardwalk. The reconditioned park offers 12 rides, including 5 for kids. Unlike many parks along the coast, the rides here are mostly portable rides and are taken down each fall and put up in the spring.

Open daily from Easter Sunday through Labor Day. Free admission, with rides on a pay-as-you-go basis (no pay-one-price available).

Clementon Amusement Park
Route 534, Berlin Road
Clementon, NJ (609) 783-0263

The 15-acre Clementon Lake provides the centerpiece for this well-kept traditional park. Several old buildings date back to the park's founding in 1907 and give the 50-acre park a nostalgic ambience.

Among the 25 rides is the second oldest operating wooden roller coaster in North America. There are 8 kiddie rides in an appealing little shaded kiddieland.

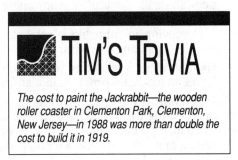

TIM'S TRIVIA

The cost to paint the Jackrabbit—the wooden roller coaster in Clementon Park, Clementon, New Jersey—in 1988 was more than double the cost to build it in 1919.

Food service: 5 snack and fast-food outlets, with a large outside terrace seating area. Food—but no alcohol—may be brought into the park.

Entertainment: Clowns, jugglers, face painter, high divers, and a disk jockey on weekends.

Extras: Softball; volleyball and basketball courts; many large picnic pavilions.

Special events: Fireworks, July 4.

Season: Late April through Labor Day.

Operating hours: Noon to 10:00 P.M., Tueday through Sunday; closed Monday.

Admission policy: Pay-one-price, under $10. After–5:00 P.M. discount. Free parking.

Top rides: Jack Rabbit, a circa-1919 wooden roller coaster; a circa-1919 Philadelphia Toboggan Company carousel; a Whip; Neptune's Revenge, a log-flume in the lake; Sea Dragon, a pirate ship.

Plan to stay: 5 hours.

Best way to avoid crowds: Tuesdays are least crowded.

Directions: Take Exit 3 off the New Jersey Turnpike. Go south 4 miles on Route 168 to Route 534. Go east on 534 for 4 more miles; the park is on the right.

Nearby attractions: Edmund Scientific Company, in nearby Barrington, sells unusual and hard-to-find scientific equipment; open to the public and well worth the trip.

Fantasy Island
320 West Seventh Street
Beach Haven, NJ (609) 492–4000

Victoriana—that's what this pleasant park is all about. From the brick sidewalks and immaculate landscaping to the Tiffany lights in the arcade, the atmosphere here is Victorian.

Occupying an entire block just 2 blocks from the beach, the park has 16 rides, including 9 for kids.

Food service: 3 locations: food court, Sugar Shack, and Fantasy Delights, an ice-cream parlor. Indoor and patio seating available.

Entertainment: Jugglers, clowns, and costumed characters at various times during the day. Scheduled entertainment includes a reptile show and a magic presentation. For one month each summer, the Mechanical Man, a mime that acts like a robot, performs.

Extras: Miniature golf, extra charge.

Special events: Every Friday night, a pay-one-price special discount with live entertainment; Fireworks, July 4; Soap Opera Festival, date varies from year to year.

Season: Park is open Memorial Day through Labor Day; the arcade, year-round on weekends and daily during summer.

Operating hours: The park opens at 5:00 P.M. during the week and at 1:00 P.M. Friday through Sunday; it closes at varying times, depending on crowds and weather. The arcade opens at noon.

Admission policy: Free admission, with rides and attractions on a pay-as-you-play basis. Pay-one-price specials on Friday night. Parking at meters nearby.

Top rides: Sea Dragon, a swinging pirate ship; bumper cars; kiddie boats; a train ride; a carousel.

Plan to stay: 4 hours.

Best way to avoid crowds: Come on a sunny day; everyone else is at the beach.

Directions: Take the Garden State Parkway to Exit 63 (Route 72). Take Route 72 east until it dead-ends on Long Beach Island. Turn right and go 7 miles; the park is on the right.

Nearby attractions: Plenty of water activities nearby—the beach is 2 blocks away and the bay 1 block down the street.

Fun City Amusement Park, see page 101.

Fun Town Pier, see page 101.

Hunts Pier, see page 108.

Jenkinson's Pavilion, see page 101.

Keansburg Amusement Park
75 Beachway
Keansburg, NJ (201) 495-1400

This neat little seaside park, overlooking the Atlantic Ocean, is a mecca for the entire family. With 25 of the 41 rides especially for kids, it's no wonder the park is a favorite among local families. In all, there are more than 150 rides, games, eateries, and attractions located along the ¼-mile walkway adjacent to the beach.

Food service: 14 locations, including 2 sit-down restaurants featuring seafood and Italian cuisine.

Entertainment: There is no regularly scheduled in-park entertainment.

Extras: Go-carts, water slides, batting cages, a mirror maze, miniature golf, and an Olympic-sized swimming pool, all at an extra charge.

Special events: Fireworks, July 3; Anniversary Celebration, featuring discounted prices and a fireworks show, a Monday in August.

Season: Palm Sunday through mid-October.

Operating hours: Opens daily at noon; closes at 11:00 P.M. during the week and at midnight on weekends.

Admission policy: All rides and attractions on a pay-as-you-play basis (no pay-one-price available). Fridays from 6:00 to 9:00 P.M., all rides 50 percent off. Kiddie rides are 25 cents each and adult rides are 50 percent off every Tuesday from noon to 6:00 P.M. Parking charge in lot or park at meters on street.

Top rides: Spook House, a ride-through dark ride; Screamin' Demon, a compact steel roller coaster; bumper cars; a Himalaya ride; Trabant.

Plan to stay: 4 hours.

Best way to avoid crowds: Mondays are the slowest; spring weekends are very seldom crowded.

Directions: Take Exit 117 off the Garden State Parkway. Follow Route 36 east for 4 miles. Turn right at the sign for Keansburg Beach and go 1½ miles; the park is on the left. Located just south of the New York State line.

Nearby attractions: Telegraph Hill, a park; Gateway National Recreation Area; Sandy Hook Lighthouse; Fort Hancock.

The following four seaside amusement parks are all located along the wooden boardwalk in Wildwood. Like similar boardwalk parks, they are surrounded by many restaurants, arcades, and shops.

Hunts Pier
2700 Boardwalk
Wildwood, NJ (609) 522–2429

The great thing about this pier is the lineup of custom rides that the original owners had built each summer. A few remain, including Hunt's Horror, a dark ride: Golden Nugget Mine Train, combining an indoor coaster and a dark ride; and the Keystone Kops, a ride-through.

These unique rides are joined by 14 additional adult rides and 10 for kids. Other rides of note are the Kamikaze, a five-inversion steel roller coaster; a log flume; bumper cars; and a small raging-rapids raft ride. A rooftop miniature golf course, located across the boardwalk, is also owned by the park.

The park is open from Easter Sunday through mid-September. Admission is free, with rides and attractions on a pay-as-you-play basis. A pay-one-price wristband is available and is good for both this park and Nickel's Midway Pier, just down the boardwalk.

Mariner's Landing
Boardwalk at Schellenger Avenue
Wildwood, NJ (609) 729–0586

The park's huge Ferris wheel, located halfway out on the pier, has become a Wildwood landmark, and at night, when its lights are on, it can be seen for miles. This 6½-acre park, high above the sandy beaches of the Atlantic, has 32 rides, including a Zyklon roller coaster and the Sea Serpent boomerang roller coaster. In addition, the park has bumper cars and a nice family carousel.

Because space is at a premium along the coast, every inch is used, which accounts for a unique structure here that houses a miniature golf

New Jersey

course, water slides, and a go-cart track, all intertwined. It's a great use of space and adds a different experience to all three attractions.

The park is owned by the same family that runs Morey's Pier (see below); the prices, hours and season are the same as listed for that entry.

Morey's Pier
Boardwalk at Twenty-fifth Street
Wildwood, NJ (609) 522-5477

It's amazing how many fun things a person can squeeze into a small space. Here you'll find the widest variety of attractions on any amusement pier in the United States, including a three-tiered log flume and a multilevel water park at the ocean end of the facility. Counting all three built-up levels, there are about 6½ acres of usable space on the pier.

A total of 29 rides includes a compact steel roller coaster, a dark ride called Dante's Inferno, a high-flying Condor, and a giant slide. The theme of the miniature golf course is the history of Wildwood.

Open from Easter Sunday through mid-September. Admission is free, with rides and attractions on a pay-as-you-go basis. Pay-one-price also available, under $15. All tickets are good at this park and at Mariner's Landing, which is owned by the same family. Water-park admission on both piers is separate.

Nickel's Midway Pier
Boardwalk at Schellenger Avenue
Wildwood, NJ (609) 522-2542

On the land side of the boardwalk, this pier has the state's only remaining walk-through haunted castle, complete with flaming torches at the entranceway. Called Castle Dracula, the place is also one of the most popular attractions along the boardwalk.

The 23 rides consists of 18 for kids and 5 that the entire family can enjoy, such as the Dragon, a roller coaster; bumper boats; bumper cars; and the ever-popular 4X4 trucks.

Open during peak season from noon to midnight, the operation begins each spring on Easter Sunday and closes at the end of September. Free admission, with rides and attractions on a pay-as-you-go basis. Pay-one-price also available, under $10. Every Wednesday is "Wacky Wednesday," when pay-one-price passes are discounted.

Tickets purchased here are also valid on Hunts Pier.

During peak season, rides open at noon and close at various times, depending on weather and crowds.

■ ■ ■

Playland, see page 102.

Children of all ages enjoy the scaled-down version of a 1910 American Mercer at Old Tucson Studios, in Tucson, Arizona.

Six Flags Great Adventure
Route 537
Jackson, NJ (201) 928–2000

This is the largest amusement park facility along the East Coast and gets much of its business from the New York and Philadelphia markets.

The 1,100-acre park has no overall theme, but some of the individual sections do, including the Old West, Bugs Bunny Land, and a games area called Good Times Square. In addition to the ride park with 43 rides, is a drive-through safari, considered the largest such facility in the world.

Several fantasy buildings were constructed when the park was built in 1974, including the Yum Yum Palace, a giant tipi and a huge covered wagon. These are unique and make great photos—especially the Yum Yum Palace, shaped like an ice-cream sundae.

Food service: 32 eateries, plus mobile stands and carts during peak periods. There are 3 sit-down, buffet-style restaurants, including the Yum Yum Palace, ice cream; Best of the West, barbecue and chicken; and Gingerbread Fancy, chicken and biscuits.

Entertainment: 8 shows, including a dolphin/sea lion exhibition; fireworks every Friday, Saturday, and Sunday night; a magic show; high divers; and a movie at the Adventure Theatre. In addition, there are street performers and Looney Tunes costumed characters.

Extras: Big-name entertainers are brought into the Great Arena throughout the summer; the admission is included in the pay-one-price ticket.

Special events: Kidsfest, July and August; Oktoberfest, late September to mid-October; Halloweekends, last two weekends in October.

Season: Late March through Halloween weekend in October.

Operating hours: Opens at 10:00 A.M.; closes at 10:00 P.M. on weekdays and at 11:00 P.M. on Saturdays and Sundays.

Admission policy: Pay-one-price includes park and safari, under $25. A safari ticket may be purchased separately. An evening discount goes into effect at 4:00 P.M. Make sure you get your ticket validated for $5, and it will be good for another admission anytime during the season. Parking charge.

Top rides: Great American Scream Machine, a 173-foot-tall, looping steel roller coaster; Shockwave, a stand-up roller coaster with two loops; Roaring Rapids, a raging-rapids ride; Lightnin' Loops, a pair of interlocked shuttle-loop coasters; Parachuter's Perch, a 250-foot-tall parachute drop; a circa-1890 Savage Gallopers carousel that runs clockwise; Adventure Rivers, a series of 10 wet/dry raft-ride experiences.

Plan to stay: All day and into the evening, 8 to 10 hours.

Best way to avoid crowds: Avoid weekends if you want to stay out of crowds. Come early during the week or just before dinnertime. Ride the big rides first. Pick up a free park map when you enter, and plot your course.

Directions: Take Exit 7A off the New Jersey Turnpike, go east on I–195 to Exit 16, and head south on Route 537 for 1½ miles. Follow signs to the park. Located 50 miles from Philadelphia and 60 miles from New York City.

Storybook Land
Black Horse Pike
Cardiff, NJ (609) 641–7847

You'll be greeted by a very tall Mother Goose as you approach this intriguing park. Opened in 1955, it has become a tradition in the area. Kids who came here long ago are now bringing their own children to enjoy the fun.

This wonderful world of fantasy has 8 kiddie rides, including a train, a carousel, antique cars, and a flying elephant. A petting zoo and costumed characters are also part of the experience. A special month-long "Fantasy with Lights" Christmas celebration features more than 200,000 lights in the park and Mr. and Mrs. Santa in their home to welcome the kids.

Admission is pay-one-price, under $10. Hours vary; call first.

Tivoli Pier
Brighton Avenue and Boardwalk
Atlantic City, NJ (609) 340-3444

Inside the Trop World Casino, this two-level, 2-acre park has an Old Atlantic City theme. Nostalgic settings surround you when you enter, with the shows, rides, and restaurant reflecting the theme.
There are 5 rides that the entire family can ride.

Food service: Red Lips Saloon is a sit-down eatery serving a full menu of food items and beer and wine. The Drinkart serves snack foods and drinks.

Entertainment: The Red Lips Saloon Stage Show is a 65-minute musical revue. The Cavalcade of Stars is an animated show.

Season: Weekends only, September through June; daily, July and August. Closed for about 4 weeks in January or February for renovation and maintenance.

Operating hours: Summer: Opens at 4:00 P.M.; closes at 10:00 P.M. during the week and at midnight on the weekends. Winter: noon to 8:00 P.M.

Admission policy: Pay-one-price, under $10. A shows-only ticket available for half-price. Parking free with casino validation.

Top rides: Biggest Six, a Ferris wheel; Tivoli Plunge, a compact steel coaster; On The Boardwalk, a dark ride with an Atlantic City theme; Boardwalk Bumpers, bumper cars.

Plan to stay: 4 hours.

Best way to avoid crowds: Saturdays are most crowded.

Directions: Take the Atlantic City Expressway east to the end. Once in the city, turn right on Arctic Avenue. Go 8 blocks to Brighton Avenue; turn left and go 3 blocks to Boardwalk and Trop World.

Nearby attractions: Numerous casinos; Ocean One Mall, shopping; other boardwalk attractions and restaurants; beach and ocean.

Wonderland Pier, see page 102.

New Mexico

**Amusement Village
In Presidents Park
Muscatel Avenue off Highway 62–180
Carlsbad, NM (505) 887–0512**

Nestled against the scenic Pecos River, just four blocks from downtown Carlsbad, this little park has 20 rides, including 10 for kids. Rides include a Tilt-A-Whirl, Ferris wheel, and a train ride. The park also operates the *George Washington* paddle-wheel boat, a circa-1858 cruise vessel, and the smaller *Centennial Princess,* both offering tours of the diverse river environment.

A swimming beach, paddleboat rentals, games arcade, and concessions stands are also available. There are plenty of shaded picnic tables in and around the park.

Open daily during the summer midmorning to early evening, admission is free, with rides on a pay-as-you-go basis. Look for discount coupons for special pay-one-price promotions at local businesses.

Cliff's Amusement Park
**4800 Osuna NE
Albuquerque, NM (505) 881–9373**

Pinks, tans, and browns—the traditional Southwest colors are the dominant shades here, as is adobe architecture with a touch of frontier motif. Located in the middle of the city, in the middle of the desert, this 15-acre park doesn't have to work too hard to achieve its southwestern theme.

There are 21 rides, including 10 just for the wee ones, set in a separate kiddieland.

Food service: 8 food and drink locations, serving fast food and typical amusement park "fun" food. The nachos here are delicious; they're made in the park and are about as fresh and tasty as you'll find anywhere. Food may be brought into the park.

Entertainment: 3 shows daily: a musical revue, a comedy song-and-dance presentation, and a juggler.

Extras: A large game room and a midway lineup of carnival games.

Season: Mid-April through mid-October.

Operating hours: Weekdays, 6:00 to 10:00 P.M.; weekends, opens at 1:00 P.M and closes at 11:00 P.M. on Saturday and 9:00 P.M. on Sunday.

Admission policy: General admission fee includes all entertainment, with rides and attractions on a pay-as-you-play basis. Pay-one-price available on weeknights, under $15. Free parking.

Top rides: Rocky Mountain Rapids, a log flume; Yo-Yo, flying swings; Galaxy, a compact steel roller coaster; bumper cars.

Plan to stay: 4 hours.

Best way to avoid crowds: Come on weeknights early in the week.

Directions: Take the San Mateo exit off I–25 and go south on San Mateo for a short distance to Osuna. Turn left on Osuna; the park is a short distance.

Nearby attractions: Putt-Putt, miniature golf; Rio Grande Zoo; aerial ride up the Rocky Mountains; Indian Museum; Albuquerque Museum.

New York

Adventureland
2245 Broadhollow Road, Route 110
East Farmingdale, NY (516) 694–6868

The last thing you expect to see as you're driving along this crowded highway, known as the "downtown area of Long Island," is a first-class major amusement park.

TIM'S TRIVIA

Six Flags Great Adventure, in Jackson, New Jersey, has the largest drive-through safari outside Africa.

Located on 10 acres, this beautifully landscaped park has decorative brick sidewalks and is especially pretty at night. A large kiddieland is at one end of the park and offers 12 rides. In addition, there are 12 major rides and an 18-hole miniature golf course with a unique floating hole.

Food service: 1 large, 400-seat, line-service restaurant serves a wide menu of items. In addition, 5 others serve snacks and fast food.

Entertainment: A costumed-character mascot, Albert Adventureland, strolls the midway. Live concerts are booked in at various times during the summer.

Extras: The large arcade and restaurant are open year-round.

Season: Palm Sunday through Labor Day.

Operating hours: Noon to 11:00 P.M.

Admission policy: Free admission, with rides and attractions on a pay-as-you-go basis. Pay-one-price also available, under $15. Parking is free if you show a receipt for anything purchased at the park.

Top rides: 1313 Cemetery Way, a ride-through haunted house; Capt. Willy's Wild Water Ride, bumper boats; Looping Star; a compact steel roller coaster.

Plan to stay: 4 hours.

Best way to avoid crowds: Come any weeknight during the season and you'll rarely have a long wait.

Directions: Take Exit 49 (Route 110) off the Long Island Expressway and head south for 1½ miles. The park is on the left.

Nearby attractions: Splish Splash, a water park, owned by the same company that runs the park; Long Island Game Farm; Jones Beach, Fire Island, and other beach activities.

Astroland Amusement Park
1000 Surf Avenue
Brooklyn/Coney Island, NY (718) 372-0275

Ahh, Coney Island. This is where it all started, a long, long time ago. Amusement park roots lie under these sandy beaches. Today, the entertainment area of Coney Island is comprised of this park and various other clusters of rides, games, and attractions along the boardwalk.

Astroland consists of 22 rides, including for 14 kids. Among the 8 adult rides is the world renowned Cyclone wooden roller coaster. Built in 1927, it's the last operating coaster of the many that used to be along these boardwalks, including the Switchback Railway, the first roller coaster built in the United States, in 1884.

Food service: The park itself has 2 walk-up, fast-food stands, but within a few blocks are many other eateries, including the original Nathan's hot-dog stand, serving the most fantastic hot dogs in the world.

Entertainment: No regularly scheduled in-park entertainment.

Special events: Air Show, during the July 4 holiday period; Mermaid Parade, sponsored by a local historical group, June.

Season: Palm Sunday through September.

Operating hours: Noon to midnight.

Admission policy: Free admission with rides on a pay-as-you-go basis. Pay-one-price also offered, under $15. Though parking is available at meters along street, recommended parking is in the New York Aquarium parking lot adjacent to the park; the parking fee during the day includes admission to the aquarium.

Top rides: Cyclone, a wooden roller coaster, designated a New York Historic Landmark; a log flume; Dante's Inferno, a dark ride; Music Express; Breakdance.

Plan to stay: 3 hours.

Best way to avoid crowds: The last two weeks in June are the least crowded during the season. Come early to avoid the big after-work crowd.

Directions: Take Exit 7 South (Ocean Parkway South) off the Belt Parkway. Ocean Parkway curves onto Surf Avenue. Follow Surf to West 10th Street; the park is on the left.

Nearby attractions: Coney Island Beach and Boardwalk; Coney Museum, on boardwalk; other smaller ride areas scattered throughout the immediate area; New York Aquarium.

Darien Lake Theme Park
Route 77
Darien Center, NY (716) 599–4641

Billing itself as the state's largest entertainment and recreational complex, this park is located on 1,500 acres, which includes a 2,000-site campground.

There are 52 rides here, including 12 for kids, located in a separate area called Adventureland. The park is clean, easy to get around in, and offers a great deal of activity. A separate water park, Barracuda Bay, has 15 rides and activities and requires an additional fee.

Food service: 3 sit-down, table-service restaurants and 30 additional snack and fast-food outlets. Among the eateries are Maria's Italian Restaurant, Gold Dust Cafe, Ann's Country Chicken, Perry's Fountain Ice Cream parlor, and Señor Taco.

Entertainment: 7 different shows, including Cinema 2000, a Broadway musical revue, various music shows, a bird show, and a costumed-character production. There is also strolling entertainment.

Extras: The campground is an original: You can bring your own RV, or rent one of theirs. A general store is located within the camping area. Paddleboats, miniature golf, and go-carts are available for an additional fee.

Special events: Opening Day celebration, Memorial Day weekend; Custom Car Show, early June; July 4 fireworks and activities; in-park Triathlon, mid-July; Fiddling Championships, mid-July; Christian Fest, late August; International Festival, Labor Day weekend.

Season: Memorial Day through Labor Day.

Operating hours: 10:00 A.M. to 10:00 P.M. daily, except in June, when it closes at 5:00 P.M. on weekdays.

Admission policy: Pay-one-price, under $15. Discount tickets available at Tops Markets throughout the area. Parking charge.

Top rides: Predator, the state's largest wooden roller coaster; The Viper, a looping, corkscrew steel roller coaster; Grizzly Run, a raging-rapids ride; Giant Wheel, a 165-foot-tall Ferris wheel; and Ranger, a looping ship ride.

Plan to stay: 4 hours—6 if you go to Barracuda Bay.

Best way to avoid crowds: Come early in the day on all days. Mondays and Tuesdays are the slowest.

Directions: Located midway between Rochester and Buffalo. Take Exit 48A off the New York State Thruway and head south 5 miles on Route 77.

Nearby attractions: Holland Purchase Historical Museum; Niagara Falls, about 45 minutes away.

Deno's Wonder Wheel Park
1025 Boardwalk
Brooklyn/Coney Island, NY (718) 372–2592

The giant Wonder Wheel is another survivor of the old Coney Island rides lineup and has been officially declared a New York Historic Landmark. There are 23 rides here, 16 of them for kids. The circa-1920, 135-foot-tall, oceanside Wheel is the main attraction and the only one of its kind in the world. While most of the additional rides and attractions are relatively new, the Spook-a-Rama is an old dark ride.

Located along the boardwalk and adjacent to Astroland, the park is close to all other Coney Island attractions, rides, and food outlets. Pay-one-price is available, under $10. The park is open from noon daily and is in operation from mid-April through October.

The Enchanted Forest
Route 28
Old Forge, NY (315) 369–6145

If there's an amusement park in America that can be described as "way off the beaten path," this is it. Nestled in the heavily wooded hills of the Adirondack Mountains in the upstate area, the park can't be seen from the parking lot, because of the dense woods.

The 50-acre facility is a wet/dry park with a combination of water-park and amusement park rides. It's divided into four themes: Water Safari, the water park; Storybook Lane, a walk through the land of several storybook characters; Animal Lane, a petting zoo; and the Yukon, a western village.

There are 14 mechanical rides, including 7 for kids, and 24 water slides and activities, including a wave pool.

117

Food service: The Saloon and the Oasis Cafe are the 2 main eateries. Also here are an ice-cream shop and additional snack-food locations.

Entertainment: The circus has two shows daily, and the bear mascot, dressed in beachwear, can be seen walking the park throughout the day.

Extras: A large statue of Paul Bunyan, plus narrated visits to the cottages of some of the most famous storybook characters of all times, free with admission.

Season: Memorial Day through Labor Day.

Operating hours: 9:30 A.M. to 6:00 P.M.

Admission policy: Pay-one-price, under $15. "Siesta Savings" plan allows for next day free when you pay after 3:00 P.M.

Top rides: Tilt-A-Whirl; a Ferris wheel; bumper cars; a carousel; and Scrambler.

Plan to stay: 8 hours if you play in the water park.

Best way to avoid crowds: Come during early summer or midmorning during the peak season.

Directions: Located 1 hour north of the New York State Thruway (I–90). Take Exit 31 (Route 12) off I–90 near Utica, and go north on Route 12 for about 25 miles to Alder Creek. Take Route 28 north to Old Forge; the park is on Route 28, on the north side of the village.

Hold onto your hats! The Old West comes alive at Knott's Berry Farm, in Buena Park, California. (© 1991 Knott's Berry Farm)

Nearby attractions: Old Forge Lake Cruises, boat tours of the Fulton chain of lakes; camping and water activities, including boating, fishing, and swimming throughout the area on the various lakes; Nutty Putty, miniature golf. You can also visit the local landfill and see the bears, or you can take a chairlift to the top of a local ski mountain, where people go to see deer.

Falls Street Faire
235 Rainbow Boulevard
Niagara Falls, NY (800) 223–2557

Take a walk down a cobblestone street while you gaze into shops and restaurants with turn-of-the-century facades. Then take a rest and lean against one of the antique streetlights for a while.

That's what you'll be able to do when the doors to this new indoor entertainment center open. Modeled after a 1900s-style village street, the park will have 10 rides, including 4 just for kids; a large food court; a games arcade; and retail shops. The park was scheduled to open by the time this book went to press.

Plans call for a MotionMaster, wide-screen film, wherein the seats move in conjunction with the scenes on the screen; Krazy Kars, bumper cars; Tilt-A-Whirl; and an Allan Herschell carousel.

Fantasy Island
2400 Grand Island Boulevard
Grand Island, NY (716) 773–7591

It's hard to pinpoint the exact theme of this "something for every member of the family" park. A lot of parks claim it, but this 80-acre facility truly does have something for everyone.

It's a ride park, a water park, a western town, a storybook park, and a fantasyland all tied together. Each of its five areas has a theme: Fantasyland, Western town, Midway, Water World and Festival Picnic Grounds. There's a great children's area, containing many of the 18 kiddie rides. In total, the park offers 36 rides.

Food service: 3 major restaurants, including the Laughing Giraffe and the 1950s Boppers; 10 others offer foods ranging from chicken and barbecued rib dinners to ice cream. Food may be brought into the park, and picnic tables are plentiful.

Entertainment: 10 shows, including a rainmaker, Cinema 180, a puppet show, high divers, a variety of musical shows and a gunfighter/stunt show. A kid's game show called "Do You Dare?" is a big hit.

Extras: Miniature golf, paddleboats, and a petting zoo are all included in the admission price. The Coronation Coach ride is pulled by matched ponies around a large castle; during the ride, a princess tells stories (cost included in admission).

Special events: Sneak-a-Peak, a park preview, with special rates, Memorial Day weekend; Christian Music Weekend, late June.

Season: Late-May through mid-September.

Operating hours: 11:30 A.M. to 8:30 P.M.

Admission policy: Pay-one-price, under $15. Free parking.

Top rides: Old Mill Scream, a log flume; Devil's Hole, an indoor rotor whereby the floor drops out during the ride; Wildcat, a compact steel coaster; Splash Creek, an active lazy-river raft ride.

Plan to stay: 6 hours.

Best way to avoid crowds: Come during the week and plan your visit around the show schedule.

Directions: Take Exit N19 off Highway 190, go west on Whitehaven Road to Baseline Road, turn left, and go to Grand Island Boulevard. The park can be seen from the highway.

Nearby attractions: Niagara Falls; Niagara Splash, a water park; a factory outlet mall; Buffalo Zoo.

Great Escape
Route 9
Lake George, NY (518) 792–6568

Nestled into the Adirondack Mountains, this park is one of the prettiest in the county. In addition to the colorful landscaping, a clear river, numerous bridges, and huge shade trees, the 140 acres hold 31 rides, including 10 just for kids; a participatory play area called Smallfry Funworld; and several walk-through attractions.

There are six separate areas: Fantasy Rides, where most of the rides are located; Ghost Town, an Old West area and one of the oldest sections in the park; International Village, offering shopping from around the world and including a Tiffany shop and a quality toy shop; Jungle Land, a tropics-oriented area; Arto's Small World, a child-size version of a town, with walk-through buildings; and Alice in Wonderland, where one enters the area through the famed rabbit hole that Alice fell through to reach her dream.

Food service: The Texas Rib Pit, serving outstanding barbecued beef and pork ribs; The Beer Garden, having a German theme and serving beer, German potato salad, and sandwiches; and a number of other eateries throughout. Make sure you stop by the Gingerbread House—

you'll be amazed at the number of sweet things that can be made. Food may be brought into the park, and there are inviting picnic areas in which to spread out your blanket.

Entertainment: 7 shows, including a full-scale circus with lions, tigers, and aerialists. Other shows feature high divers, a rainmaker, magic, puppets, animated animals; and street gunfights and stunts.

Extras: Miniature golf, no additional charge. The Cinderella Carriage Coach is a horse-drawn coach ride during which a princess tells stories.

Special events: Scout Month, June.

Season: May through Labor Day.

Operating hours: 9:30 A.M. to 6:00 P.M.

Admission policy: Pay-one-price, under $20. Come in after 3:00 P.M., next day free. Free parking.

Top rides: Giant Wheel, a gondola-style Ferris wheel; Steamin' Demon, a single-loop, double-corkscrew steel roller coaster; Desperado's Plunge, a log flume; Raging River, a raging-rapids ride; Condor.

Plan to stay: 5 hours.

Best way to avoid crowds: Come during the early part of the week.

Directions: Located a few miles outside Lake George on Route 9, between Exits 19 and 20 of the Adirondack Northway (I–87).

Nearby attractions: Lake George Zoological Park, an exotic-animal petting zoo; Lake George Steamboat Company, cruises on the lake; Lake George Village, a tourist area with a plethora of shops, restaurants, and attractions.

Hoffman's Playland
Route 9
Newtonville, NY (518) 785-3735

With its small family park, the Hoffman family caters to the local market and it's not unusual, especially during the day, for most of the people in the park to know one another.

The 16 rides include a 1952 Allan Herschell carousel, an iron horse (train), a Ferris wheel, a compact steel roller coaster, and extremely well maintained bumper cars. A large arcade and a video-game room feature a diversity of games including Skee-ball. And both a miniature golf course and a driving range are adjacent to the park.

Open from Easter Sunday through mid-September. Park hours are noon to 10:00 P.M. daily; admission is free, with rides and attractions on a pay-as-you-go basis.

Kids Kingdom
3351 Route 112
Medford, NY (516) 698–3384

This Long Island kiddieland birthday park has its parties under a giant tent next to the rides midway. In addition to its 15 kiddie and family rides, the park offers costumed characters, live music, puppet shows, and a good selection of fast food, including gyros.

Open daily, from April through October, 10:00 A.M. to 1:00 A.M. The park has a free gate, with rides and attractions on a pay-as-you-go basis; pay-one-price ticket is also available.

Lake George Ride and Fun Park
Route 9
Lake George, NY (518) 668–5459

Rides and family fun are the emphasis at this well-maintained park on the edge of the village, close to Lake George. The 7½-acre park is full of willow and maple trees, has lots of grassy areas, and offers 18 rides.

Food service: The major eatery is Tiffany's Cafe, a walk-away that features hamburgers, fish sandwiches, and hot dogs. The Pizza Trolley serves pizza and beer, and the park has an authentic antique popcorn wagon. There are also several snack stands and a fudge shop. Many say the fudge made here is the best of any found in amusement parks nationwide.

Entertainment: Various circus-type acts on an outside stage, plus an animated band show.

Extras: The park is very attractive after dark, with its neon signs and many traveling lights on rides and buildings. Don't miss the popular Disco Bumper Cars: The bumping takes place in a fog-filled, strobe-lighted building.

Season: Mid-June through Labor Day.

Operating hours: 2:00 to 11:00 P.M.

Admission policy: General admission, with rides and attractions on a pay-as-you-go basis. Pay-one-price also available, under $10. Parking charge.

Top rides: Crystal Carousel, a double-decked merry-go-round; Dragon Coaster, a compact, dragon-themed family coaster; Trabant and Flying Bobs, both spinning thrill rides; a Ferris wheel; an antique car ride; Pirate Ship, a pendulum pirate ship.

Plan to stay: 2½ hours.

Best way to avoid crowds: Come during the early part of the season—up to mid-July—or during the last part of August; the park is located in

New York

a heavy tourist area. Fridays are the most fun, with just enough people in the park to make the visit enjoyable, but not overcrowded.

Directions: Located on Route 9 (Main Street), on the south side of Lake George Village.

Nearby attractions: Fort William Henry, the original fort of the French and Indian Wars; Water Slide World, a water park; Around the World in 18 Holes, miniature golf; House of Frankenstein, a fun house and wax museum; Charlie's Saloon, an old-time restaurant and bar, offering food, beer, and live music.

Magic Forest
Route 9
Lake George, NY (518) 668-2448

Set in a pine forest a few miles from Lake George, Magic Forest is a family park with a Christmas and holiday atmosphere. It's divided into three areas: Christmas Village, Storybook, and a ride section. In addition to the bird show, the magic show, and a high-diving horse, the park offers 13 kiddie rides and 7 adult rides, including a Tilt-A-Whirl and a Ferris wheel.

Open daily from Memorial Day through early September; call for hours. Admission is pay-one-price, under $10.

Midway Park
Route 430
Maple Springs, NY (716) 386-3165

When this turn-of-the-century park opened in 1898, William McKinley was president and there had never been a World Series. People came by steamboat, train, and trolley car. Today, that nostalgic, trolley park atmosphere is being preserved, and a step into this park is a step back in time. Midway Park is a scenic, well-designed facility on the banks of Lake Chautauqua. It has 17 rides, including 8 for kids, and features a roller-skating rink—complete with a view of the lake—on the second floor of a seventy-five-year-old building.

Food service: 4 snack bars. Food may be brought into the park.

Entertainment: No regularly scheduled in-park entertainment.

Extras: Museum highlighting the park and the trolley and railroad companies that started it, free. Roller skating, miniature golf, go-carts, bumper boats, and pontoon boat excursions on the lake, all for extra charges.

Special events: July 4 picnic and celebration.

Season: Memorial Day weekend through Labor Day weekend.

Operating hours: 1:00 or 2:00 P.M. until dusk.

Admission policy: Free admission to the park, with rides on a pay-as-you-go basis. Pay-one-price available on weekends. Wednesdays are 10-cent kiddie days, when popcorn and most rides cost a dime.

Top rides: Tubs of Fun, a spinning ride; Tilt-A-Whirl; a giant slide; Dragon Coaster, a compact steel roller coaster.

Plan to stay: 2 hours.

Best way to avoid crowds: Come during the week and be there when the rides open.

Directions: Located on Route 430 on Lake Chautauqua in Maple Springs.

Nearby attractions: *Chautauqua Belle,* a paddle-wheeler; Longpoint State Park, swimming, and hiking.

Nellie Bly Park
1824 Shore Parkway
Brooklyn, NY (718) 996–4002

Other than the beach, this may well be the most delightful place in Brooklyn to take the kids. It's a compact, friendly family park with 14 rides, including 9 just for the wee ones.

Located 5 blocks from the Coney Island district, the park was named after the country's first female newspaper reporter. The theme of the fun house is Bly's world travels.

Food service: 4 locations for snacks and fast food, including ice cream, cotton candy, and hot dogs.

Entertainment: Jugglers and magicians perform at various times in a small entertainment pavilion.

Extras: Walk-through haunted house. Go-carts, extra charge.

Season: Easter through October, or as long as the weather holds out.

Operating hours: Noon to 10:00 or 11:00 P.M.

Admission policy: Admission is free, with rides and attractions on a pay-as-you-play basis. Pay-one-price available on Tuesday and Thursday from 11:00 A.M. to 2:00 P.M., under $10. Free parking.

Top rides: The Flash, a compact steel coaster; Convoy, a kiddie truck ride; Red Baron, a kiddie plane ride; a carousel; Tilt-A-Whirl.

Plan to stay: 2 hours.

Best way to avoid crowds: Wednesdays are the slowest days.

Directions: Take Exit 5 off the Belt Parkway and travel ½ mile to 25th Street; the park is on the right.

Nearby attractions: Coney Island Beach and Boardwalk; Gateway National Recreation Area; Fort Tilden.

Playland
Playland Parkway and the Beach
Rye, NY (914) 921–0370

There's so much preserved nostalgia here that the entire park has been listed as a National Historic Landmark. The combination of original Art Deco elements of the late 1920s with rides of the 1990s provides a wonderful experience.

This 279-acre, county-owned complex features a boardwalk along Long Island Sound, a large beach, an 80-acre lake, picnic groves, and a nicely shaded and landscaped ride park. The 45 rides include 7 original, circa-1929 rides that are still in great working shape. The 20 kiddie rides are located in a separate kiddieland.

Food service: 28 food locations, including Roast Beef at Rye, a walk-up stand that specializes in roast beef sandwiches.

Entertainment: A 1950s musical show is presented on weekends during spring and into June. Starting in mid-June, a musical revue runs daily through Labor Day.

Extras: Olympic-size swimming pool, miniature golf, paddleboats, rowboats, beach swimming, all extra. Nature preserve, free.

Special events: Fireworks and marching-band performance, opening day and every Wednesday, plus shows and concerts throughout the summer on the outdoor stage.

Season: Mid-May through Labor Day.

Operating hours: Opens at noon and closes at various hours during the evening, depending on crowds and weather. Closed Mondays.

Admission policy: Free admission, with all rides and attractions on a pay-as-you-go basis (no pay-one-price available, but officials are thinking about starting one). Parking charge.

Top rides: Dragon Coaster, a wooden roller coaster; Whirlwind, a steel corkscrew coaster; Flight Trainer, a participatory flight simulator; Giant Gondola Wheel; Auto Scooter, bumper cars; Derby Racer carousel, one of only two still operating in the nation (the other is at Cedar Point in Ohio).

Plan to stay: 4 hours.

Best way to avoid crowds: Tuesdays are the slowest, but Wednesdays are the most fun. Come early, have dinner, hear the band concert, and see the fireworks. You'll have small crowds to contend with but will have a great old-fashioned time.

Directions: Take Exit 19 (Playland Parkway) off I-95. Follow the parkway 1½ miles to the beach where the road dead-ends at the park.

Nearby attractions: U.S. Tobacco Museum; Stamford Museum and Nature Center; Bartlett Arboretum; Bruce Museum; plus all New York City attractions.

Seabreeze Amusement Park
4600 Culver Road
Rochester, NY (716) 323–1900

High on the bluffs overlooking Lake Ontario, this is a beautiful, well-kept traditional park. Founded in 1879, this 30-acre step back into time offers 23 rides, plus a water park. It's also a good place to be on a hot day—the temperature is usually 10-degrees cooler up here than in the city.

With most of its buildings dating back to the turn of the century, the park provides a fine blend of nostalgia and technology, the latter evident in the sophisticated water rides within Raging Rivers water park. Especially nice is the park's Victorian entranceway.

Food service: 1 major restaurant, plus 10 additional locations serving traditional park food—hot dogs, hamburgers, pizza, ice cream. And remember those crispy sugar waffles that would break into a zillion pieces when you took a bite? The ones served here have a reputation for being the best in the country. Food and beverages may be brought into the park.

Entertainment: No regularly scheduled daily entertainment, but the Seabreeze Strutters, the house Dixieland band, performs every weekend. Radio station promotions throughout the season bring in other entertainment.

Extras: The Goofy House, an optical-illusion walk-through, is free with park admission. The Historic Carousel Museum is also free to park guests and includes the park's history, and that of carousel carving. There's a carver's shop set up, with several horses in varying stages of completion.

Special events: Grand Opening celebration, bands and fireworks, opening day weekend in May; Kid's Weekend, featuring circus acts, clowns, and costumed characters, late June.

Season: Early May through Labor Day.

Operating hours: Noon to 10:00 or 11:00 P.M.

Admission policy: General admission, with rides and attractions on a pay-as-you-go basis. Pay-one-price also available; includes all rides and water park, under $10. Discounted Night Rider pass available every night after 6:00 P.M. Free parking.

Top rides: Jack Rabbit, a circa-1920 wooden roller coaster; a circa-1915 Philadelphia Toboggan Company carousel, in beautiful shape; Wildwater, a log flume; bumper cars; Tilt-A-Whirl.

Plan to stay: 6 hours.

Best way to avoid crowds: Come any weekday, at any time.

Directions: Take I-490 off the New York State Thruway (I-90) to I-590. Go north toward Lake Ontario. Take a left at the Seabreeze traffic circle;

then take the next right onto Culver Road. The park is a few blocks down on the right.

Nearby attractions: Port of Rochester, a waterfront area with a circa-1905 Dentzel carousel; International Museum of Photography at the George Eastman House; Strong Museum.

Sylvan Beach Amusement Park
Park Avenue, Route 13
Sylvan Beach, NY (315) 762-5212

Some of the best amusement parks in our history were established near summer resorts, as was this one. These early parks were important gathering places for the community and provided a constant in the area.

This one, on the east shore of Oneida Lake, has survived pretty much intact and is a good example of a traditional Northeast resort park. A village park and a public swimming beach are located next door.

A 1940 Art Deco building houses traditional midway games like Fascination and Skee-ball and imparts a sense of nostalgia. There are 19 rides, including 10 for kids and a super slide.

Food service: 2 food stands serve fast food, and 3 others feature snacks and drinks. Food may be brought into the park.

Entertainment: A clown roams the park every Wednesday afternoon passing out gifts and doing face painting. Reduced rates for rides while the clown is in the park.

Special events: Old Fashioned Weekend, observed opening weekend in April, with all rides 25 cents each; Thank You Weekend, last weekend of the season, with all rides 25 cents each.

Season: May through September.

Operating hours: Noon to 11:00 P.M.

Admission policy: Free gate, with rides and attractions on a pay-as-you-go basis. Free parking.

Top rides: Bumper cars; Bumper Boats; Laffland, a classic Pretzel dark ride; Tilt-A-Whirl; and a classic Philadelphia Toboggan Company teacup ride.

Plan to stay: 2 hours.

Best way to avoid crowds: Since rides are on a pay-as-you-go basis, there usually isn't a crowd rushing from one ride to another. The pace is slower here; the park is very seldom overcrowded.

Directions: Located in the Village of Sylvan Beach on Route 13, 4 miles north of Route 31. About halfway between Utica and Syracuse.

Nearby attractions: Vernon Downs, horse racing; Chittenango Falls State Park; plus the beaches and activities that surround Oneida Lake.

North Carolina

Carowinds
Carowinds Boulevard
Charlotte, NC (704) 588-2606

The Old South is alive and well and living in this park. You enter through Plantation Square, and everywhere you look you see the traditional South. You'd swear you were on a Charleston waterfront.

This 83-acre park can also claim something no other park can. It has the North Carolina–South Carolina state line running right down the middle of its main street. There's a marker on the street, where you can catch some great photos of you and yours standing in both states.

In addition to the park's 35 rides, including 18 for kids, the 6-acre Riptide Reef area contains a number of water slides and a wave pool, these activities included in the admission price.

Food service: 2 major sit-down restaurants, Casey's Grill and Country Kitchen, offer a full menu that includes some of the best fried chicken and barbecue sandwiches you've ever eaten. There are about 50 additional fast-food and snack outlets in the park.

The 360-degree looping Frenzoid in the foreground at Carowinds, in Charlotte, North Carolina, makes the Thunder Road roller coaster in the background almost look tame.

Entertainment: 6 shows, including a Cinema 180, several kids' shows featuring costumed characters, a major Broadway musical revue, and many other productions that highlight nostalgia and country music.

Extras: The Paladium Amphitheatre books in top-name entertainers throughout the summer, extra charge. There are also 207 campground sites adjacent to the park.

TIM'S TRIVIA

Carowinds, located just south of Charlotte, North Carolina, has the North Carolina–South Carolina state line going right through the middle of the park. While a unique distinction for the park, it creates its share of headaches, including different state-mandated break times, employment procedures, and state income tax rules.

Special events: Varsity cheerleading championships, March; Chorale Festival, April weekends; July 4 celebration, entire week of the holiday.

Season: Mid-March through the first weekend of October.

Operating hours: 10:00 A.M. to 8:00 P.M. Stays open until 10:00 P.M. on Saturdays. Closed Fridays.

Admission policy: Pay-one-price, under $20. Reduced-rate 2-day tickets also available. Parking charge.

Top rides: Goldrusher, a mine-train roller coaster; Thunder Road, twin racing wooden roller coasters; Rip Roarin' Rapids, a raging-rapids ride; Frenzoid, a looping pirate ship; Carolina Cyclone, a multielement steel coaster; Skytower, a 340-foot-tall observation tower.

Plan to stay: 10 hours.

Best way to avoid crowds: Come on weekends during the morning hours and ride the popular rides before the midday crunch arrives.

Directions: Take Exit 90 (Carowinds Boulevard) off I–77, 10 miles south of Charlotte.

Nearby attractions: Several small, quaint towns with great antiques shopping nearby, as well as all the attractions in Charlotte.

Crystal Beach
White Lake Road at the Beach
White Lake, NC (919) 862–4326

The main draw here is the crystal-clear, spring-fed lake and the sandy white beaches. When the beaches close at night or when the sky is overcast, that's when you'll find vacationers enjoying the 10 family rides this park has to offer.

The Crystal Beach Restaurant, with indoor and outdoor seating, overlooks the lake and offers a full menu, including the famous White Lake unpeeled french fries. There's a teenage dance every weekend, 2 games arcades, and a go-cart track.

In operation from early April through Labor Day. Peak season hours are 9:00 A.M. to 11:00 P.M.; the rides are open late afternoon and evenings. Free admission, free parking, and free use of the beach. Rides and games on a pay-as-you-go basis.

Emerald Pointe
3800 South Holden Road
Greensboro, NC (919) 852-9721

Mechanical rides were added to this successful water park in 1990, and the locals loved them. Now the area has not only the finest water park around but also an outstanding array of rides to choose from.

There are 10 dry rides here in the Dockside Park section, including a Ferris wheel, a carousel, a Round-Up, and a Paratrooper.

There are 4 for kids. Make sure you bring your bathing suit so you can cool off after riding the rides.

A pay-one-price admission, under $15, includes all wet and dry activities in the park. Call for hours and days of operation.

Ghost Town in the Sky
U.S. Route 19
Maggie Valley, NC (704) 926-1140

What an amazing place this is! To get to the park, you have to take a chair lift or an incline railway to a plateau most of the way up the side of a mountain. Then you climb aboard a bus that takes you the rest of the way up to the attractions.

Begun in 1961 as a ghost-town attraction, the facility has added rides and other elements through the years. There are 20 rides, including 8 for children. But the best attraction of all is the splendid view of the Great Smoky Mountains.

Divided into four sections, the park offers the original Ghost Town, Fort Cherokee, Crafters Village, and the Mile High Ride area.

Food service: 7 buffet-style restaurants and 7 snack bars.

Entertainment: 7 shows, including gunfights, Indian dancers, cloggers, country music shows, cancan dancers, comedy shows, and a one-man band.

Extras: Sunday church services are held in Ghost Town. The Mystery Shack is a unique gravity house, free with admission. A large crafts area for watching and buying is always in action.

Special events: Oktoberfest, first week of August.

Season: May through October.

Operating hours: 9:00 A.M. to 6:00 P.M. The chair lifts and incline quit taking guests up to the park 2 hours before the official closing time.

Admission policy: Pay-one-price, under $15. Free parking.

Top rides: Red Devil, a single-loop steel coaster built into the side of the mountain (you leave the station and drop off the side of the mountain; the lift-hill is at the end); Global Swings, flying swings in a metal globe; Black Widow, an indoor Scrambler.

Plan to stay: 4 hours.

Best way to avoid crowds: The smallest crowds come in late May and late August. Monday is the slowest day of the week.

Directions: Located on Highway 19, west of Maggie Valley. The park is 35 miles from Asheville via I–40 and 90 miles east of Knoxville, Tennessee, via I–40.

Nearby attractions: Cherokee Indian Reservation.

Goldston's Beach and Pavilion
White Lake Road at the Beach
White Lake, NC (919) 862–4064

Adjacent to Crystal Beach, this park's major draw is also the free, white sandy beach. Located on 15 acres, the park offers 12 rides, miniature golf, a large video-game and games-of-skill arcade, cottages, and a motel.

In addition to 2 restaurants, the park has a Dairy Queen franchise.

The entire facility is open from 9:00 A.M. to midnight, with the rides in operation only during the evening. Admission is free, with a pay-as-you-play policy for the rides and attractions.

Jubilee Park
Highway 421
Carolina Beach, NC (919) 458–9017

Built around a pond about 2 blocks from the oceanside boardwalk, this 8½-acre park has 20 rides, including 9 for kids. Flat, paved walkways between the rides makes this an easy park to get around in.

Food service: 1 fast-food location and 1 outlet for snack food and drinks. Food and beverages may be brought into the park; a nice shaded picnic pavilion is available for guest use.

Entertainment: No regularly scheduled in-park shows.

Extras: Go-carts, miniature golf, water slides, speed slides, and a kiddie play pool, all at extra charge.

Special events: Fireworks, July 4.

Season: Easter through mid-October.

Operating hours: July is considered peak season, with hours 11:00 A.M. to 11:00 P.M.; rest of the season, 1:00 to 10:00 P.M.

Admission policy: Free admission, with rides on a pay-as-you-go basis. Pay-one-price also available, under $10.

Top rides: A carousel, Tilt-A-Whirl; a Ferris wheel; Trabant, a spinning platform; bumper cars; Scrambler.

Plan to stay: 3 hours.

Best way to avoid crowds: Tuesdays are the slowest days. July is the busiest month.

Directions: Located on Highway 421, about 1 mile past the Pleasure Island Bridge, 17 miles east of Wilmington.

Nearby attractions: Fort Fisher, a Confederate fort; Putt-Putt, miniature golf; plus boardwalk shops, attractions, games, and restaurants.

Santa's Land
Route 1
Cherokee, NC (704) 497–9191

Santa is always on duty at this cool, 16-acre park, located in the Great Smoky Mountains. Flower and vegetable gardens throughout the facility add a great deal of color, and the large shade trees and grassy areas enhance comfort. Bring your Christmas shopping list—there's terrifc shopping here, in addition to the 9 rides.

Food service: 4 food outlets, serving fast-food and snack items. The operation makes its own fudge in the fudge shop.

Entertainment: 6 shows, including a chance to talk with Santa; 4 animated shows, and a magic production.

TIM'S TRIVIA

In keeping with its musical roots, the Opryland theme park in Nashville, adjacent to the Grande Ole Opry, has named many of its rides along musical lines: Little Deuce Coupe, Rock 'n' Roller Coaster, Wabash Cannonball, Tennessee Waltz, Old Mill Scream, and the Country Bumpkin.

Extras: Paddleboats, playground equipment, a petting zoo, all free. Don't miss the Nativity scene or the giant snowman. And the employees may wear the neatest costumes of any park in the country . . . some are dressed as elves.

Special events: Harvest Festival, weekends in October and the first weekend in November.

Season: May through the first weekend of November.

Operating hours: 9:00 A.M. to 8:00 P.M.

Admission policy: Pay-one-price, under $10. Free parking.

Top rides: Rudicoaster, a Rudolph-themed family roller coaster; a train ride, a mile-long jaunt; paddleboats; a Ferris wheel.

Plan to stay: 3 hours.

Best way to avoid crowds: Weekdays are least crowded. Park officials say the best time to visit is during the Harvest Festival.

Directions: 3 miles north of Cherokee, on U.S. Highway 19.

Nearby attractions: Cherokee Indian Reservation. And the entire region is a tourist area, having a varied lineup of attractions and activities.

Tweetsie Railroad
Highway 221/321
Blowing Rock, NC (704) 264-9061

Billing itself as the state's first theme park, this unique place opened in 1956 as a train excursion. Today, not only is that train ride aboard a full-size, coal-fired steam locomotive just as popular as ever, but the owners have created a neat little theme park around it.

The overall atmosphere is one of an Old West railroad town. You enter the park through an old depot building and proceed down a western-style street. Specific areas include Tweetsie Square, Mouse Mountain, and Country Fair, where the 7 family rides are located.

Apart from the rides and the train, a chair lift takes you up to Mouse Mountain, where you can pan for gold, visit a petting zoo, or take a miniature train ride through Mouse Mine and see small, animated mice busy at work.

Food service: 2 main restaurants and numerous fast-food and snack locations. Sparky's BBQ serves barbecue sandwiches; The Feed and Seed, hamburgers, hot dogs and chicken.

Entertainment: 4 shows: country music, a rainmaker, clogging, and a saloon music and cancan presentation.

Extras: Wild West, a coin-operated shooting gallery, and the Railroad Museum. During the 3-mile train ride, guests get robbed by bandits and attacked by Indians.

Special events: Railroaders Day, late June; July 4 Week celebration; High Country Arts and Crafts festivals, late July and mid-October; Music Festival, featuring country, bluegrass and gospel music, mid-July; Clogging Jamboree, August.

Season: Memorial Day through October.

Operating hours: 9:00 A.M. to 6:00 P.M. daily.

Admission policy: Pay-one-price, under $15. Free parking.

Top rides: A chair lift to Mouse Mountain; bumper cars; a Ferris wheel; bumper boats; a train ride; a carousel.

Plan to stay: 5 hours.

Best way to avoid crowds: Come at opening time on a Monday or a Friday. Try to avoid weekends and holidays if you can.

Directions: Located 3 miles from Blowing Rock and 3 miles from Boone, on Highway 321/221.

Nearby attractions: Magic Mountain, miniature golf; Mystery Hill; The Blowing Rock; Grandfather Mountain.

North Dakota

Lucy's Amusement Park
Highway 83 South
Minot, ND (701) 839–2320

With a slogan of "Fun is our business," how can you pass up Lucy's? Located on 3 acres, ½ mile outside the city limits, the park has 6 kiddie rides, a giant slide, an 18-hole miniature golf course, and a circular go-cart track with intersecting crossroads.

Although you'd think the park would be mainly for kids, 75 percent of its business comes from adults playing miniature golf.

Nicely laid out in a treed, grassy area, the park has free admission, with all rides and attractions on a pay-as-you-play basis. It is open daily, from midmorning to 10:00 or 11:00 P.M. The golf course stays open later than the rides.

Ohio

Americana Amusement Park
5757 Middletown–Hamilton Road
Middletown, OH (513) 539–7339

Surrounding a 22-acre, man-made lake, this traditional park is southeast Ohio's premier corporate picnic park, hosting more than 500 outings a year. This fact alone says something about the local reputation the park enjoys. Founded in 1921 as LeSourdsville Lake, the facility was renamed in 1978.

The shaded picnic grove is directly inside the gate to your right, with most of the 47 rides, including 19 for kids, to your left and across the lake.

Food service: 1 major restaurant and a 300-seat, mall-style food court with a Gold Star Chili franchise. Additional stands serve fast food, snacks, and drinks.

Entertainment: No regularly scheduled daily shows. Special concerts and musical events, however, are held during the season.

Extras: Olympic-size swimming pool, included in park admission. Miniature golf, extra charge.

Special events: July 4 celebration.

Season: May through September.

Operating hours: 10:00 A.M. to 8:00 P.M.

Admission policy: Pay-one-price, under $15. After 4:00 P.M., half-price special. Parking charge.

Top rides: Raging Thunder, a log flume; Screechin' Eagle, a circa-1927 wooden roller coaster; The Serpent, a compact steel roller coaster; The Galleon, a swinging pirate ship; Demolition Derby, bumper cars.

Plan to stay: 5 hours.

Best way to avoid crowds: Come during the week; mornings are the least busy.

Directions: Take Exit 29 (Monroe-Lebanon) off I–75 to Route 63 West, proceeding to the intersection of State Route 4; the park is at the intersection, about 5 miles from the interstate. Located 30 miles north of Cincinnati, 30 miles from Dayton, 100 miles from Columbus.

Nearby attractions: Miamisburg Mound State Park; Voice of America radio station; Fort Ancient State Memorial Park; Sugarcreek Ski Hills; Caesar Creek State Park.

Cedar Point
On a Lake Erie Peninsula
Sandusky, OH (419) 626–0830

Overlooking Lake Erie, this turn-of-the-century park is the finest traditional amusement park in the country. With its 54 rides, including 10 roller coasters, it is also the largest ride park on the continent.

Although some areas have themes, Cedar Point is not a serious theme park. It is a good old-fashioned ride park with a great deal of nostalgia.

The 364-acre park, with its tall rides presenting a bird's-eye view of Lake Erie, is heavily wooded and spread out. A walk to Frontier Town in the back of the park is about a mile's hike. Along the Frontier Trail you'll find numerous craftspeople and log cabins.

Utilize the park's transportation system to get around and save a few steps. The skyride provides a one-way trip between the front and back of the park, and the Cedar Point and Lake Erie Railroad has a stop in Frontier Town.

135

The Cedar Point and Lake Erie Railroad at Cedar Point, Sandusky, Ohio, is more than just a great, nostalgic train ride. It's a viable transportation system within this huge park.

Food service: 14 sit-down restaurants, with 5 of them providing table service. An additional 35 food outlets offer various foods, including the famous Cedar Point french fries. Children's menu at most restaurants features peanut butter and jelly sandwiches and chicken snacks.

Entertainment: 5 major theaters, presenting live musical productions, from bluegrass to Broadway; animal shows, held in Jungle Larry's Safari; dolphin and sea lion shows, held in the Oceana Marine-Life Stadium; IMAX Theater.

Extras: The park's marina is one of the finest on Lake Erie. Docking for boats of all sizes is available just 500 feet from the park's entrance. Swimming in Lake Erie with lifeguard supervision and bathhouse facilities, is included in admission. Soak City, a water park, charges an additional hourly admission. The park's history is chronicled in the Town Hall Museum, free.

Special events: CoasterMania, a day for the enthusiasts, early June; Cleveland Browns Day, come out and meet the players, mid-June; Corvette Show, mid-June; in-water boat show, September.

Season: May through September.

Operating hours: 9:00 A.M. to 10:00 P.M. or midnight.

Admission policy: Pay-one-price, under $25. Extra day for an additional $10. Parking charge.

Top rides: The Magnum XL200, a steel roller coaster that's listed in *Guinness* as the country's tallest and fastest coaster (*Note:* The Steel

Phantom steel coaster at Kennywood, in West Mifflin, Pennsylvania, opened in early 1991 and is now faster than the Magnum and has a longer drop, but the Magnum is still the tallest); Blue Streak, a wooden roller coaster; Thunder Canyon, a raging-rapids ride; Disaster Transport, a space-themed indoor toboggan coaster; Giant Wheel, a 15-story-tall Ferris wheel with gondola-style seating; Mean Streak, the world's tallest and fastest wooden roller coaster.

Plan to stay: A 2-day visit is a must, in order to enjoy the park to its fullest.

Best way to avoid crowds: Come before mid-June or during the last week in August. Be there early; the causeway leading out to the park becomes a bottleneck once the masses start arriving.

Directions: Located midway between Toledo and Cleveland. Take Exit 7 off the Ohio Turnpike (I–80), go north on Route 250 into Sandusky, and then follow the signs to the causeway.

Nearby attractions: Ferries to popular Lake Erie Islands; Follett House, an 1837 mansion; Historic Lyme Village, a restored nineteenth-century settlement; Great Lakes Historical Society Museum; Carousel Museum.

Coney Island
6201 Kellogg Avenue
Cincinnati, OH (513) 232–8230

With the name Coney Island, this park along the banks of the Ohio River had a lot to live up to in the early days. Founded in 1886, the park, often referred to as Coney Island West, had little but its name in common with the famous Brooklyn, New York, area. But it was every bit as popular, with thousands of people coming weekly by steamboat to play, swim, dance, and ride.

Most of the park was dismantled in 1972 when Kings Island was developed by the same owner. Today, however, this pretty little park is starting to make a slow comeback. A large swimming pool and water slides have kept its gates open. There are now several kiddie rides, paddleboats and bumper boats, bumper cars, and a Ferris wheel—plus a miniature golf course and a games-of-skill-midway.

Big band, jazz, and nostalgic rock-and-roll offerings are scheduled weekly in the historic Moonlight Gardens, the original ballroom of Coney Island. The Balloon Festival, with dozens of hot-air balloons, is held the last weekend in May each year, and the Appalachian Festival, featuring crafts and music of the area, takes place the second week of May.

Erieview Park
5483 Lake Road
Geneva-on-the-Lake, OH (216) 466–8650

Located on a bluff overlooking Lake Erie, this 18-ride park may be the best-kept secret in this part of the state: Its rides are "hidden" behind the stores and restaurants on the commercial strip of this resort community.

In Geneva-on-the-Lake, Ohio, they make their own wine at Erieview Park's Firehouse Winery.

But that's a plus once you're in the park. The hustle and bustle of the street and real life are left behind, and usually only the sounds of boats on the lake can be heard above the sounds of the rides.

Founded in 1945, the 3-acre park has, in addition to its mechanical rides, a two-flume water slide and a large arcade.

Food service: Being on the commercial strip, there are myriad eateries within a block of the park itself. On park property, you'll find Time's Square Restaurant, serving fast-food items, and the Firehouse Winery, offering a full menu. Also on the property but not run by the park is a Chinese restaurant and a pizzeria. And ample shade and nice views of the lake make picnicking on the well-kept lawns enticing as well.

Entertainment: Live bands are booked into the Firehouse Winery nightly. The Swiss Chalet Night Club, along the strip adjacent to the park, also has live entertainment nightly.

Extras: A palm reader and a large shooting gallery are directly adjacent to the park entrance. The Firehouse Winery makes its own wine.

Special events: Ghost Town USA comes alive each October in the park: The area under the water slides is turned into a series of haunted mazes, and the entire park adopts a haunted theme.

Season: Mother's Day through Labor Day.

Operating hours: Opens during the week at 5:00 P.M.; on weekends, 10:00 A.M. Closes nightly at 10:00 P.M.

Admission policy: Free gate, with rides on a pay-as-you-go basis. An all-day "ride and slide," pay-one-price ticket is available, under $10. Parking free if you buy ride tickets.

Top rides: A Ferris wheel; Roll-O-Plane; a dark ride; bumper cars; a carousel.

Plan to stay: If you intend to use both rides and water slides, plan to stay 4 to 5 hours.

Best way to avoid crowds: Come early in the week or at midday on weekends. The park is busiest in the evening, when the town itself is hopping.

Directions: Take the Geneva-on-the-Lake exit (Route 534 North) off I-90 and drive north about 7 miles into the village. The park is on your left, with parking next to the water slide and Woody's World Arcade.

Nearby attractions: Old Mill Winery; Ashtabula History Museum; Putt-Putt, miniature golf; Fascination game room; Fun Karts, a go-cart track.

Fantasy Farm Amusement Park
5885 Hamilton–Middletown Road
Middletown, OH (513) 539-8864

Heavily wooded and full of fun, this park provides the perfect outing for a family with kids 12 years of age and younger. You won't find any so-called thrill rides here. Small kids can ride them all, and half the 25 rides in operation are solely for little tots.

Located directly next to the larger Americana Amusement Park, Fantasy Farm has chosen to remain a small, family-oriented park that's a laid-back and traditional place to visit.

Food service: 1 sit-down, air-conditioned restaurant serving full meals and platters, plus 4 additional outlets providing snacks and beverages. Food and beverages may be brought into the park; picnic tables are situated throughout.

Entertainment: No regularly scheduled, daily in-park entertainment; however, Big Red, the park's costumed rooster, shows up often. On holidays, musical concerts and puppet shows are occasionally offered.

Extras: Train ride and pony ride, extra charge. Swimming pool and petting zoo, included in admission.

Special events: Great American Picnic, July 4. In addition, a local radio station broadcasts from the park on holidays during the season and usually brings along entertainment.

Season: April through September.

Operating hours: 10:00 A.M. to 6:00 P.M.

Admission policy: Pay-one-price, under $10. Special carload admission prices in effect 2 days a week. Parking charge.

Top rides: Haunted House, a dark ride; Elephant, a Dumbo-style children's ride; Tilt-A-Whirl; bumper cars; Scrambler.

Plan to stay: 4 hours.

Best way to avoid crowds: Weekends are generally slower than weekdays because there are few weekend group picnics. Holidays are always busy because of special promotions.

Directions: Take Exit 29 off I–75 and go west on Route 63 for about 5 miles. The park is at the intersection of Route 63 and Highway 4.

Nearby attractions: Same as Americana Amusement Park (see above listing).

Geauga Lake
1060 North Aurora Road
Aurora, OH (216) 562–7131

A lakeside location, plenty of old buildings, rides and games, and trees and colorful landscaping make a trip to this traditional park a good fun investment. Today the facility is one of the state's finest parks, offering the latest in rides, shows, and attractions.

Located on Geauga Lake, across from Sea World, the 47-acre park is reminiscent of the old-time family fun parks once so plentiful in this part of the country. The place is also a good example of a wet/dry park, wherein water-park elements and mechanical amusement rides coexist in a total environment, creating a great entertainment bargain for the whole family. There are more than 40 "dry" rides and 15 "wet" rides, all included in the park admission price.

Food service: The 30-plus food outlets include a full-service nautical restaurant called the Funtime Sail Company. In addition, the Wharf (a seafood cafeteria) and the Engine House serve up full meals.

Entertainment: Live shows include a Broadway-style musical revue, a country music show, and a magic presentation. There is also a Cinema 180 film.

Extras: Large games-of-skill arcade. Miniature golf and paddleboats available at additional charge.

Special events: Octoberfest, third weekend in September.

Season: May through September.

Operating hours: 11:00 A.M. to 10:00 P.M.

Admission policy: Pay-one-price, under $15. After 5:00 P.M. reduced ticket available. Parking charge.

Top rides: Raging Wolf Bobs, a wooden roller coaster; Big Dipper, a circa-1924 wooden roller coaster; Double Loop, a two-loop steel roller coaster; Gold Rush, a log flume; Rocket Ships, a classic circular swinging ride; a circa-1918 Illions Supreme Carousel.

Plan to stay: 6 hours.

Best way to avoid crowds: Wednesdays and Thursdays are the least crowded days. Take a ride up the observation tower and see what the park layout looks like and where the crowds are congregating; then plan your attack accordingly.

Directions: Take Exit 13 off the Ohio Turnpike (I–80) and go north 9 miles on North Aurora Road (Highway 43). The park is 30 miles southeast of Cleveland and 26 miles north of Akron.

Nearby attractions: Dankorana Winery, wine tasting and tours; Mario's International Health Spa complex; Aurora Farms, an outlet mall complex.

Kings Island
Kings Island Drive
Kings Island, OH (513) 398–5600

The people of Ohio love their amusement parks, and they're sure lucky to have this one. With more than three million visitors yearly, Kings Island is one of the two most popular seasonal amusement parks in America. (Cedar Point, also in Ohio, is the other.) The park's entrance is nothing short of breathtaking: At the end of a 320-foot-long-by-80-foot-wide water fountain stands a magnificent, 330-foot replica of the Eiffel Tower, complete with observation deck. That's a good

TIM'S TRIVIA

Two parks premiered Arrow Development's new Log Flume during the 1963 season: Six Flags Over Texas, Arlington; and Cedar Point, Sandusky, Ohio.

place to start your visit. With map in hand, search out what you want to do from high atop everything else.

And there's *a lot* taking place on these 288 acres. There are 41 rides, for example, including 16 for children. One of those rides is the Beast, without a doubt the best wooden roller coaster in the world, and with its 4-minutes-plus ride, it's also the longest coaster ride in the United States. There's also WaterWorks, the park's water park, offering 11 additional rides and activities at no additional charge.

Food service: Several large sit-down restaurants are among the park's 40 permanent food locations. Eateries with a theme are found in each of the different parts of the park—the Festhaus German restaurant, where you can eat, drink, and watch an ice-skating presentation, is one example. The Coney Cafe offers a giant Thrillburger; blue ice cream can be found where the Smurfs hang out; and Skyline Chili franchise serves the best chili money can buy in or out of an amusement park.

Entertainment: 8 different shows, including ice skating, a musical magic show, Cinema 180, a puppet show, a dolphin show, and an assortment of costumed characters and strolling entertainers. Nightly fireworks.

Extras: Wild Animal Habitat offers a 2-mile monorail trip into an area of roving wild animals, extra charge. The TimberWolf Amphitheatre offers top-name concerts throughout the summer, additional charge.

Special events: Winterfest, Thanksgiving through New Year's Eve.

Season: Mid-April through mid-October.

Operating hours: 9:00 A.M. to 11:00 P.M.

Admission policy: Pay-one-price, under $25. A specially priced second-day ticket is available. Parking charge.

Top rides: The Beast, number-one wooden roller coaster in the country (others may disagree with me, but I'm writing this and they're not); Flight Commander, a participatory flight ride; Rushing River, an inner-tube wet ride in the water-park section; Vortex, a steel looping coaster; Amazon Falls, a spill-water raft ride; Smurfs' Enchanted Voyage, a slow boat ride through the land of Smurfs; a circa-1926 Philadelphia Toboggan Company carousel; Adventure Express, a mine-train roller coaster.

Plan to stay: 10 hours.

Best way to avoid crowds: Work your way around the circular layout and finish each area as you go; doubling back is time-consuming. Use a map to plan your voyage.

Directions: Located 24 miles north of Cincinnati, 80 miles south of Columbus, off I–71. Take the Kings Island Drive exit and go east to the park entrance.

Nearby attractions: College Football Hall of Fame; The Beach, a water park; Jack Nicklaus Sports Center.

Memphis Kiddie Park
10340 Memphis Avenue
Cleveland, OH (216) 941–5995

The manager who helped open this park in 1952 is now the owner, and the 11 rides that were running on opening day are still the only rides in the park. Things haven't changed much here. In fact, the rides still look new and the cotton candy is still fluffy and delicious.

In a state filled with megaparks, this quaint little traditional kiddie park is a breath of fresh air. Dedicated to the "little people" of the Cleveland area, the facility is adjacent to a metropolitan park and across the street from a drive-in theater.

Open daily from 11:00 A.M. to 10:00 P.M., April through October. It's pay-as-you-go for the rides, games, and miniature golf.

Sea World of Ohio
1100 Sea World Drive
Aurora, OH (216) 995-2121

Shamu is alive and well and living in Ohio. This 90-acre marine-life park is one of the four Sea World parks and the only "northern" facility of the group. In addition to the regular Sea World attractions, this park has one major claim to fame: It's now home to Kalina, the first killer whale to be born and raised in captivity. She was born at Sea World of Florida and for several years was commonly known as Baby Shamu.

Food service: 17 eateries, serving a wide variety of foods, from fried chicken dinners to the latest rage in snack foods.

Entertainment: 5 major shows, including the Shamu Killer Whale production, sea lion shows, high divers, and a waterskiing show. Mime acts and banjo sing-alongs are offered as preshow entertainment for the larger shows.

Extras: Dolphin feeding and petting; the Penguin Encounter, an Antarctic exhibit; and sea lion feeding—all free with admission.

Special events: Summer Nights celebration offers additional shows, laser-light productions, and fireworks during the peak summer months.

Season: Mid-May through the first week of September.

Operating hours: 9:00 A.M. to 11:00 P.M.

Admission policy: Pay-one-price, under $20. Half-price discount after 6:00 P.M. Free parking.

Top rides: No mechanical rides at park; Cap'n Kids World offers a 3-acre participatory play area for children.

Plan to stay: 5 hours.

Best way to avoid crowds: Come during the week right at opening time or come at about 5:00 P.M. and stay until closing.

Directions: Located 30 miles southeast of Cleveland on Route 43. Take Exit 13 (Route 43) off the Ohio Turnpike (I–80) and go north 9 miles to Sea World Drive.

Nearby attractions: See attractions at end of Geauga Lake listing, above.

Time Out on the Court
Indoors at the Forest Fair Mall
I–275 and Winton Road
Cincinnati, OH (513) 671-8008

Colorful banners, an 18-hole miniature golf course, and the grand carousel lets you know when you've entered this nice, clean family entertainment center. With 5 rides total, the area also offers a large video-game room and a games-of-skill midway.

The park, adjacent to the mall's large food court, is open during mall hours. There's no admission charge; rides and attractions are on a pay-as-you-go basis.

Tuscora Park
Off Tuscora Avenue
New Philadelphia, OH (216) 343–4644

You'll see the colorful Ferris wheel from the road as you drive down Tuscora Avenue, a few blocks from downtown. Other than that, you'd have no idea a small ride park was nestled into the corner of this 37-acre, city-owned recreation area.

The park has a total of 8 kiddie rides, including a circa-1929 Herschell-Spillman carousel in beautifully restored condition. And the place offers an 18-hole miniature golf course, a swimming pool, and picnic facilities.

Open daily at noon, Memorial Day through Labor Day. The rides are on a pay-as-you-go basis.

Wyandot Lake
10101 Riverside Drive
Powell, OH (614) 889–9283

Don your bathing suit and spend the day—this park exemplifies the way in which wet and dry amusement rides can work together successfully. Here you can ride and scream on a roller coaster and then walk a few yards and go bodysurfing in a wave pool, all for one admission price.

With 17 mechanical rides (including 9 kiddie rides) and 8 major water elements, there's plenty to keep you busy. Swimsuits need not be changed before riding the dry rides, but shoes are required.

Food service: Gasper's Pizzeria, featuring Italian food and alcoholic drinks, is the major eatery. Additional outlets located throughout park.

Entertainment: A magic show and a puppet show are featured daily.

Extras: Miniature golf and go-carts, extra charge.

Special events: Drive-in Movies and Teen Dance parties, Friday nights in August.

Season: Mid-May through mid-September.

Operating hours: 10:00 A.M. to 8:00 or 9:00 P.M.

Admission policy: Pay-one-price, under $15. Parking charge.

Top rides: A circa-1914 Mangels-Illions carousel; Sea Dragon, a circa-1956 Philadelphia Toboggan Company junior wooden coaster; Canoochie Creek, an active lazy river–type inner-tube adventure.

Plan to stay: 7 hours if both wet and dry activities are to be experienced.

Best way to avoid crowds: Much of the crowd comes and rides the rides first and then hits the water elements to cool off. Reverse this pattern and you'll have no problems with crowds.

Directions: Located adjacent to the Columbus Zoo on Route 257. Take the Sawmill Road exit off I–270 and follow the signs to the park and to the zoo.

Nearby attractions: Columbus Zoo; Ohio State University; historic Worthington.

Oklahoma

Bell's Amusement Park
3900 East 21st Street
Tulsa State Fairgrounds
Tulsa, OK (918) 744–1991

There's a lot of fun packed onto these 10 acres. Bob Bell, who founded the park in 1951, has taken those acres and created a 26-ride family amusement park. Needless to say, it's compact, but it's also well run and quite popular among the locals. There's even room left over for trees, flower beds, and shaded rest areas.

This may also be the only park in the country where senior citizens (age 60 and over) always get in and ride for free. Bell has informed his employees that these special guests are to be treated "just like Mr. Bell."

Food service: 5 to 8 locations, depending on the crowds. All locations offer traditional amusement park fare, including corn dogs, hamburgers, french fries, and fried chicken.

Entertainment: No shows are scheduled on a regular basis, but sponsorship tie-ins with local country and Christian music radio stations result in quite a bit of in-park entertainment during the season.

Extras: Miniature golf, free with pay-one-price admission. Make sure you see where the Zingo roller coaster goes under one side of a concession stand and out the other. The park becomes part of the carnival midway during the Tulsa State Fair.

Special events: Fireworks and Music Festival, July 4.

Season: Mid-April through mid-October. Season ends with the closing of the Tulsa State Fair in October.

Operating hours: Weekdays, 6:00 to 10:00 P.M.; weekends, 1:00 to 11:00 P.M.

Admission policy: Small general admission fee, with rides on a pay-as-you-go basis. Pay-one-price available for all rides and miniature golf, under $15; children's pay-one-price available for kiddie rides only, under $4. Free parking.

Top rides: Phantasmagoria, a dark ride; Zingo, a wooden roller coaster; White Lightning, a log flume; Wildcat, a compact steel roller coaster; 1001 Nights, a 360-degree swinging pendulum ride where the rider stays upright the entire time.

Plan to stay: 3 hours .

Best way to avoid crowds: Mondays and Thursdays are the least busy days. Although this is a small park, its rides are high-capacity and seldom entail a wait of more than 10 minutes, even on the busiest day.

Directions: Take the Harvard Street exit off I–244, go south 1¾ miles, turn east on 17th Street, and go ⅓ mile and to the fairgrounds.

Nearby attractions: Big Splash, a water park; Gilcrease Museum and Philbrook, both art museums.

Frontier City
11601 Northeast Expressway
Oklahoma City, OK (405) 478–2414

You might think you're walking onto a TV-western set when you enter the front gates of this 40-acre park. It's a replica of an 1880s western town, with all architecture and environs reflecting that genre.

In keeping with the image, the owners call the park the "territory of fun." The kiddie rides are located in the O.K. Kid's Korral, as are a petting zoo and special games, shows, and activities.

Food service: 7 sit-down restaurants and numerous fast-food and snack locations throughout the park. Eateries include the Chicken Ranch, fried chicken dinners; Two Johns Saloon, drinks and snacks; Santa Fe Grill, barbecue; Sweet Sioux's, ice cream; and Mustard's Last Stand, hot dogs. One of the eateries is located next to the Wildcat coaster and provides diners with a great view through a glass wall.

Entertainment: 9 shows, including nightly fireworks, street gunfighters, a saloon musical presentation, Cinema 180, a rainmaker, a magic show, and a medicine-man show.

Extras: A large games complex houses a full array of video games and games of skill. The wooden roller coaster was moved here from the now-defunct Fairyland Park in Kansas City.

Oklahoma

Unusual stage shows await guests at Universal Studios Hollywood. This is a scene from the park's Riot Act, an action comedy stunt show.

Special events: Easter Egg Hunt, April; July 4 Extravaganza; Kid's Fest, July; Christian Family Nights, July and August; Back to School Party, mid-August; Music Fest, all through September.

Season: Mid-April through September.

Operating hours: Opens at 5:00 P.M. Tuesday through Friday and at 10:00 A.M. or noon on weekends; closes most nights at 10:00 P.M. Closed Mondays.

Admission policy: Pay-one-price, under $15. Parking charge.

Top rides: Nightmare, an indoor compact steel coaster; Mystery River, a log flume; Silver Bullet, the state's only looping coaster; Prairie Schooner, a swinging pirate ship; Renegade, a raging-rapids ride; Raging Riptide, a sled ride down a water trough; Wildcat, a wooden roller coaster.

Plan to stay: 6 hours.

Best way to avoid crowds: Come on weekdays or on Sunday afternoons.

Directions: Take the 122d Street exit off I-35, about 20 minutes north of downtown Oklahoma City. The park is just south of 122d Street on the west side of the interstate.

Nearby attractions: National Cowboy Hall of Fame and Heritage Center; Oklahoma City Zoo; Kirkpatrick Planetarium.

Oregon

Enchanted Forest
8462 Enchanted Way SE
Turner, OR (503) 363-3060

Truly a child's paradise, Enchanted Forest is a heavily forested park, with storybook characters' homes as the main attraction. Walk through the Seven Dwarfs' Cottage or the Alice in Wonderland area, or take a stroll past a life-size gingerbread house.

In addition to the storybook activities, are two other attractions, a walk-through haunted house and the Ice Mountain Bobsleds.

Food service: 2 eateries in a Tudor-style village. Food may be brought into the park.

Entertainment: Fantasy Fountain, a computerized dancing-waters show, and a live stage production of a childhood story.

Season: Mid-March through September.

Operating hours: 9:30 A.M. to 6:00 P.M.

Admission policy: Pay-one-price, under $5. Ice Mountain Bobsleds and Haunted House cost extra.

Top rides: Only ride is the Ice Mountain Bobsled, a themed roller coaster ride that goes through tunnels.

Plan to stay: 2 hours.

Directions: Located 7 miles south of Salem, just off Exit 248 of I-5.

Oaks Park
Southeast Oaks Parkway
Portland, OR (503) 233-5777

Once you see this 44-acre family park along the banks of the Willamette River, you'll know how its name came about: Huge oak trees are everywhere.

First opened in 1905 to coincide with the Lewis and Clark World's Expo, the park now has 25 rides, as well as some of the original buildings, including those housing a roller skating rink, skooters, and a carousel.

Food service: 2 locations, selling hot dogs, hamburgers and a wide variety of snack and fast foods, including the popular Jo-Jo potatoes; an additional eatery is located inside the skating rink. Picnics may be brought in, and picnic areas along the banks of the river are numerous.

Entertainment: There is no regularly scheduled in-park entertainment; however, Chipper the Squirrel, the park's mascot, visits often. During summer, local bands are often booked in, and a couple of times each summer, a beer garden with entertainment is set up. Although not run by the park, the Ladybug Theatre is a children's participatory theater that offers regularly scheduled shows throughout the year.

Extras: Miniature golf, extra charge. Bingo is played every Friday evening and Sunday afternoon, year-round.

Special events: Fireworks, July 4; Sculling Race, collegiate competition, October; plus several other sponsored events during the season.

Season: Mid-March through October. Roller skating rink is open year-round.

Operating hours: Opens during the week at 1:00 P.M. and closes at 10:00 or 11:00 P.M. Opens on weekends at noon and closes at 11:00 P.M. on Saturday and 8:00 p.m on Sunday. Closed nonholiday Mondays.

Admission policy: Free admission, with rides and attractions on a pay-as-you-go basis. During July and August, various promotions offer a pay-one-price deal. Free parking.

Top rides: Monster Mouse, a compact steel coaster; bumper cars; Scrambler; a Ferris wheel; Tornado, a compact steel coaster; a circa-1924 Philadelphia Toboggan Company carousel; Haunted Mine, a dark ride; a train ride around the park and along the river.

Plan to stay: 5 hours.

Best way to avoid crowds: Visit Tuesday or Friday during the day or on weekends before Memorial Day or after Labor Day.

Directions: Take the Corbett Road exit off I-5 and follow the signs to Lake Oswego, which will take you to Macadam Avenue. Proceed south on Macadam until you get to the Sellwood Bridge. Cross the bridge and make a left on 6th Avenue; the park is on your left. Located 8 miles from downtown.

Nearby attractions: Portland Metro Zoo; International Rose Test Gardens.

Pennsylvania

Bland's Park
Route 220
Tipton, PA (814) 684-3538

The people of Pennsylvania are indeed lucky—their state is full of wonderful traditional family parks, and this is one of the finest. Although small, the park packs a lot of fun into its 8 acres. Kids Kingdom is a separate little kiddieland with 11 rides, and 10 additional adult and family rides are spread throughout the park.

Food service: 3 walk-up eateries with patio seating. Carts are added during the peak seasons. Don't leave the park without trying Bland's potato salad; it's made fresh daily and is delicious.

Entertainment: The Lidell Circus performs daily for a week in early June. Additional shows are booked in during special events and celebrations.

Extras: Live pony rides, included in pay-one-price admission.

Special events: Mother's Day, mothers ride free; Father's Day, fathers ride free; Fireworks, one of the largest displays in the state, July 4; Harvest Festival, with big-name entertainers, late September.

Season: May through September.

Operating hours: Noon to 10:00 P.M. Closed Mondays.

Admission policy: Free admission, with rides and attractions on a pay-as-you-go basis. Pay-one-price available, under $7.50.

Top rides: Space Odyssey, an indoor caterpillar with a sound and light show; Zyklon, a compact steel coaster; Scrambler; Dodgem's, bumper cars; a circa-1924 Herschell-Spillman carousel, with a Wurlitzer band organ.

Plan to stay: 4 hours.

Best way to avoid crowds: Tuesdays are the least crowded. Small crowds and beautiful weather prevail on weekends in spring and fall.

Directions: Take Exit 23 (Highway 220) off I-80. Follow Highway 220 south for 35 miles; the park is on the right, 3 miles south of Tyrone.

Nearby attractions: Indian Caverns; Etna Furnace; railroad industry's famous Horseshoe Curve.

Conneaut Lake Park
Highway 618
Conneaut Lake Park, PA (814) 382–5115

The owners here own not only the park, but the town bearing its name. In fact, the town *is* the park, and the park *is* the town—rides, attractions, and summer cottages are all mixed together in this traditional resort setting.

TIM'S TRIVIA

Crooner Perry Como was "discovered" while cutting hair at the Conneaut Lake Hotel at Conneaut Lake Park, Pennsylvania.

The park is a wet and dry park, with several water-park elements blended in with the 38 mechanical rides. The facility, located on the north side of the lake, also encompasses a swimming beach, boat excursions, boat rentals, and a marina.

Food service: The Log Cabin serves open-pit grilled hamburgers, fries, and steak sandwiches; American Pie features pizza, finger foods, baked potatoes, subs, spaghetti, and salads; and the Conneaut Lake Hotel, on the grounds, has a full-service, full-menu dining room. Fifteen more outlets are located throughout the park. And the ice-cream parlor serves excellent ice cream.

TIM'S TRIVIA

The tunnel of the Blue Streak roller coaster in Conneaut Lake Park (Pennsylvania) is a favorite hideout for skunks, which raid the nearby picnic grounds each night. So many skunks have been run over by the coaster that it is now known as Skunk Tunnel.

Entertainment: The park began offering in-park entertainment in 1990 and is still experimenting with which type of mix goes over best with visitors. Several shows are scheduled daily. In addition, the American Pie books in nationally known rock-and-roll oldies acts on Saturday nights.

Extras: The Lakeland Museum, located within the park, highlights the history of the park as well as the entire lake area. Live pony rides and miniature golf available, extra charge. Campground.

Special events: Two antiques shows, end of May and first week of September; two Penn-Ohio Polka festivals, first weekend of June and middle weekend of August; Conneaut Lake Jazz Festival, late August; fireworks, July 4 and Labor Day weekend.

Season: Mid-May through Labor Day.

Operating hours: Opens daily at noon; closes at 9:00 P.M. on weeknights and 10:00 P.M. on weekends. Closed all nonholiday Mondays.

Admission policy: Small admission fee, plus rides on a pay-as-you-go basis. Pay-one-price also available, under $15. Special discounts after 7:00 P.M. Parking charge.

Top rides: Blue Streak, a wooden roller coaster; Sea Dragon, a swinging pirate ship; a circa-1905 D. C. Muller & Brothers carousel; Tumble Bug; a Ferris wheel; bumper cars; Whip; Yo-Yo, flying swings; Hell Hole, a rotor; The Ultimate Trip, an indoor Scrambler.

Plan to stay: 6 hours.

Best way to avoid crowds: Come at opening time during the week or around dinnertime.

Directions: Take Exit 36B off I–79 and go west on Highway 6/322 to Highway 18. Go north on Highway 18 to Highway 618 and follow it around the north end of the lake to the park.

Nearby attractions: Conneaut Lake, for fishing, swimming and boating; Conneaut Cellars Winery; McMinley Miniature Golf.

Dorney Park
3830 Dorney Park Road
Allentown, PA (215) 398–7955

There isn't much this park *doesn't* have to offer. From a contemporary, full-scale, top-notch water park (Wild Water Kingdom) to a traditional amusement park, Dorney Park has a host of activities for the entire family.

Opened as a fish weir and summer resort in the 1860s, the park now has 44 rides, including 14 for kids. The older part of the park still has some of the original buildings left and several of the early classic rides, including Journey to the Center of the Earth, one of the last remaining mill-chute rides in operation in the world today.

Food service: 17 food and beverage outlets, including the Memories restaurant, a table-service eatery with lots of memorabilia from historic Dorney Park. The Fest Haus is a German walk-up facility with a covered eating pavilion.

Entertainment: 5 shows, including a marionette show, a Care Bears animated presentation, a German band in the Fest Haus, and 2 music shows. Teen dances are held every Friday night in the Stargazer Showplace.

Extras: 2 miniature golf courses, speedboats, bumper boats, race cars, tank tag, boat tag, and gallery guns, all extra.

Special events: Kidsfest, mid-June through July 4.

Season: Third weekend in April through Labor Day.

Operating hours: 10:00 A.M. to 10:00 P.M.

Admission policy: Pay-one-price, under $20, includes both the ride park and the water park. Separate pay-one-price tickets also available for one or the other. Special after-5:00 P.M. rate saves $10 per admission.

Top rides: Hercules and Thunderhawk, each a wooden roller coaster; Lazer, a two-loop steel coaster; Skyscraper, a 90-foot-tall Ferris wheel; Thunder Creek Mountain, a log flume; a Zephyr train, offering a classic train ride; bumper cars, using vintage Lusse cars.

Plan to stay: 10 hours if you visit both parks.

Best way to avoid crowds: Most people visit the ride park until noon, next go to the water park until around 5:00 P.M., and then go back to ride park until closing. To avoid the crowds, do the opposite. Monday is the slowest day of the week.

Directions: Take Exit 16 (Route 222) east off Highway 309 and follow the signs to the park.

Nearby attractions: Liberty Bell Shrine; Moravian Historic Area; Allentown Art Museum; Lost River Caverns.

Dutch Wonderland
2249 Route 30 East
Lancaster, PA (717) 291–1888

Although the name would lead you to believe the park has a strong Dutch theme, don't be fooled. This park *is* in the middle of the Pennsylvania Dutch area, but it doesn't have a major theme—instead, it has several small themed areas, each beautifully landscaped and, all told, containing more than 100,000 exotic plants and shrubs.

The 44-acre park has a great deal of water, lots of trees, lots of walk-through attractions, and 20 family-oriented rides. You enter the park through a castle. Once you're inside, the paved paths take you through an Indian Village, past the Old Woman's Shoe, the Church in the Dell, and Bossie the Cow, and across a bridge to an international-themed botanical garden.

Among the unique rides is a gondola boat ride that takes visitors on a trip past the Eiffel Tower, Big Ben, and a Japanese pagoda. It also takes riders past another unique ride: a kiddie Ferris wheel built to resemble a Dutch windmill.

Food service: 2 major restaurants, including the Castle Coffee Shop, specializing in homemade pot pies and bean soup. The Park Place Pavilion serves some of the best broasted chicken in the state. An additional 5 stands offer snacks and fast-food items. Picnics may be brought in; areas along the creek banks are designated as picnic grounds.

Entertainment: High divers and an animated musical bear show run daily; storytelling by Chief Halftown takes place on weekends.

Extras: The Wonder House is a fascinating attraction: The guest sits still while the whole room spins, making it feel like you're tumbling. Other extras, also included in admission, are a giant slide inside a barnyard silo and an opportunity to milk a make-believe cow.

Special events: Grandparent's Day, late September.

Season: Easter weekend through Labor Day.

Operating hours: Opens at 10:00 A.M. Monday through Saturday and at 11:00 A.M. on Sunday; closes at 7:00 P.M. daily.

Admission policy: Pay-one-price, under $15. A limited pay-one-price ticket is available for 5 attractions, under $10. Free parking.

Top rides: Flying Trapeze, flying swings; Skyride, going from the front to the back of the park; Turnpike Ride, antique cars; Monorail, a trip around the park; Tug Boat Ride; River Boat Ride.

Plan to stay: 3½ hours.

Best way to avoid crowds: Come early in the week; take the skyride to the back of the park and work your way forward.

Directions: Located on Route 30, 4 miles east of Lancaster.

Nearby attractions: Weavertown One-Room Schoolhouse; Abe's Buggy Rides; Robert Fulton Birthplace; National Wax Museum.

49th Street Galleria
Indoors in the Franklin Mills Mall
1563 Franklin Mills Circle
Philadelphia, PA (215) 281–0895

As an anchor tenant in a huge mall, this entertainment complex truly has something to keep all family members busy. The ride area consists of a Gravitron, a carousel, and a couple of kiddie rides. Additional elements are: batting cages, a roller-skating rink, a 40-lane bowling alley, a miniature golf course, and Photon Laser Tag. Moreover, the place has its own food court, consisting of a Dairy Queen franchise, an Orange Julius franchise, and 3 additional food and snack locations. Regularly scheduled concerts and dances take place in the main court of the complex.

Free admission, with rides and activities on a pay-as-you-go basis, or a custom pay-one-price pass is available for various activities. Hours are basically the same as the mall's, with weekend closing times being extended.

Hersheypark
100 West Hersheypark Drive
Hershey, PA (717) 534–3824; (800) HERSHEY

Beautiful—that's the word to sum up this 87-acre, well-landscaped park. The wonderful old trees, the rolling terrain, and the myriad shaded resting areas make this park one of the nicest in the country.

Founded in 1907 by Milton Hershey as a recreation area for his chocolate-factory workers, the park now contains 52 rides, including 16 for children. And contrary to expectations, the park does *not* have a chocolate theme!

Yet, there *is* intricate theming in seven areas: Tudor Square, a seventeenth-century English village; Music Box Way, an 1800s-style Pennsylvania Dutch settlement; Tower Plaza, featuring the

TIM'S TRIVIA

Hersheypark's "Carrousel," in Hershey, Pennsylvania, was spelled wrong by the original sign painter and the name is still used today.

330-foot-tall Kissing Tower observation ride; Rhineland, an early German town; Carousel Circle, a circle of smaller rides around the antique carousel; and Zooamerica, an 11-acre walk-through zoo.

Food service: 50 locations, including 10 walk-up eateries with patio seating. The Tudor Rose Tavern is a table-service, indoor restaurant. Make sure you ask for a nutrition guide that lists every food and drink item sold in the park by calories, fat, and so on.

Entertainment: 8 hours of shows daily, including musical presentations, a children's show, a dance revue, and a dolphin/sea lion show.

Extras: Miniature golf and paddleboats, extra charge. Chocolate World, located next to the park, presents a ride-through tour of how chocolate is made (free). The streetlights in the town of Hershey are shaped like Hershey chocolate kisses.

Special events: Character Parade, in which the resident chocolate-costumed characters invite other mascots over for a party, June and July; World Wrestling Federation Day, in which wrestling stars walk the park, meeting and greeting visitors the day a wrestling event is being held next door at the Hersheypark Arena, date varies; LifeFair, health checkups, third Saturday in August; Contemporary Christian Day, August; Paddleboat Races, mid-August.

Season: May through September.

Operating hours: 10:00 A.M. to 10:00 P.M.

Admission policy: Pay-one-price, under $20, includes admission to Zooamerica. Sunset admission, after 5:00 P.M, saves $6. In fall when park is closed, a separate admission is available for Zooamerica.

Top rides: Coal Cracker, a log flume; Comet, a wooden roller coaster; Sooperdooperlooper, a single-loop roller coaster; Canyon River Rapids, a raging-rapids ride; a circa-1919 Philadelphia Toboggan Company carousel, the second largest this company ever made; Giant Wheel, a double Ferris wheel with gondola seating; Sidewinder, a steel boomerang roller coaster.

Plan to stay: 8 hours.

Best way to avoid crowds: Monday and Tuesdays are the slowest days during the season. Avoid weekends. The park opens a half-hour before the rides do; come early, stake your claim on your favorite ride, and go from there.

Directions: Take Exit 20 off the Pennsylvania Turnpike to Route 322. Follow Route 322 to Hershey and take Route 39 West to Hersheypark Drive; the park is on the right.

Nearby attractions: Indian Echo Caverns; Hershey Adventure, miniature golf; Gettysburg National Military Park; Pennsylvania Dutch country.

Idlewild Park
Route 30
Ligonier, PA (412) 238–3666

This 90-acre park, located in the mountain woodlands of Central Pennsylvania, is considered America's most beautiful amusement park by most aficionados. It's more than a hundred years old and has kept its traditional amusement park flavor.

Yet it has not stood still. The 27 rides, including 11 for kids, are top-notch contemporary rides. The park is divided into four sections: H-2-Ohhh Zone, a water park; Hooting Holler, Wild West territory; Jumpin Jungle, a participatory play area; and the Story Book section, where kids can walk through Little Red Riding Hood's woods and visit other book stars' homes.

All the kiddie rides are located in Raccoon Lagoon.

Food service: 1 major sit-down restaurant and 10 snack-food stands. The Potato Patch serves the world's best french fries. (See the listing for Kennywood Park, West Mifflin, Pennsylvania. Owned by the same people, that park also has the same potato-cooking secret.)

Entertainment: 2 different live shows: a comedy variety show and a musical revue.

Extras: Miniature golf, paddleboats, and rowboats, extra fee.

Special events: Old Fashion Days, mid-July; Ligonier Highland Games, September (the Scottish games are sponsored by an outside group, not the park, but they are held annually).

Season: Mid-May through the first week of September.

Operating hours: 10:00 A.M. to dusk. Closed Mondays.

Admission policy: Pay-one-price, under $15. Free parking.

Top rides: Mister Rogers' Neighborhood, a one-of-a-kind trolley ride through the neighborhood of make-believe popularized by TV's Fred Rogers; Rafters Run, a twin-tube water slide; a circa-1931 Philadelphia Toboggan Company carousel; Black Widow, a Spider ride.

Plan to stay: 6 hours.

Best way to avoid crowds: Come early afternoon on any weekday.

Directions: From the Pennsylvania Turnpike, take Exit 9 and go north on Route 711 to Route 30; turn right and go 3 miles west to the park.

Nearby attractions: Fort Ligonier, a restored fort from the French and Indian Wars, 3 miles west of the park on Route 30.

Kennywood
Route 837
West Mifflin, PA (412) 461–0500

This popular park is one of the best traditional parks in the country. High on the bluff overlooking the Monongahela River, the park sits on 40 acres and has 50 rides, including 15 for kids.

Founded in 1898 as a trolley park, it has a long-standing reputation as a superb picnic and family park. It's one of two parks in the country that has been listed as a National Historic Landmark. Kennywood received that status for the preservation of traditional park elements. (Playland in Rye, New York, is the other park.)

Two of the original turn-of-the-century buildings are still standing, and the tunnel of love ride dates back to the early 1920s.

TIM'S TRIVIA

During an average season of 163 operating days, guests at Six Flags Over Georgia in Atlanta consume 200,000 pounds of hamburger, 100,000 pounds of cheese, 250,000 pizzas, 200,000 giant pretzels, and 5,000,000 soft drinks.

The park is known nationally for its three high-ranking wooden roller coasters and for having the best amusement park french fries in the country.

Food service: 13 eating establishments, including the Patio Cafe, for salads, sandwiches and spaghetti; the Golden Nugget, for ice cream and snacks; and the Potato Patch, home of the great french fries.

The Patio is located in the original 1898 Casino building. Food may be brought into the park.

Entertainment: 7 shows, including circus acts, musical revues, and nostalgic musical performances.

Extras: Noah's Ark, a dark, walk-through fun house, free with admission. Available for an extra charge are a miniature golf course and paddleboats.

Special events: Christian Music Weekend, Labor Day; plus a dozen different ethnic community days throughout the summer. The different nationalities come out, cook and sell food, have their own entertainment, and draw visitors from a three-state area.

Season: Mid-May through Labor Day.

Operating hours: Noon to 11:00 P.M.

Admission policy: General admission fee, with rides on a pay-as-you-go basis. Pay-one-price also available, under $15. Free and paid parking.

Shamu is the king of the killer whales at the four Sea World facilities. Each of the parks offers an action-packed whale show several times a day.

Top rides: Log Jammer, a log flume; Raging Rapids, a raging-rapids ride; Steel Phantom, a multielement steel roller coaster that is considered to be the fastest and to have the steepest drop of all coasters in the world; Thunderbolt, Jack Rabbit, and the Racer, wooden roller coasters; Turtle, the classic Tumble Bug ride; Haunted Hideaway, a ride-through tunnel of love in wooden boats; a circa-1926 Dentzel carousel with band organ.

Plan to stay: 7 hours.

Best way to avoid crowds: Come on weekdays. This is not a tourist park, and so crowd patterns do not reflect tourist patterns. It's wise to call ahead to learn when the major groups are booked in so that you can avoid those days.

Directions: Take Exit 9 (Swissvale) off I–376 (Penn-Lincoln Parkway). Go south, across the river, until the road dead-ends. Turn left on Highway 837 and go about 1½ miles. The park is on your left; free parking is on your right. Located 8 miles from downtown Pittsburgh. *Note:* The park is famous for its big yellow arrows pointing the way.

Nearby attractions: Sandcastle, a water park and entertainment complex; Pittsburgh Zoo; Pittsburgh Childrens Museum; Monongahela Incline Railroad.

Knoebels Amusement Resort
Route 487
Elysburg, PA (717) 672-2572

This family-owned and -operated facility is amazing. Though situated in the middle of nowhere, it offers just about anything you could ever want in an amusement park.

Roaring Creek meanders through a pine forest that shelters most of the 37 rides. It was this creek that started it all back in the early 1900s, when a swimming hole attracted people to Knoebels Groves. The first rides and attractions were added in 1926, and thankfully, the family has not attempted to create a theme for the park. The lovely natural setting provides its own theme.

Just walking onto the grounds gives one an "old-fashioned" feeling. The shaded, hilly walkways and the old buildings are beautifully maintained, as are both old and new rides. The attractions, plus the state's largest swimming pool, the large picnic grounds, rental cabins, and a campground, make this a true family resort.

Food service: The Alamo Restaurant, located indoors, and offering table service, is the park's largest eatery. The Phoenix Junction Steak House serves fantastic steaks, and Cesari's Pizza has what is without a doubt the best pizza found in any U.S. amusement park. More than a dozen additional food service outlets are situated throughout the park.

Entertainment: All entertainment is free and includes stage shows, a saloon show, life-size animated bear presentation, a marionette show, and a live interactive show, for kids. Kosmo, the park's mascot, can be found in Kosmo's Kiddieland.

Extras: A crafts demonstration area, the Anthracite Coal Museum, and 4 working band organs are all free. Miniature golf, 4 water slides and the ¾-million-gallon swimming pool are all available for a fee.

Special events: Covered Bridge Festival, first weekend in October; Christmas in September, mid-September; Appreciation Day, September 1; Senior Citizens Day, one in June, one in July; Crafts Fair, fourth week of July.

Season: Mid-April through mid-September.

Operating hours: 11:00 A.M. to 10:00 P.M.

Admission policy: Free gate, with rides and attractions on a pay-as-you-go basis. Pay-one-price available only during the week, under $15 (does not include the Haunted Mansion). After–5:00 P.M. specials. Free parking.

Top rides: Phoenix, a wooden roller coaster; Haunted Mansion, the best haunted ride-through outside the Disney parks; Scooter, bumper cars that still use original Lusse cars; a log flume; and you can still grab for the brass ring on the Grand Carousel, a circa-1913 Kramers Karousel Works/Carmel machine with band organ.

Plan to stay: 6 hours is the average, but if you plan to swim and eat here, add a couple of hours—you'll probably want to make it an all-day affair.

Best way to avoid crowds: Mondays are the slowest, followed by other early-in-the week days. Weekends are busiest, but because of the number of high-capacity rides, most lines move swiftly.

Directions: Located on Highway 487 between Elysburg and Catawissa, in the east central part of the state. Take Exit 33 (Danville) off I-80 and head to Danville on Highway 54. Follow Highway 54 when it turns toward Elysburg; then turn left onto Highway 487 North. Bear right at the large, colorful Knoebel's billboard/sign; the park is ½ mile down the road from the main highway. About 45 minutes northeast of Harrisburg.

Nearby attractions: Covered Bridge Tour; Pioneer Mine Tunnel Tour.

Lakemont Park
Routes 220 and 36
Altoona, PA (814) 949–7275

Leap The Dips, the country's oldest wooden roller coaster, is located here, and if things go according to plan, it should be renovated and in operating order shortly. Lakemont Park—founded in 1894 and located on the south side of the city—is currently undergoing a few changes and realignments, including a slight reduction in mechanical-ride offerings and an increase in water-related activities.

Once the changes are made, the park will have about 25 rides, including a Mad Mouse, a compact steel coaster, and the Skyliner, another wooden roller coaster.

It is open daily, with a pay-one-price admission. Hours vary during the season.

Sesame Place
New Oxford Road
Langhorne, PA (215) 752–7070

Big Bird, Bert, Ernie, and all the other members of the "Sesame Street" gang are here to greet and entertain you at what is absolutely the finest children's park in the country. The facility has plenty of color, unique activities, and first-rate supervision; its familiar characters make the experience great fun for the kids, especially the younger ones.

Although the park has no mechanical rides, it does offer more than 40 outdoor physical play activities, including several water-oriented "rides." (Be sure to bring swimsuits for the entire family.) Familiar sights, including scenes from the popular TV show, make this park feel like home to the little tykes.

Food service: The emphasis is on "good foods for you." Even standing in line for food is an education here. The facilities have been designed so that food preparation is done behind glass walls, enabling all to watch. Eateries include the Sesame Food Factory, Sesame Sandwich Shop, and Captain Ernie's Cafe. Menu items range from peanut butter and jelly sandwiches to flame-broiled burgers. In keeping with the health theme, the park uses sesame seeds instead of salt on the soft pretzels.

Entertainment: Audience participation shows, a strolling brass band, a special-effects-participatory video production show, and bird shows.

Extras: Educational computer games arcade, extra charge. The Sesame Neighborhood is a full-size replica of the storefronts and buildings seen on the TV show.

Special events: Career Days, in which members of various careers visit the park and talk to kids about their jobs, May.

Season: May through October.

Operating hours: 9:00 A.M. to 8:00 P.M.

Admission policy: Pay-one-price, under $20. This is about the only park in the country where a parent's admission fee is lower than a 5-year-old's. A special twilight discount begins at 5:00 P.M. Parking charge.

Top rides: Big Bird's Rambling River is the only "family" ride. It's a lazy-river raft ride around the facility.

Plan to stay: 5 hours.

Best way to avoid crowds: Come early morning or just before dinnertime during the week.

Directions: Located on New Oxford Valley Road off U.S. Route 1 near Oxford Valley Mall, 7 miles southwest of Trenton and 20 miles northeast of downtown Philadelphia.

Nearby attractions: Several revolutionary war buildings, including the Barracks, the Douglas House, and the Trent House, are open to the public. The entire area is very historical, with many museums, galleries, and antiques shops.

Waldameer
Route 832
Erie, PA (814) 838–3591

The entrance to this wonderful traditional park is about as low-key as you can get: A small sign on the highway tells you the park is here, but that's the last sign you'll see. Just follow the crowds through the small opening in the fence in the corner of the parking lot and you'll be inside. (And before you even get to the parking lot, you'll undoubtedly spot the tall towers of the facility's water park.)

Directly adjacent to the gate are heavily wooded picnic groves, and the first signs you see of the ride park itself are the roller coaster and a beautiful carousel off to your right. Waldameer, founded in 1896 as a trolley park, has kept much of its old-time charm. In addition to the popular water park (separate admission), Waldameer offers 25 rides.

Food service: 7 locations, serving various fast-food and snack items. Pizza, cookies, fudge, caramel corn, and French waffles are all made from scratch and are among the most popular items sold. Food may be brought into the park.

Entertainment: A stage in the middle of the park features "homegrown" talent, including high school and college students. The schools use the park as a place for their students to gain experience before an audience. Shows include singing, dancing, and a sampling of the entire arts field.

Extras: Pirates Cove, a walk-through fun house.

Special events: Fireworks five times a year: July 3 and 4, Sunday and Monday of Memorial Day weekend, and Labor Day Sunday; plus several specially sponsored community days.

Season: Mother's Day through Labor Day.

Operating hours: The ride park is open from 1:00 to 10:00 P.M.; the water park, from 11:00 A.M. to 8:00 P.M. Both facilities closed Mondays.

Admission policy: Free gate, with rides and attractions on a pay-as-you-go basis. Pay-one-price also available, under $10; combination ticket with water park also available. Free parking.

Top rides: Train ride, a scenic, 15-minute ride; Comet, a junior wooden roller coaster; Old Mill, a boat ride; Wacky Shack, a two-decker dark ride; a carousel; a flying coaster ride, one of only three or four left in operation.

Plan to stay: 4 hours if you only go on the rides; 7 hours if you also visit the water park.

Directions: Take Exit 5N off I–90 and go north on Route 832 for about 8 miles. The park is on the left, just before you enter the parkway to Presque Isle State Park.

Nearby attractions: Planetarium; Erie Zoo; Putt-Putt, miniature golf; Presque Isle State Park, swimming, hiking, fishing, and picnicking.

Williams Grove Amusement Park
Off Route 74 on Williams Grove Road
Mechanicsburg, PA (717) 697–8266

What does a park that first opened to the public more than 130 years ago look like? Visit this quaint little park and you'll find out. Located in a heavily wooded, rural area, the park has a stream and a small lake on its property. A display of steam-driven vehicles is at the entrance, and a steam locomotive gives rides around the park.

Among the nostalgia and the well-kept old buildings are 20 rides, including 7 just for kids. Also here are a miniature golf course and paddleboats. You can bring in your own food and beverage and enjoy a nice shaded picnic, or you can eat in the park's cafeteria or one of its fast-food and snack locations.

Country music and magic shows are usually scheduled throughout the season. The park is open from Memorial Day through Labor Day. Call for hours and days of operation and admission prices. It is located about 20 miles north of Gettysburg.

Rhode Island

Enchanted Forest
Route 3
Hope Valley, RI (401) 539–7711

Founded in 1962 as a kiddie attraction, this 17-acre park has been able to maintain its original storybook theme through the years. A walk along the path through the woods takes you to many storybook characters' homes, including the Three Little Pigs' house and the Little Red Schoolhouse.

In addition, there are 11 rides, all kiddie and family oriented, and a go-cart skid track.

Food service: Snack bar, featuring homemade pizza. Food may be brought into the park.

Entertainment: Magic shows daily.

Extras: Miniature golf is included in admission. Go-cart skid cars and batting cages cost extra.

Season: May through September.

Operating hours: The park is open from 10:00 A.M. to 5:00 P.M.; golf, batting cages, and game room, from 10:00 A.M. to 10:00 P.M.

Admission policy: Pay-one-price, under $10. Free parking.

Top rides: Airplanes; a merry-go-round; a kiddie roller coaster; kiddie pony carts, originally from Coney Island, New York.

Plan to stay: 2 hours.

Directions: Take Exit 2 off I–95 to Route 3; proceed to the park, in Hope Valley. About 30 miles south of Providence.

Rocky Point Park
Rocky Point Avenue
Warwick, RI (401) 737-8000

Overlooking Narraganset Bay, this 128-acre traditional park is a well-kept facility with a great selection of rides and games. Through the years, the park has maintained its quality and, in so doing, has retained a strong local support. Dating back to the mid-1800s, the park is now entertaining the fourth and fifth generations of its original family visitors.

The park has 33 rides, including 10 for kids.

Food service: The Shore Dinner Hall, which seats 4,000 at one time, is considered the world's largest such establishment. Its specialties include Rocky Point Chowder and clam cakes. An additional 15 eateries can be found along the midway.

Entertainment: Musical variety shows on the midway throughout the day. Concerts by various national and regional groups every Friday night on the midway.

Special events: July 4 fireworks show.

Season: April through September.

Operating hours: Noon to 10:30 P.M.

Admission policy: General admission, plus rides, or pay-one-price, under $10. After–6:00 P.M. discount on pay-one-price. Free parking.

Top rides: Loop-Corkscrew, a steel looping coaster; Free Fall; Flume, a log flume; House of Horror, a dark ride.

Plan to stay: 3 hours.

Best way to avoid crowds: Come midweek during midafternoon.

Directions: Take Exit 10 off I-95; go east on Route 117 about 5 miles to Rocky Point Avenue.

Nearby attractions: Tourist town of Newport, Rhode Island.

South Carolina

Myrtle Beach Pavilion and Amusement Park
Ocean and 9th Avenues
Myrtle Beach, SC (803) 448-6456

The largest seaside ride park south of New Jersey, this 10-acre complex is smack-dab in the middle of the city's downtown area. It serves as the hub of a 5-block area of beachside entertainment attractions, shops, and restaurants.

The park, in business since 1949, is intersected by Ocean Avenue. The pavilion, teenage club, arcade, miniature golf course, boardwalk games, shops, and restaurants are located on the beach side of the avenue, while the amusement park, including its 31 rides, is located on the other.

Although this is not a traditional seaside park, there are more than enough attractions here to keep you active and happy. As you enter the park, one element will jump out at you—the green asphalt. To help keep the heat down in the park, a tennis court coating is put over the blacktop each season. It also adds some nice color.

Food service: 21 food outlets, including 5 with seating. Menus are traditional—hot dogs, hamburgers, nachos, soft drinks, and the like.

Entertainment: Every night, weather permitting, a 1900 Ruth (German) band organ, with paper rolls, is played in a small amphitheater in the middle of the park. The organ has 400 pipes and 98 keys, with hand-carved wooden figures.

Extras: Miniature golf, extra charge. The large arcade is open from 8:00 A.M. to 2:00 A.M. daily. The Pavilion has an 1,800-seat auditorium that is regularly used as an alcohol-free teenage club. On occasion, name entertainment is booked in.

Special events: Beginning of Year Appreciation Day, early March; End of Year Appreciation Day, late September; Canadian-American Day, first day of the season; Sun Fest, held in conjunction with the city's chamber of commerce, first week of June.

Season: March through September.

Operating hours: Rides are open from 1:00 P.M. to midnight. Miniature golf and boardwalk shops and attractions are open from 8:00 A.M. to 2:00 A.M.

Admission policy: Free gate, with rides on a pay-as-you-go-basis. Pay-one-price available, under $15. Discount ride ticket books also available. Parking charge.

Top rides: A circa-1915 Herschell-Spillman carousel with band organ; Haunted Inn, a dark ride; Super Skooter, bumper cars; The Corkscrew, a steel corkscrew roller coaster; Siberian Sleigh Ride, a Himalaya; Scrambler, set up inside with lights, fog, and sound; Caterpillar, with canvas top.

Plan to stay: 3½ hours.

Best way to avoid crowds: Most of the people who come here come for the beaches and play at the park when they can't be on the beach. Therefore, daytime hours are the least crowded. Business picks up when the sun goes down or when the sky is overcast.

Directions: Take Route 17 to Myrtle Beach. Turn east on 8th Avenue and go 4 blocks to Ocean Avenue. The park is located between 8th and 9th avenues, on Ocean Avenue.

Nearby attractions: Wild Rapids Waterslide, a water park; 2001, a dance club; Myrtle Beach Grand Prix, miniature golf and motor tracks; South Carolina Hall of Fame; Brookgreen Gardens.

South Dakota

Flintstones Bedrock City
West Highway 16 and Highway 385
Custer, SD (605) 673–4079

"Hey Wilma, look here—I've found a nifty amusement park named after me!" Yes, that's Fred Flintstone, whom you'll meet if you stop by this colorful little park. You'll also get a chance to meet Fred's neighbor, Barney Rubble.

Founded in 1966, the park replicates Bedrock, the Flintstones' hometown. Visitors can peek into the twenty Flintstone-style buildings or romp in the prehistoric playground, which features dinosaurs and huge birds made just for climbing.

A miniature train ride takes guests around the park. Two old Volkswagens converted into Flintstone-style cars also give visitors a ride around the town. In the movie theater, you'll find a continuous showing of Flintstone cartoons; on the stage, an animated trio singing a happy song.

Food available at the Bedrock Drive-in—where Wilma and Betty work—includes Bronto Burgers, Dino Dogs, and Chick-a-Saurus sandwiches.

Open mid-May through mid-September. Admission is pay-one-price, under $5. Hours vary; call first.

Tennessee

Dollywood
700 Dollywood Lane
Pigeon Forge, TN (615) 428–9488

Co-owned by country singing superstar Dolly Parton, this 100-acre, heavily wooded Smoky Mountain theme park has a lively selection of the arts, crafts, food, music, and customs of the mountains. There's nothing like this park's Craftsmen Valley in any other park in the country.

Dolly grew up in this area, and she does whatever she can to promote and showcase the region. She has an apartment at the park and is here many times each year. Many of her family members work and perform at the park.

There are 15 rides, including 4 just for the little ones. Other attractions include a replica of Dolly's childhood home and the Dolly Parton Story museum.

Food service: 9 full-menu restaurants and many additional fast-food/ snack outlets offer everything from ham and beans served in a sourdough bread bowl to smoked babyback ribs to fresh pork rinds. The best pork barbecue you'll find in any park in the world is smoked and served here. After 4:00 P.M., a good-priced, all-you-can-eat plan is offered at many of the restaurants.

Entertainment: Lots of free music throughout the park. Several live shows each day feature nostalgic rock-and-roll, bluegrass, country, and gospel music. Country music superstars perform twice daily in the DP Celebrity Theatre, additional charge. There are live birds-of-prey shows and eagle exhibits in the park's huge aviary.

TIM'S TRIVIA

Dolly Parton owns Dollywood, in Pigeon Forge, Tennessee, but her singing buddy Kenny Rogers doesn't own Kennywood, in West Mifflin, Pennsylvania. That park is more than fifty years older than Rogers.

Extras: Black-powder gun shooting and gold panning available for additional charge.

Special events: American Quilt Showcase, May; National Crafts Festival, October; Smoky Mountain Christmas, featuring 300,000 lights, Thanksgiving through New Year's Day.

Season: Late April through October. Reopens the day after Thanksgiving for its Christmas celebration.

Operating hours: 8:30 A.M. to 6:00 or 9:00 P.M.

Admission policy: Pay-one-price, under $20. All rides and shows, except in Celebrity Theatre, are included. Parking charge.

Top rides: Smoky Mountain Rampage, a raging-rapids ride; Thunder Express, a mine-train roller coaster; Mountain Slidewinder, a fast, downhill toboggan run in a rubber boat; Dollywood Express, a 5-mile excursion up the mountain on a 110-ton, coal-fired steam train; a circa-1924 Dentzel carousel in beautiful, original condition; Blazing Fury, a combination roller coaster, dark ride, and water ride that takes riders through a burning town.

Plan to stay: 5 hours.

Best way to avoid crowds: Come on Mondays, Thursdays, or Fridays. The park has an "in after 3:00 P.M., next day free" policy: Come for a few hours, go rest, and come back the next day free.

Directions: Located 1 mile east of Highway 441 in Pigeon Forge, about 5 miles north of Gatlinburg. Turn at the Dollywood Information Center, located below the area's largest billboard and beside a 110-ton Dollywood Express locomotive.

Nearby attractions: Waltzing Waters, a water show; The Track Recreation Center; Ogles Water Park; Dixie Stampede Dinner Attraction.

Libertyland
Mid-South Fairgrounds
940 Early Maxwell Boulevard
Memphis, TN (901) 274–1776

It is appropriate that this patriotic theme park opened on July 4, 1976, the country's bicentennial. The 26-acre park has a colonial feel to it, with the buildings and landscaping following that theme. Various colonial icons, including Independence Hall and the Liberty Bell, are replicated, as is the Statue of Liberty.

TIM'S TRIVIA

The Zippin' Pippin wooden roller coaster at Libertyland, in Memphis, Tennessee, not only is the oldest operating roller coaster in the country, but also was Elvis Presley's favorite. Elvis would rent out the entire park so that he and his family could enjoy the coaster, as well as the rest of the rides, without being bothered by fans.

Nine of the park's 25 rides are located in Kiddie Korner and on Tom Sawyer's Island, where costumed characters, including D. J. Foxx and Hound Dog, perform daily.

Food service: 2 sit-down restaurants, featuring fried catfish and southern cooking, as well as gourmet hamburgers. Ten additional snack-food stands are located throughout park.

Entertainment: 2 major musical shows and a street show featuring the costumed characters. The park is known for its top-quality musical revues and many of its performers have gone on to musical careers.

Special events: Libertyland Remembers Elvis, mid-August (Elvis Presley lived in Memphis and would rent the park out for his daughter and her friends); Christian Family Days, July; July 4 Birthday Party, featuring a tea party and a ride by Paul Revere.

Season: Mid-April through September.

Operating hours: Opens at 10:00 A.M. or noon and closes at 9:00 P.M. Closed Mondays.

Admission policy: General admission, plus rides, or a pay-one-price ticket is available, under $10; some rides are included in the general ad-

Tennessee

mission ticket. A Twilight ticket purchased after 4:00 P.M. saves half the price of general admission.

Top rides: Zippin' Pippin, considered the oldest operating wooden roller coaster in the country (it was Elvis's favorite); Revolution, a corkscrew coaster; Surf City Slide, a double water slide on fiberglass sleds; Grand Carousel, a circa-1909 Dentzel carousel.

Plan to stay: 4 hours.

TIM'S TRIVIA

The best French fries in the world, inside or outside an amusement park, can be found at the Potato Patch fry stand at Kennywood Park, West Mifflin, Pennsylvania, and its sister facility, Idlewild Park in Ligonier, Pennsylvania.

Best way to avoid crowds: Come on Tuesday or Wednesday and plan your rides around the show schedule.

Directions: Located 7 miles from downtown Memphis, on the fairgrounds. Take the Airways exit off I–240 to East Parkway. The park entrance is 2 miles north, between Central and Southern.

Nearby attractions: Graceland Mansion, Elvis Presley's home and shrine; Memphis Zoo; Mud Island, a Mississippi River museum, water park, and concert venue; the pyramid.

Magic World
Highway 441
Pigeon Forge, TN (615) 453–7941

High on a hilltop, this family park was founded in 1971 and has grown to include 35 rides, shows, and attractions. There are 13 mechanical rides, including several just for children. Most rides can be ridden by the entire family.

A participatory play area for kids offers a crawling maze, Crawl-a-Pillar, an air bounce, a ball swim, and super slides.

Food service: Several food outlets, serving sandwiches and snacks.

Entertainment: 3 live shows, including a magic show.

Season: Mid-April through September.

Operating hours: 10:00 A.M. to 10:00 P.M.

Admission policy: Pay-one-price, under $10. Free parking.

Top rides: Dragon Coaster, a compact steel coaster on the side of the hill overlooking Pigeon Forge; Giant Spider Ride; Tilt-A-Whirl; a Ferris wheel; antique cars; bumper boats; Magic Carpet, a unique suspended dark ride.

Plan to stay: 2½ hours.

Directions: Located along the strip of attractions on the west side of U.S. Highway 441, next to the Ice Cream Factory. The park is on the hill and you'll see the rides.

Nearby attractions: Kid's Country, miniature golf and kiddie rides; Carousel Fun Center, kiddie rides; Spinnin' & Grinnin', bumper boats and kiddie rides.

Opryland
2802 Opryland Drive
Nashville, TN (615) 889–6600

It's music everywhere you go here at Opryland. The music show park, located adjacent to the historic Grand Ole Opry, also has 22 grand ole rides and a well-supervised, shaded kiddieland area. The wooded park is divided into various theme sections, including Do Wah Diddy City, Grizzly Country, New Orleans, Hill Country, and State Fair.

Food service: 6 sit-down restaurants with line service and one with table service, plus snack stands and portable carts throughout.

Entertainment: Country, nostalgic rock-and-roll, and showtune music are all featured in 12 different productions; strolling musicians keep guests entertained while waiting in lines; and the park's 3,000-seat amphitheater features top-name country entertainers, for no additional charge, throughout the season.

Extras: Free petting zoo. Near Grizzly Country, there's a display showing country entertainer Roy Acuff's gun collection. Outside the gates, museums honoring the life and careers of Roy Acuff and Minnie Pearl are open to the public. Acuff lives next to his museum, on the park's grounds.

Special events: Gospel Jubilee, Memorial Day weekend; Blue Grass Extravaganza, July 4; plus many one-season-only special events.

Season: Late March through October.

Operating hours: 9:00 A.M. to 9:00 P.M.

Admission policy: Pay-one-price, under $25. Parking charge. Second-day ticket can be purchased for $5 additional.

Top rides: Chaos, an indoor roller coaster with 3-D visual and sound effects; Grizzly River Rampage, a raging-rapids ride; Wabash Cannonball, a corkscrew coaster; Old Mill Scream, a spill-water raft ride; Opryland Railroad, with vintage locomotives, providing a trip through the park.

Plan to stay: 6 hours.

Best ways to avoid crowds: Come midmorning during midweek and stay late. Big rush at opening time.

Directions: 9 miles northeast of downtown Nashville. Take the Briley

Parkway exit north from U.S. Route 40, or take the Briley Parkway exit east from I–65. Well-marked, separate exit off Briley Parkway for the park.

Nearby attractions: *General Jackson,* a paddle-wheel showboat; Grand Ole Opry; Grand Ole Golf, miniature golf; Nashville Toy Museum; Wax Museum; Nashville Palace, live music and southern cooking.

Texas

AstroWorld
9001 Kirby Drive
Houston, TX (713) 799–1234

Talk about an oasis of plant life! This 75-acre Six Flags park contains more than 600 varieties of plants and shrubs and is home to the world's largest hanging basket, holding 5,000 flowering plants. The landscaping has been beautifully designed to fit into the park's twelve theme areas, each representing a classic culture and era of America's past. Also blended nicely into the surroundings are the park's 30 rides.

Food service: 7 restaurants, including Gabby's Bar-B-Que and the Chat-n-Chew, serve up menu items ranging from platters to burritos to pizza; 28 additional locations serve fast-food and snack items.

Entertainment: 11 shows, including high divers, gunfights, nostalgia musical revues, animated cowboys, and a dolphin presentation. Special children's shows are presented in the Enchanted Kingdom area of the park. Sid and Marty Krofft have produced the extravagant stage show "Blast."

Extras: The Southern Star Amphitheater books in top-name entertainers all season long; some shows carry an additional surcharge.

Special events: Fright Nights, during which the park adopts a Halloween motif, weekends in late October; Holiday in the Park, special Christmas and holiday activities, Thanksgiving through December.

Season: March through October.

Operating hours: Opens daily at 11:00 A.M.; closes at 11:00 P.M. Sunday through Thursday and at midnight on Friday and Saturday.

Admission policy: Pay-one-price, under $25. Special discounts available after 4:00 P.M. Parking charge. Special combination ticket available for AstroWorld's sister park, WaterWorld.

Top rides: Alpine Carousel, a circa-1895 Dentzel carousel; Texas Cyclone, a wooden roller coaster; XLR-8, a suspended steel roller coaster; Tidal Wave, a spill-water raft ride; Astroway, a cable-car ride 100 feet above the park; Ultra Twister, a twisting steel roller coaster.

Six Flags' AstroWorld in Houston, Texas, has America's only Ultra Twister roller coaster. Riders reach speeds of 68 feet per second.

Plan to stay: 8 hours.

Best way to avoid crowds: Come during the week. The park is easy to get around in: Though spread out, it has a circular pattern. Take your time, see things as you go, and you won't have to double back.

Directions: Take the Kirby Drive exit off I–610; go north on Kirby to the park's parking lot.

Nearby attractions: WaterWorld, a water park also owned by the Six Flags Corporation; Malibu Grand Prix; Museum of Natural Science; Lyndon B. Johnson NASA Space Center; Houston Zoo; Houston Children's Museum.

Clown Around
702 East Safari Parkway
Grand Prairie, TX (214) 263–0001

It's amazing how much fun can be packed inside one building. Here are 9 mechanical kiddie rides, a ball crawl, a concessions stand, and a video-game and games-of-skill arcade.

And there is never an admission charge. A pay-one-price is always available, under $10, or you can pay-as-you-go. The park is closed on Mondays and Tuesdays but otherwise is open year-round for family outings and birthday parties. Hours vary; call first.

Fiesta Texas
Loop 1604 and I–10
San Antonio, TX (512) 697–5000

Being created in an abandoned stone quarry about 15 miles northwest of the city, this 200-acre park is expected to open to the public in the spring of 1992. The theme will be the music, culture, and history of the area and of the entire Southwest. The park promises to be an original, with rides, shows, and attractions being situated around the steep cliffs of the quarry. The park will open with 13 rides including the Gully Washer, a raging rapids ride; Power Surge, a spill-water raft ride; and a world-class wooden roller coaster. It is co-owned by Opryland (in Nashville), so expect the same first-class shows and attractions that you find there.

Funland Amusement Park
2006 Southwest Parkway
Wichita Falls, TX (817) 767–7911

Family fun at reasonable prices is what you'll find at this small, attractive traditional park on the outskirts of town. Started in 1960 as a kiddieland, the well-maintained park now caters to young families with kids from 3 to 14. It has 14 rides, including 6 just for the wee ones.

Food service: 1 large concession stand, serving hot dogs, french fries, corn dogs, and typical amusement park snack food.

Entertainment: Funland Freddie, the park's costumed-character, canine mascot, shows up on occasion to entertain the kids.

Extras: Miniature golf and a games-of-skill arcade. The city-operated park next door has a picnic pavilion and a child's playground.

Special events: End of School Party, mid-June; Back to School Party, late August.

Season: April through October.

Operating hours: Opens Tuesday through Friday at 6:30 P.M. and Saturday and Sunday at 2:00 P.M.; closes nightly at 10:00 P.M. Closed Mondays.

Admission policy: Free admission, with rides and attractions on a pay-as-you-go basis. Pay-one-price available, under $10. Free parking.

Top rides: Tilt-A-Whirl; Paratrooper; a Ferris wheel; bumper cars; and a miniature train.

Plan to stay: 2 hours.

Best way to avoid crowds: This isn't a tourist park, so crowds aren't usually a problem. Weeknights are generally less crowded than weekends.

TIM'S TRIVIA

The word fun appears in more amusement park names than any other descriptive word.

Directions: Take the Southwest Parkway exit from Highway 281 and go west 2 miles to the park. Located about 5 miles from downtown.

Nearby attractions: Putt-Putt, miniature golf; Wichita Falls Museum and Arts Center.

Joyland Amusement Park
McKenzie State Park
Lubbock, TX (806) 763–2719

Located in McKenzie State Park on its own 10-acre site, Joyland has been serving up entertainment to the area since the early 1940s. The midway is bright and clean with a nice "local amusement park" feeling to it.

The entire park, including the rides, is well maintained by the Dean family, who have owned it since 1973. It has 22 rides, including 9 for kids.

Food service: 2 concession stands, serving short-order meals like hamburgers, burritos, and french fries. Lots of tables around the park.

Entertainment: No regularly scheduled in-park shows.

Special events: Weeknights at the park are sponsored by local businesses that offer special discounts, ranging from two-for-ones to family nights when parents ride free.

Season: Mid-March through mid-September.

Operating hours: Opens at 7:00 P.M. during the week and 2:00 P.M. on weekends; closes nightly at 10:00 P.M.

Admission policy: General admission, plus rides on a pay-as-you-go basis; pay-one-price also available, under $10. Free parking.

Top rides: Musik Express; Mad Mouse, a compact steel roller coaster; a skyride; Paratrooper; Galaxy, a compact steel roller coaster.

Plan to stay: 3 hours.

Best way to avoid crowds: Tuesday nights are the least crowded.

Directions: Take Fourth Street exit off I-35 and enter the state park. Follow the signs to Joyland.

Nearby attractions: Prairie Dog Town, in McKenzie State Park; Putt-Putt, miniature golf; Texas Tech Museum; Ranching Heritage Center, a restored ranching village.

Jungle Jim's Playland
Bellaire at Southwest Freeway
Houston, TX (713) 995-JIMS

Jungle Jim's is a Texas-based chain of indoor family entertainment centers that have a jungle theme and are professionally run. Everyone under 18 must be accompanied by an adult.

This location is in its own building, adjacent to the Sharpstown Mall. There are 7 mechanical kiddie rides, including a mini-Himalaya ride and an elephant ride. And there's Jungle Play, a huge participatory play area, as well as a games-of-skill and video-games arcade.

Admission is by pay-one-price only, under $10. Adults always ride free. Hours vary; call first.

Jungle Jim's Playland at Memorial City
Gessner at Katy Freeway
Houston, TX (713) 932-PLAY

This is the largest of the Jungle Jim's locations. Inside the huge Memorial City mall are four separate sections: a roller-skating rink with a jungle theme, an arcade room, a games-of-skill redemption area, and the traditional Jungle Playland, with 7 mechanical kiddie rides, an air bounce, and a Jungle Play participatory play area.

Pay-one-price admission, under $10 for the ride area only. Hours of operation are the same as the mall's but are extended on weekends.

Jungle Jim's Playland
521 Campbell Road
Richardson, TX (214) 234-JIMS

In the heart of the Dallas–Ft. Worth metroplex, this indoor family fun facility is located in a shopping center and has its own storefront. With

8 mechanical kiddie rides, including a safari adventure jeep ride, this park also has the trademarked Jungle Play participatory play area and a games-of-skill and video-games arcade.

Admission is pay-one-price, under $10, with adults always riding free. Everyone under 18 must be accompanied by an adult.

Jungle Jim's Playland
Bitters Road at Highway 281
San Antonio, TX (512) 490-9595

This is the Jungle Jim's that started them all—the original location. There are 8 mechanical kiddie rides, including a Ferris wheel, a mini-Himalaya ride, and a jungle train ride. Also here are a games-of-skill and video-games arcade and Jungle Play, the company's trademarked participatory play area. Food service includes hot dogs and pizza, and activities encompass birthday parties and a Jungle Jim costumed character.

Admission by pay-one-price only, under $10, with adults riding free at all times. Hours vary; call first.

Kiddie Park
3015 Broadway
San Antonio, TX (512) 824-4351

Well known throughout the area, this park is now entertaining its fourth generation of kids. Established in 1925 adjacent to the sprawling Brackenridge City Park, Kiddie Park has 10 rides, including a circa-1918 Herschell-Spillman carousel.

Admission to the 1-acre park is free, with rides on a pay-as-you-go basis. A pay-one-price ticket is also available, under $5. Open year-round, 10:00 A.M. to 10:00 P.M.

Note: If you're still eager for some action after you've done everything at Kiddie Park, cross the street to the city park, where you can enjoy pony rides, train rides, an aerial ride, and the San Antonio Zoo.

Neff's Amusement Park
Neff's Way, Riverpark Mall
San Angelo, TX (915) 653-3014

The action in this wonderful little city takes place down by the river. And this small family park is located downtown on 3 acres along the river. Situated next to the boardwalk, the park is divided by a walkway that runs from the street. The 7 kiddie rides are on one side, the 7 adult and family rides on the other.

The entire area around the park is being developed into a riverside park, complete with a band shell, benches, walkways, and shopping areas.

Food service: 1 major concession stand, serving ice cream, hot dogs, popcorn, and similar items.

Entertainment: No regularly scheduled shows. A few concerts and dances, including senior dances, take place during the season.

Extras: Paddleboats, extra charge. Arcade games.

Special events: Fiesta Celebration, June; July 4 fireworks and celebration.

Season: March through October.

Operating hours: Opens at 6:00 P.M. during the week and 1:30 P.M. on weekends. Closes nightly at 11:00 P.M.

Admission policy: Free admission to the park, with rides on a pay-as-you-go basis. Pay-one-price available on certain days, under $15. Free parking.

Top rides:. A train ride, taking you out of the park and along the river; bumper cars; a Ferris wheel; a circa-1906 Parker carousel.

Plan to stay: 2 hours.

Best way to avoid crowds: Tuesday nights are the least crowded.

Directions: Located on the river between the Okes and Chadbourne bridges. Take Neff's Way off either of those avenues and follow it to the parking lot. Follow the path to the park.

Nearby attractions: Fort Concho, a restored military fort; Putting Course, miniature golf.

Penny Whistle Park
10712 East Northwest Highway at Plano Road
Dallas, TX (214) 348–6470

If there's a granddaddy of the indoor family entertainment center, this is it. Founded in 1975, Penny Whistle was one of the first such establishments in the country. The park has 8 indoor kiddie rides, as well as an outdoor participatory play unit that's set up only during summer months.

Wednesday and Thursday nights are family nights, with reduced pay-one-price ride tickets, under $5. Other times, there is free admission and rides are on a pay-as-you-go basis. Open year-round, but closed on Mondays during the summer and on Mondays and Tuesdays the rest of the year.

Sandy Lake Amusement Park
1800 Sandy Lake Road
Dallas, TX (214) 242-7449

"We don't cater to tourists or the rich people. We're here for the working families." Of course, both are welcome, but that's how the owner explains his family's park in the Dallas suburb of Carrollton. It's also the only outdoor amusement park in Dallas County.

Spread out over 112 acres, the park features 20 rides, clustered in groups under large pecan and oak trees. There are resting spots galore and a 2-acre lake. Probably the biggest draw here, though, is the "Texas-size" swimming pool: The largest in the area, it holds 1.5 million gallons of filtered water.

Food service: 4 concession stands, selling hot dogs, nachos, ice cream, and other fast-food and snack items; no fried foods are served. The park has 1,200 picnic tables, and guests are allowed to bring in their own food. Beer may be brought in but is not sold.

Entertainment: No scheduled in-park entertainment.

Extras: Miniature golf, paddleboats, live pony rides, and horse-drawn stagecoach rides, all available for extra charge.

Special events: Easter Parade, when 40,000 plastic eggs are dropped from a helicopter, Easter weekend; FunFest, when more than 1,000 school bands, choirs, and choral groups compete for trophies, April and May.

Season: Easter through mid-September.

Operating hours: Daily, 10:00 A.M. to 6:00 P.M. (The park has never been open after dark.)

Admission policy: General admission, plus rides. Free parking.

Top rides: Fun House, a classic Pretzel dark ride; a train ride around the park; Tilt-A-Whirl; Scrambler; a kiddie roller coaster; bumper cars.

Plan to stay: 3 hours.

Best way to avoid crowds: Come on Sunday afternoons, when crowds tend to be moderate—just enough people to make things interesting, but not so many as to slow you down.

Directions: 15 miles north of Dallas at the Sandy Lake exit off I-35.

Nearby attractions: North Lake city park; Grapevine Recreational Area; University of Dallas.

Sea World of Texas
10500 Sea World Drive
San Antonio, TX (512) 523-3600

This is the largest and the newest of the Sea World parks. In fact, with 250 acres, it's the world's largest marine zoological park.

When built in 1988, the park created a Cypress Gardens West area, forming a 16-acre oasis of plant and tree life. Although the section is not nearly as beautiful or significant as the original in Florida, it does offer much in the way of relaxation.

A 4-acre kiddie section called Cap'n Kid's World is a children's participatory play area.

Food service: 4 sit-down, air-conditioned restaurants and 12 snack bars. The nonalcoholic frozen drinks available at the Daiquiri Factory are fantastic!

Entertainment: 5 shows, including the trademark Shamu Killer Whale show, as well as ice skating, waterskiing, and sea lion/otter shows.

Extras: Texas Walk, enabling you to walk through state history in a garden containing statues of sixteen famous Texans. A 90-minute behind-the-scenes tour is available, extra charge.

Season: March through November.

Operating hours: 10:00 A.M. to 11:00 P.M.

Admission policy: Pay-one-price, under $25. Free parking.

Top rides: 2 water rides: Texas Splashdown, a flume, and the Rio Loco, a raging rapids ride.

Plan to stay: 7 hours.

Best way to avoid crowds: Come during the week, just before dinnertime.

Directions: Located 16 miles northwest of downtown San Antonio, off State Highway 151 between Loop 410 and Loop 1604, on Sea World Drive.

Nearby attractions: San Antonio River Walk, shopping and dining; the Alamo; San Antonio Zoo; Ripley's Believe It or Not! and Plaza Theatre of Wax.

Six Flags Over Texas
2201 Road to Six Flags
Arlington, TX (817) 640-8900

This 205-acre park is the mother ship of the Six Flags organization. In fact, it not only was the first Six Flags park to open (1961) but also the first major regional theme park in the country.

Beautiful at night because of the colorful lights, and beautiful in the day because of the colorful flowers and landscaping, the park has a total of 30 rides, including 6 for kids housed in Bugs Bunny Land.

TIM'S TRIVIA

There's enough lumber in Texas Giant, the roller coaster at Six Flags Over Texas in Arlington, to build thirty houses.

The mature, well-grown-in facility has six different areas reflecting the architecture and atmosphere of life under "the rule of the six flags": Spain, France, Mexico, the Confederacy, the Republic of Texas, and the United States.

Food service: 35 locations throughout the park, including Chubby's Diner and The Food Court, both with indoor, air-conditioned seating.

Entertainment: 7 shows, including a dolphin presentation, a magic show, 2 musical revues, gunfights, and shows in the Music Mill Amphitheater by top-name entertainers. The Looney Tunes characters call this park their home, as they do all the other Six Flags facilities.

Extras: Two of the original attractions are still in operation: the Casa Magnetica (a tilt house) featuring gravity illusions, and the Six Flags Railroad, taking visitors on a trip around the park.

Special events: Holiday in the Park, Thanksgiving through New Year's Day; Fright Nights, the last three weekends in October; Music and Crafts Fair, September; Christian Family Day and Texas Music Fest, their dates varying from year to year.

Season: April through October. Reopens for Holiday in the Park.

Operating hours: Opens daily at 10:00 A.M.; closes at varying times all season long, from 6:00 P.M. to midnight.

Admission policy: Pay-one-price, under $20. Parking charge.

Top rides: Texas Giant, a wooden roller coaster; Flashback, a steel boomerang roller coaster; Roaring Rapids, a raging-rapids ride; Splashwater Falls, a spill-water raft ride; Oil Derrick, an observation tower; Silver Star Carousel, a circa-1926 Dentzel carousel.

Plan to stay: 8 hours.

Best way to avoid crowds: Come on Sundays in fall or spring, or come early in the day during midweek in peak season. Avoid Saturdays any time of the year if you want to stay out of crowds.

Directions: In Arlington, halfway between Dallas and Ft. Worth, off I–30. Signs will give you fair warning that the exits to the park are approaching, and a huge electronic sign and the observation tower will mark the spot quite nicely.

Nearby attractions: Wet 'n Wild, a water park; Arlington Stadium; Billy Bob's, a world-renowned country music nightclub; Dallas Zoo.

It's OK to stand up on this roller coaster. In fact, that's the only way you can ride Kings Dominion's Shockwave, in Doswell, Virginia.

Sunshine Park
2834 Roosevelt Avenue
San Antonio, TX (512) 532–5255

If you're unfamiliar with the area, it's easy to be surprised as you drive down Roosevelt Avenue: All of a sudden, there beside a convenience store is Sunshine Park. A family park with 8 kiddie rides and 5 adult and family rides, the facility is open only on Thursdays, Fridays, Saturdays, and Sundays.

Thursday night is Family Night, when all rides, popcorn, and sodas go for 25 cents each. Among the popular rides is a haunted house, bumper cars, Tilt-A-Whirl, a kiddie roller coaster, and a Ferris wheel. Admission is free, with rides on a pay-as-you-play basis.

Western Playland
6900 Delta
El Paso, TX (915) 772–3953

As the Ferris wheel stops and you're at the top, don't kiss. Instead, look out over the river and you'll see Mexico. That's how close this park is to the border. Located in Ascarate County Park, the facility has 30 rides, including 10 for kids, on 20 acres.

With its Spanish motif, the park features an abundance of colorful gardens, shade trees, benches, and adobe buildings.

Food service: 4 snack bars, serving hot dogs, hamburgers, ice cream, and other snack and fast-food items.

Entertainment: No regularly scheduled in-park shows. Special concerts are booked into the park's amphitheater several times a season.

Extras: Go-carts, additional fee.

Special events: July 4 fireworks and celebration.

Season: March through mid-October.

Operating hours: Opens at 6:30 P.M. during the week and at 2:00 P.M. weekends. Closes nightly at 10:00 P.M. Closed Mondays.

Admission policy: Pay-one-price, under $10. Also general admission, plus rides on a pay-as-you-go basis. Free parking.

Top rides: Splashdown, a log flume; El Bandito, a Zyklon compact steel roller coaster; Big Cheese, a Mad Mouse roller coaster; a train ride, a 2½-mile trek around the park; Gold Nugget, a dark ride.

Plan to stay: 4 hours.

Best way to avoid crowds: Come on weekday nights or Sunday afternoons.

Directions: Take the Trobridge exit off I–10. Go left and proceed through three traffic lights, turning right onto Delta. The park is located about a mile after you cross over an overpass.

Nearby attractions: Tigua Indian Reservation; San Elezario, a restored Spanish village with an old mission.

Wonderland Park
Highway 287 North
Amarillo, TX (806) 383–4712

This truly is a family park—the family that started it in 1951 still owns and operates it for the families of Amarillo. Located in the city's largest greenbelt, Thompson Park, Wonderland has 24 rides, including 5 for the little folks.

Founded as a kiddie park, the facility has grown and is now a popular place for the entire area. A flat, paved midway is lined with trees and flowers and contains lots of benches.

Food service: 1 large walk-away stand, with tables and umbrellas nearby, plus 3 small stands offering additional snacks and fast food.

Entertainment: No scheduled in-park shows.

Extras: Miniature golf, extra fee.

Season: Mid-March through September.

Operating hours: Opens during the week at 7:00 P.M. and on weekends at 1:00 P.M.; closes nightly at 10:30 P.M.

Admission policy: General admission, plus rides, or a pay-one-price ticket is available for weeknights, under $10, and on weekends, under $15 (the looping coaster and the dark ride are not included in the pay-one-price). Free parking.

Top rides: Texas Tornado, a two-loop steel roller coaster; Rattlesnake River, a raging-rapids ride; Zyklon, a compact steel roller coaster; Fantastic Journey, a dark ride; Big Splash, a log flume.

Plan to stay: 3 hours.

Best way to avoid crowds: Come during June. Thursday evenings are the slowest times.

Directions: Located in the Texas Panhandle. Take the 24th Street or River Road exit off Highway 287; the park is located inside Thompson Park and is easily visible from the road.

Nearby attractions: Thompson Park's zoo, swimming pool, tennis courts, and miles of walking trails.

Utah

49th Street Galleria
4998 South 360 West
Murray, UT (801) 263–2987

There's something for everyone in this huge indoor family fun center— several kiddie rides, batting cages, a roller-skating rink, a 40-lane bowling alley, and a miniature golf course. There's also an entertainment stage, featuring regularly scheduled concerts, dances, and family shows. Food service includes The Patio restaurant, The Creamery ice-cream parlor, Leonardo's Pizza, and an Orange Julius.

Free admission, with rides, games, and attractions on a pay-as-you-play basis. Opens Monday through Saturday at 10:00 A.M.; closes at 11:00 P.M. on weeknights and at midnight on Fridays and Saturdays. Closed Sundays.

Lagoon Park
I–15 and Lagoon Drive
Farmington, UT (801) 451–0101

Summertime fun is both plentiful and varied in the state's largest amusement facility. From thrilling roller coasters to a charming pre-1900 pioneer village to a cool water park, there's enough here to keep the whole family busy.

There are 40 rides, including 12 for kids in Mother Gooseland. The 15-acre Pioneer Village features crafts, foods, and architecture from the pre-1900 Utah frontier, while Lagoon A Beach is a 6-acre water park offering a bevy of water activities.

Once located on the shores of the Great Salt Lake, this park moved inland to its own 9-acre lagoon and changed its name from Lake Park to Lagoon Park. The merry-go-round, skating rink, saloon, and cafe went along with the park. Today, all that remains from that 1896 move is the wonderfully Victorian Lake Park Terrace, used as one of the picnic terraces for group outings.

Food service: The Gaslight Burger Palace is the park's major sit-down restaurant, featuring a full menu, including chicken, fish, and steak dinners. Ten walk-away locations offer traditional fast-food and snack items. The park advertises that it has the "Best Fried Chicken in Utah." And whatever you do, don't miss the freshly baked cinnamon rolls; they're big and sweet.

Entertainment: Several different shows, including a major musical revue, a Wild West shoot-out, and the marching and playing of the popular Lagoon Marching Band. The clown band calls itself the L.A. Goon Band and can be found wandering throughout the park. The Lagoon Opera House is a summer theater venue offering daily performances, usually for an additional fee.

Extras: Paddleboats on the lagoon, free with admission, and an 18-hole miniature golf course called Putter Around the Park, extra charge, that features miniature versions of amusement park attractions, including a roller coaster hole.

Special events: Clogging Championships, several weekends in May; School Days, May; fireworks, Memorial Day, July 4, and Labor Day; Utah's Pioneer Days, a state holiday, July 24.

Season: April through early October.

Operating hours: 11:00 A.M. to midnight.

Admission policy: Pay-one-price, under $20; includes water park and "dry" rides. Parking charge.

Top rides: Dracula's Castle, a dark ride; Flying Carpet, a 360-degree swinging platform; Tidal Wave, a pendulum pirate ship; Roller Coaster, a wooden roller coaster; Colossus Fire Dragon, a two-loop steel coaster; a circa-1900 Herschell-Spillman carousel; a train ride around the lagoon and through a small zoo.

Plan to stay: 8 hours.

Best way to avoid crowds: Sunday and Monday are the slowest days of the week. Saturday is the busiest.

Directions: Located off I-15, 17 miles north of Salt Lake City and 17 miles south of Ogden. Take the Lagoon Drive exit.

Nearby attractions: Raging Waters, a water park; Seven Peaks, a water park; Cherry Hills, camping, miniature golf, and batting cages; the Great Salt Lake; Temple Square, Mormon Temple and Tabernacle.

Vermont

Santa's Land
Route 5
Putney, VT (802) 387-5550

"Where the Spirit of Christmas is a way of Life"—that's the slogan of this little park in the foothills of the Green Mountains. The alpine architecture throughout lends a fine touch to making this a fun outing for the entire family.

In addition to a train ride through a joyful Santa's Tunnel, the park offers a carousel, an iceberg-shaped giant slide, a petting zoo, horse-drawn sleigh rides, a playground, and an animatronic show of animals preparing for Christmas.

What's more, Christmas movies and cartoons are constantly being shown in the Little Red Schoolhouse, and Santa and his elves are ready to greet visitors in his elegant home at the back of the park.

The Igloo Pancake House, housed in three white igloo-shaped buildings, serves delicious pancakes and waffles; of course, real Vermont maple syrup is on every table. Several Christmas shops, too, provide top-notch shopping.

Open from May through Christmas; closed Thanksgiving and Christmas days. Pay-one-price, under $10.

Virginia

Busch Gardens, The Old Country
Route 60
Williamsburg, VA (804) 253-3350

With its 360 acres of heavily wooded, rolling hills, this is the most beautiful large theme park in the country. The architecture in each of the nine Old World European hamlets looks as though it has been there for years; hats off to the designers. It's not easy to build things that look 400 years old and at the same time make 39 modern rides look like they belong in the setting. But they did it here, quite nicely.

Food service: Das Festhaus is a German beer house complete with costumed waitresses and German oompah bands. The Three Rivers Smokehouse offers barbecued beef, spareribs, and chicken. An additional 5 sit-down restaurants and 40 fast-food and snack stands serve just about any Old World treat you can think of.

Entertainment: There's myriad Renaissance merriment here, as live shows abound throughout the park, offering all sorts of musical treats, from bluegrass to Broadway to Italian. Additional shows include a computerized animated production, an ice show, a bird show, and strolling street entertainers.

Extras: The Royal Preserve Petting Zoo is free with admission. Top-name entertainers are scheduled in the Royal Palace Concert Theatre all summer for an extra charge in addition to park admission. And self-guided brewery tours at the adjacent Anheuser-Busch Brewery offer free samples at the end. A special "Shopper's Pass" is available if you want to enter only to shop in the stores.

Special events: Story Telling Festival, end of May.

Season: April through October.

Operating hours: 10:00 A.M. to 10:00 P.M. or midnight.

Admission policy: Pay-one-price, under $25. An after–5:00 P.M. twilight ticket discount is available, as is a second-day pass, for an additional $5. Parking charge.

Top rides: Loch Ness Monster, a double-looping steel coaster; The Big Bad Wolf, a suspended roller coaster ride through a Bavarian village; Roman Rapids, a raging-rapids ride; Le Scoot, a log flume; Questor, a fantasy-themed simulator attraction; a scenic boat cruise down the Rhine River; a 1919 Allan Herschell carousel.

Plan to stay: 10 hours.

There's all sorts of medieval fun awaiting the family at Busch Gardens, The Old Country, in Williamsburg, Virginia.

Best way to avoid crowds: Come in spring or fall, when crowds are fewer. During the season, midweek is best. Check the concert schedule; the park is generally much more crowded on big concert days.

Directions: Take I–64 east into the Williamsburg area, follow the signs to get onto Route 60, and follow that route until you get to the park.

Nearby attractions: Historic Colonial Williamsburg; Williamsburg Pottery; Mariner's Museum; Chrysler Museum; Water Country USA, a water park; Williamsburg Winery.

Kings Dominion
Route 30
Doswell, VA (804) 876–5000

The excitement of a visit to this park begins as you enter the front gate. Looming 330 feet into the air in front of you is a replica of the Eiffel Tower, and a good way to start your visit is to take a trip up to its observation deck to get a feel for what the park is all about.

TIM'S TRIVIA

The Eiffel Tower exists, albeit one-third scale, in two American parks: Kings Island amusement park, near Cincinnati, Ohio, and Kings Dominion, in Doswell, Virginia.

The park is divided into five areas: International Street, Old Virginia, Wild Animal Safari, Candy Apple Grove, and the Land of Hanna-Barbera, a great little kiddie-ride area. All 43 rides, including the 10 for kids, are divided among the different sections.

Food service: 12 restaurants, including Livingston's and Victoria Gardens, serve the full gamut of food. Some of the park's best food is its country cooking, served in the Country Kitchen. Additional fast-food outlets are scattered throughout.

Entertainment: 14 shows, including a full-scale, Broadway-style musical revue; a child's participatory show; and shows featuring sea lions, puppets, and Hanna-Barbera characters. Roving performers include jugglers and mimes.

Extras: The 7,500-seat Showplace Amphitheatre offers top-name entertainers on a regular basis throughout the season. There's a charge to these concerts in addition to park admission.

Season: End of March through mid-October.

Operating hours: 9:00 A.M. to 9:00 or 10:00 P.M.

Virginia

Admission policy: Pay-one-price, under $25. Parking charge.

Top rides: Shockwave, a stand-up looping roller coaster; Rebel Yell, twin racing wooden coasters; Grizzly, a wooden coaster; The Anaconda, a multielement steel coaster that disappears under Lake Charles; White Water Canyon, a raging-rapids ride; Shenandoah, a log flume; Avalanche Bobsled, a free-moving bobsled run; a 1917 Philadelphia Toboggan Company carousel.

Plan to stay: 10 hours.

Best ways to avoid crowds: Tuesday is the least busy day. Get there early and head to the major rides first.

Directions: Located 20 miles north of Richmond. Take Exit 40 (Doswell) off I–95; the park is right there.

Nearby attractions: In Richmond: state capitol, designed by Thomas Jefferson; antebellum homes along Monument Avenue; Richmond Children's Museum.

Ocean Breeze Fun Park
849 General Booth Boulevard
Virginia Beach, VA (804) 425–1241

Big things are happening at this 80-acre family fun park. Fifteen new mechanical rides, including a large steel looping coaster and a giant Ferris wheel, are scheduled to be added prior to or shortly after this book goes to press. Other elements set for debut at the same time are several new food and game locations and a new Main Street area, where glassblowers, clock makers, and other artists will make and sell their crafts.

These new features join an already-busy and -popular park that is divided into four areas: MotorWorld, featuring 11 go-cart and Grand Prix tracks; Shipwreck Golf, a 36-hole miniature golf course whose holes represent a real shipwreck off the Virginia coast; WildWater Rapids, a water park; and Strike Zone, offering batting cages.

The park is located 1 mile south of the Virginia Beach oceanfront, and different parts of the facility are open from April through October. There is a general admission fee, with activities on a pay-as-you-go basis. Several combinations of a pay-one-price ticket are also available.

189

Washington

Fun Forest
Seattle Center
370 Thomas Street
Seattle, WA (206) 728-1585

What a festive place this is! On the site of the 1963 World's Fair, the amusement park is only a part of the entire Seattle Center, which also features the famous Space Needle.

A colorful flag pavilion and the festive architecture make this entire center a treat to visit. The ride park itself contains 19 rides, including 8 for kids in a separate kiddieland. It was built as part of the entertainment package for the fair and has been in operation ever since.

Food service: Within the ride area are a snack stand and numerous carts. Directly adjacent to the rides is the Food Circus, a year-round, indoor food court with 30 different outlets.

Entertainment: The center presents various forms of entertainment throughout the summer, although nothing is scheduled on an everyday basis.

Extras: Miniature golf and a large games arcade. The monorail runs from the center to the Westlake Mall in the downtown area of the city.

Special events: Kid's Day, reduced ride prices and special events, three times a year, April, August and October; Bite of Seattle, a food fair, mid-July; Bumbershoot, a music festival with lots of arts and crafts, Labor Day Weekend.

Season: March through mid-November.

Operating hours: Opens daily at noon; closes during the week and on weekends at 11:00 P.M., midnight or 1:00 A.M.

Admission policy: Free gate, with rides and attractions on a pay-as-you-play basis. Pay-one-price available during the week only, under $10. Parking charge.

Top rides: Wild River, a log flume; Galaxy, a compact steel coaster; Galleon, a swinging pirate ship; Enterprise; bumper boats; a carousel.

Plan to stay: 2 hours.

Best way to avoid crowds: The park gets very crowded during festivals and special events, but is less crowded during the early part of the week and during fall.

Directions: Take Exit 167 (Mercer Street) west off I-5, and continue for 1 mile. The park is located adjacent to the highly visible Space Needle.

Nearby attractions: The Pacific Science Center, which features a laser show and science exhibit; the Seattle Children's Theatre; and the Opera House are all adjacent to the amusement park. Take the monorail downtown to the Pike Place Market, a large, popular outdoor market.

Riverfront Park
North 507 Howard Street
Spokane, WA (509) 456–5512

Located downtown along the Spokane River, this 100-acre park was the site of the 1974 World's Fair. Beautifully landscaped, the park offers an IMAX theater, miniature golf, and 9 rides, including a gondola ride over the spectacular Spokane Falls. (A rainbow consistently lies on the mist around the falls, so this may be the only ride in the world that goes over a rainbow.) Additional attractions include a 1909 Looff carousel, completely restored in 1990, that lets you grab for the brass ring; Dragon, a roller coaster; and an SR-2 ride simulator.

Admission to the grounds is free, and all attractions are on a pay-as-you-go basis. Most attractions are open from March 1 through mid-October. Various attractions in the park have different hours; call first.

West Virginia

Camden Park
Route 60 West
Huntington, WV (304) 429–4231

A walk down the tree-lined midway here takes a person back to the 1940s. The architecture, the selection of rides and games, and the wonderful neon lighting make this a not-to-be-missed traditional park.

There are 28 rides, including 10 for kids, and a steamboat that offers rides on the Ohio River. This may also be the only park in the country that has an Indian burial mound within its gates. It was created 2,000 years ago by the Athena Indians.

Food service: 1 large, air-conditioned cafeteria serving a full line of menu items, plus 5 other eateries serving traditional amusement park fare. People come from miles just to eat in this park; their favorites are the fried chicken dinners and the country fried steak. Food may be brought into the park, and there's a Domino's Pizza franchise in the park that delivers to the outside world.

Entertainment: Nothing scheduled on a daily basis, but country music shows by top-name performers are set for every weekend.

Extras: A roller-skating rink is open during the winter months only.

Special events: Cartoon Day, when costumed cartoon characters visit the park, early August; Anniversary Day, featuring discount attractions and special entertainment, mid-August; Fireworks and Country Music, held every holiday weekend.

Season: April through mid-October.

Operating hours: 10:00 A.M. to 10:00 P.M.

Admission policy: Small gate fee, with rides and attractions on a pay-as-you-go basis. Pay-one-price also available, under $10.

Top rides: Thunderbolt Express, a shuttle-loop roller coaster; West Virginia Logging Company, a log flume; Big Dipper, a wooden roller coaster; a 1904 Allan Herschell carousel.

Plan to stay: 6 hours.

Best way to avoid crowds: Come on Mondays.

Directions: Take Exit 6 off I–64, go 300 yards, and turn left on Madison. The road dead-ends into the park in 3 miles.

Nearby attractions: *West Virginia Belle,* Ohio River cruises; Pilgrim Glass Company, tours; Blenko Glass Company, tours.

Wisconsin

Bay Beach Amusement Park
1313 Bay Beach Boulevard
Green Bay, WI (414) 448–3365

A favorite with locals since 1920, this park has 12 rides, including 3 for children. You'll find lots of shade around, and usually a cool breeze is blowing in off Green Bay.

This may be the only park in the world that still charges 10 cents a ride. Ten rides in the park cost a dime per ride, while two cost 20 cents.

In addition to the rides, the park offers a wading pool for the little ones, softball diamonds, volleyball courts, and a horseshoe pit for adults. Staff will even lend you the athletic equipment to play with.

Food service: 2 fast-food stands. Food and beverages may be brought into the park, and you can bring your own grill. (If you don't have one, staff will rent you one.)

Extras: A wildlife sanctuary, with nature center, year-round hiking trails, and educational programs.

Season: April through September.

Operating hours: 10:00 A.M. to 9:00 P.M.

Admission policy: Free admission, with rides on a per-ride basis. Free parking.

Top rides: A train ride through the park and along Green Bay; a giant slide; bumper cars; a merry-go-round; a Ferris wheel.

Plan to stay: 2 hours.

Best way to avoid crowds: There is rarely a large crowd here, but middays during the week you'll find the least competition for the fun.

Directions: Located on Green Bay. Take the Irwin Avenue exit off Highway 43 and follow the signs.

Nearby attractions: Naval Monument.

Circle M Corral Family Fun Park
10295 Highway 70 West
Minocqua, WI (715) 356–4441

Sheriff Parker, the mascot, is the one you have to deal with at this western family park. Family-owned and -operated, the place is clean, safe, and fun for all members of the family. Attractions include a train ride through the scenic pines and a dark tunnel, go-carts, bumper boats, miniature golf, horseback riding, a water slide, and a kiddieland with a variety of rides and attractions.

The park has a unique, pay-one-price admission system whereby you can mix and match the attractions you want access to. Hours vary; call first.

Circus World Museum
426 Water Street
Baraboo, WI (608) 356–8341

Lions and tigers and elephants once roamed this land when it was the original site of the winter quarters of the Ringling Bros. Circus. That was in 1884. Today, the place is a living museum to the circus. Parades, circus performances, outdoor circus acts, and historic demonstrations are scheduled from early May to mid-September.

Three kiddie rides, including a 1925 Allan Herschell carousel, are operated on the premises, as is a petting zoo.

Pay-one-price, under $10. Hours vary, call first.

Riverview Park
Highway 12
Wisconsin Dells, WI (608) 254–2608

Keeping busy is no problem in the Wisconsin Dells. There are literally hundreds of attractions, but this park stands out from the rest. It truly has something for everyone and is considered the state's largest "U-Drive 'Em" park.

In all, the park has 11 mechanical rides, 22 water activities, and 13 U-Drive 'Ems—all this on 35 acres. And you'll find plenty of shade and benches throughout, as well as a walk-through haunted house.

Food service: Several fast-food stands, spread out across the park. Free use of picnic shelters, and you can bring your own food and beverages into the park.

Entertainment: Magic show, three times daily in amphitheater.

Extras: The "Wilderness Trail Ride and Petting Zoo" is included in the pay-one-price admission. It's a golf-cart ride through the woods to a petting zoo and a 50-foot-high overlook.

Season: May through October

Operating hours: 9:00 A.M. to 11:00 P.M.

Admission policy: Free admission, plus attractions, or a pay-one-price ticket to "slide, ride, and drive" all day is available, under $15. Free parking.

Top rides: A Himalaya ride; a skyride; Grand Prix cars.

Plan to stay: 4 hours.

Best way to avoid crowds: Come early during the week or on weekends in spring and fall.

Directions: Located near the boat docks on Highway 12, just south of Highway 13. Take Exit 87 (Highway 13) off I–90/94 to Highway 12.

Nearby attractions: Noah's Ark, a water park; Tommy Bartlett Show, waterskiing and circus acts, plus a Laser-Rama; greyhound racing; Olde Kilbourn Amusements, miniature golf and a haunted house.

Thumb Fun Park
Highway 42
Fish Creek, WI (414) 868–3418

Nestled in the lovely countryside, this family entertainment center has 12 rides, including 5 for kids, and a magnificent haunted mansion. The highlight of the park, however, is the Wilderness Railroad, one of the nation's best in-park railroads; it takes you on a 2-mile, 20-minute ride into the wilderness of Sidewinder Gulch.

Additionally, the park offers miniature golf, go-carts, bumper boats, bumper cars, a driving range, a petting zoo, and a handful of other mechanical rides for adults and children.

The park has a general admission charge, with rides and attractions extra. A pay-one-price ticket is available and includes rides and the haunted house. Open Memorial Day through mid-October. Opens at 10:30 A.M. and closes during the early evening.

Wyoming

Wyoming Territorial Park
I–80 and Snowy Range Road
Laramie, WY (307) 745–6161

Centered on the state's circa-1872 territorial prison, this living history and re-creation park will be built to "give the visitors a hands-on idea of what the history of the American West is all about."

Scheduled to open in 1992, the enterprise will offer a few mechanical rides, a large-screen-format cinema, a stagecoach, and animal rides.

The Viper, at Six Flags Magic Mountain in Valencia, California, is the world's largest looping roller coaster. Riders turn upside-down seven times as the coaster reaches speeds of 70 miles per hour.

CANADA

Canada, like the United States, has a varied selection of amusement parks. Some are big corporate parks, others are smaller family operations, but each has its own personality and its own following.

Operation- and attraction-wise, Canadian parks don't differ much from U.S. parks. The goal is the same: to create an environment in which kids of all ages can have fun.

Following is a sampling of Canadian parks, by province, that will give you a good idea of what the country has to offer.

Alberta

Calaway Park
Trans-Canada Highway at Springbank Road
Calgary, AB (403) 240–3822

Wide-open green spaces and a breathtaking view of the Rocky Mountains are what you'll first notice at this 60-acre park, just 6 miles west of the city. In addition to Mother Nature's attractions, you'll also find 20 rides, miniature golf, a petting zoo and a host of games, shows, shops, and other offerings.

Calaway Park—founded in 1982 as western Canada's first major entertainment park—abounds with brightly hued flowers throughout the summer season. Signature attractions here include the Shoot-the-Chute, a flume ride, and the Turn of the Century Corkscrew, a roller coaster.

Musical revues are presented daily, and street entertainment is common and plentiful. The Concert Tent in the picnic area is home to top-name entertainers, festivals, and special events throughout the summer. Annual events at the park include the Cabbage Patch National Birthday Party, the Care Bears Picnic, and nostalgic fifties-style dances.

Among the 20 eateries in the park is the Terrace Garden Restaurant, the best bet for a tasty, sit-down meal in a cafe setting.

Guests have a choice of two admission plans: one provides admission and shows, with no rides included; and the other is a pay-one-price arrangement that includes admission, shows, and rides. Hours vary; call first.

Fantasyland
8770 170th Street
Indoors at West Edmonton Mall
Edmonton, AB (403) 444–5300

Advertised as the "Eighth Wonder of the World," the entire $1 billion West Edmonton Mall itself could almost be classified as an amusement park. Nevertheless, inside the mall is Fantasyland—an incredible 9-acre amusement complex that is considered the largest indoor park in North America.

Included in the park's 23 rides is a 12-story-tall, triple-looping roller coaster. Nearby in the mall are other attractions, such as: a full-scale water park with 22 slides and a wave pool; Pebble Beach, a miniature golf course; Deep Sea Adventure, featuring 4 full-size submarines; a regulation-size ice-skating rink; a dolphin show; and an authentic Spanish galleon.

TIM'S TRIVIA

There are more submarines in the "Deep Sea Adventure" attraction at Fantasyland in the West Edmonton Mall (Alberta, Canada) than in the entire Canadian navy.

Food is available on a limited basis within the park itself, but the 812-store mall offers literally hundreds of eateries. Games, souvenirs, and child-care areas are plentiful.

Admission to the park is free, with rides on a pay-as-you-go basis or a pay-one-price ticket is available, under $25. The hours are basically the same as those in the mall. Free parking.

British Columbia

Flintstones Bedrock City
53480 Trans-Canada Highway
Rosedale, BC (604) 794–7410

You'll think you've walked into a Flintstones cartoon when you enter the front gates of this wonderful little children's park, just north of Vancouver. The houses and stores of Bedrock have been re-created, complete with Fred Flintstone's car sitting in front of his house.

The 11-acre park specializes in "people-powered" rides, including paddleboats, pedal cars, and hand-powered bumper cars. Other features include a children's playground, complete with treehouse; a dinosaur park, where little ones can climb on big statues; miniature golf; a "liquid playground" where kids can help put out a fire at the Bedrock Fire House No. 1; and a cartoon train ride around the city of Bedrock.

A live music and dance show, featuring Fred, Barney, Wilma, Betty, and Dino, takes place several times each day. And when they aren't performing, the characters roam the park.

There are several walk-up food stands, and management encourages families to bring their own lunches and make a day of it. The park has a number of nice picnic areas where barbecue grills are permitted to be set up.

Open from Mother's Day through Labor Day, from 10:00 A.M. to 8:00 P.M. Admission is pay-one-price, under $10, and parking is free.

Playland Family Fun Park
East Hastings Street
In Exhibition Park
Vancouver, BC (604) 255-5161

Nearby mountains provide a picturesque backdrop to this 10-acre, well-kept traditional park. Located 6 miles from downtown Vancouver, the park becomes the cornerstone for Canada's largest fair, the Pacific National Exhibition, in late August each year.

If you can arrange your trip here to coincide with the fair, do so, for you'll find a truly amazing lineup of rides, shows, and other attractions. Be aware, though, that such timing also means you'll find the park at its busiest and most crowded.

In addition to go-carts, 2 miniature golf courses, and a good selection of standard park rides, the facility also features 3 roller coasters, including an excellent historic wooden coaster. Games of skill, 7 food outlets, strolling entertainers, and a separate, well-supervised kiddieland round out the attractions.

The park is open from Easter Sunday through September. Hours vary; call first.

New Brunswick

Crystal Palace
499 Paul Street
Dieppe, NB (506) 856-8324

Located just a few blocks from the city limits of Moncton, this free-standing indoor entertainment center is situated in the parking lot of a large regional mall.

The 1.3-acre ride area lies under a high glass dome and includes 8 mechanical rides and a large ship-themed participatory play area. Among the rides is the Bullet, a family roller coaster; a carousel; and a wave swinger. Also here are an SR-2 simulator, a large video-game and games-of-skill arcade, and a miniature golf course with a pirate theme.

Adjacent to the ride area is a food court; McGinnis Landing, a restaurant; a four-screen movie theater; and a 120-room hotel with fantasy suites.

Open daily, year-round. Admission is free, with rides on a pay-as-you-go basis. Free parking in mall lot; a shuttle bus operates between Crystal Palace and the main entrance of the mall.

Nova Scotia

Upper Clements Amusement Park
Old #1 Highway
Upper Clements, NS (902) 532-7557

The early twentieth century is the theme of this 26-acre park, located between Annapolis and Digby in a heavily wooded, rural area of the province.

Although the park opened only in 1989, it looks like it's been here for years. The buildings were either built to resemble early structures or are actual historical buildings that were moved in, such as the rare round Dutch barn. The crafts village features an assortment of local artisans, including several carousel carvers who created all the horses on the park's carousel.

And in addition to that carousel are 6 rides, including the Sississiboo Sizzler, a flume ride, antique cars, The Tree Topper, a wooden roller coaster, and a train excursion. There are several kiddie rides as well. The miniature golf course is on a Nova Scotia–shaped island in the park's lake; giving a person a chance to putt around the province!

The park offers 3 restaurants: Call of the Wild, Jake's Landing, and Kedge Lodge. All are rustic-looking facilities that serve a full menu, from salmon and steak to corn dogs. And the bakery's aroma is enough to stop you in your tracks.

Admission is pay-one-price, under $20; after 3:00 P.M. every day, admission is half-price. The park closes at dusk every night during its peak summer period.

Ontario

Canada's Wonderland
9580 Jane Street
Maple, ON (416) 832-7000

Bring your walking shoes, and make sure you get a guidebook and map at the front gate, because this is a large park. With 370 beautifully landscaped acres; 35 rides, including 8 roller coasters; and seven areas with elaborate themes, there's enough here to please every member of your family.

This is coaster heaven. There are more roller coasters here—7 in all—than in any other Canadian park, and the stand-up coaster, SkyRider, is the only one of its kind in the country.

One of the first things you'll see as you enter is the spectacular International Fountain, especially dazzling after dark, when the computerized light show begins. Just beyond the fountain is the 150-foot-high Wonder Mountain, a $5 million man-made mountain that contains the Thunder Run coaster. The Vortex suspended coaster climbs and circles the mountain and thrills riders by appearing to almost crash into the mountain.

For the kids, Hanna-Barbera Land is a complete miniature park in itself, providing 14 rides for the wee ones. And don't miss the excellent lineup of shows, including musical revues, comedy acts, and marine-life presentations.

Plan to spend the entire day if you want to see and do everything. Admission is pay-one-price, under $25. The major season runs from early May through early September.

Centreville
Centre Island
Toronto, ON (416) 363–1112

You'll need to take a ferry to Centre Island, a nicely landscaped and wooded 640-acre city park, to find this neat little park.

The 14-acre amusement park was designed to resemble a turn-of-the-century Ontario village and contains 15 family rides, including antique cars, white swan boats, a flume, and the Haunted Barrel Works. There is also a miniature golf course.

The 7 food stands in the park serve a variety of foods, from steaks to fried chicken to hot dogs. Make sure, too, to stop by the fabulous O. Bumble ice-cream parlor for a wonderful ice-cream treat.

There are many other activities on the island that you may wish to partake of while visiting. Among them are a swimming pool, bike trails, boating, and fishing.

The entire complex here is low-key and offers a good way to spend a quiet, relaxing afternoon with your family.

Call for hours and days of operation and admission prices.

Maple Leaf Village
5705 Falls Avenue
Niagara Falls, ON (416) 374–0711

Wherever you are in this city, all you have to do is survey the high horizon and chances are you'll see the Giant Wheel, this park's 176-foot-tall

Ferris wheel. Set high on a hill a short distance from the falls, this popular ride anchors a 24-ride park.

Garfield the cat is the mascot here and walks around greeting visitors. Additional rides include a Tilt-A-Whirl, Sea Dragon, Rainbow (a 360-degree ride where the passenger remains upright), a carousel and Spider.

The Falls can be seen from atop the Ferris wheel, making it a tourist attraction as well as a top-notch ride. In addition to the rides, the park offers several walk-up eateries, a games-of-skill arcade, and an indoor shopping mall housing several other attractions, including one of the best haunted houses in the area.

The Giant Wheel operates whenever the weather is good enough to provide a safe ride. As an attraction, it opens earlier in the season and closes later in the fall than the park itself and is usually in operation every morning long before the other rides get cranked up. Officials say that whenever one sees the Giant Wheel turning, it's open.

Admission to the park is free, with a pay-one-price ticket available, under $20, or tickets are available on a pay-as-you-play basis.

Marineland of Canada
7657 Portage Road
Niagara Falls, ON (416) 356–8250

Originally a marine park, this facility has added rides over the years, making it a great place to visit.

Along with the killer-whale, dolphin, and sea-lion shows, there are now 10 rides, including 4 for kids to choose from. A castlelike structure in the middle of the 300-acre grounds houses a deer-petting park, and a huge, man-made mountain in the back of the amusement park contains the Dragon Mountain, a roller coaster that has one of the most interesting ride entrances in North America, complete with cave and drawbridge. A fantasy castle is planned for another man-made mountain.

Walter Ostanek, Canada's polka king, entertains guests daily during the peak season.

Among the many eateries are the Happy Lion Restaurant, featuring an all-you-can-eat buffet, and the Hungry Lion Restaurant, a full-menu, sit-down establishment. Food may be brought into the park, and there are at least a hundred places where a nice, relaxing picnic can be enjoyed.

Pay-one-price admission, under $20, and parking is free. The marine shows are open year-round, with a special admission charge in effect. *Note:* The rides and attractions are spread out with a great deal of space in between, so you should plan to do a lot of walking.

Ontario Place
955 Lakeshore Boulevard West
Toronto, PQ (416) 965-7917

It's hard to believe you're in anything but a city park as you stroll the beautiful 96 acres of this facility. Located along the shores of Lake Ontario, the park is quiet, relaxing, green, and well kept. It's also one of the largest entertainment complexes in the city. There's an IMAX theater here, as well as two other smaller film houses. Live-action shows take place on numerous stages throughout, and street performers are everywhere.

There is an additional charge for most rides and attractions, which include the Wilderness Adventure Flume, a water slide, bumper boats, paddle boats, and miniature golf.

During the day, the emphasis is on children and the young family: A Lego Creative Play Center features more than a million Lego pieces to play with; a children's village offers a large participatory play area; and a children's theater provides entertainment for the little ones.

At night, the park turns into an adult entertainment center, one with a nightclub atmosphere. The 6 sit-down, table-service restaurant offerings range from fine dining at Trillium, to casual dining at Breakers or Jam'z. In addition, there are numerous walk-up eateries and a 6-restaurant food court.

Admission is pay-one-price, under $10. Parking fee charged. Hours vary for different attractions; call first.

Quebec

La Ronde
Ile Saint-Hélène
Montreal, PQ (514) 872-6120

The skyline of this island park is exciting. The towering, dual-track wooden roller coaster, Le Monstre, and the 150-foot-tall Ferris wheel beckon as the visitor approaches.

The park is located in the center of the St. Lawrence River on St. Helen's Island, the site of the 1967 World's Fair. And it's every bit as immaculate and colorful today as it was then, offering a distinct international flavor and a festive atmosphere.

Le Boomerang is one of the 3 roller coasters among the park's 35 rides. Make sure you ride the Ferris wheel; it provides a breathtaking view of the surrounding area, including the adjacent 21-slide Aqua Parc and the Montreal Aquarium.

There's some great food here, and you'll find just about anything you might have a craving for, even a Big Mac—a McDonald's franchise is right in the park.

Unlike most parks in North America, this one does not permit guests, once they enter, to leave and reenter. So don't leave anything in the car, expecting to get it later. Instead, use the coin lockers near the front gate, and make sure you bring a sweater or jacket, since the island gets quite chilly after dark, even in midsummer.

Rides and attractions don't open until 11:00 A.M. or noon, but they do stay open until midnight or 2:30 A.M. during peak season. The major season runs from late May through early September. Admission is pay-one-price.

WATER PARKS

The ol' swimming hole has gone high-tech and has been replaced by a new type of amusement park—the water park.

These facilities are wonderful places to play, meet friends, and, above all, stay cool during the long hot summer. With six-story-high water slides having such thrilling names as the Black Hole, The Cliff, and The Edge, they provide action that the basic community swimming pool never even thought of. Body surfing is even possible in the ones with wave pools!

Many of the best water parks in the country are within or adjacent to the amusement parks described in this book. Listed below is a sampling. Each entry is brief, but will give you a good idea of the size and scope of the facility.

The hours and days of operation listed are for peak summertime periods. Many are open weekends only during the spring and fall, with limited hours. All have changing rooms and locker facilities.

AMUSEMENT PARKS PLUS WATER

California

Raging Waters, in Lake Cunningham City Park, 2333 South White Road, San Jose, (408) 238–9900. 8 slides and flumes; adult activity pool; lazy river; Wacky Waters, children's area with activity pools and slides; food service; games arcade; beach shop. Admission is under $15. Open from Memorial Day through Labor Day, 10:00 A.M. to dusk. (See other Raging Waters parks under New Jersey and Utah.)

Florida

Shipwreck Island, adjacent to Miracle Strip Amusement Park, 12000 West Highway 98A, Panama City, (904) 234–2282. 12 slides and flumes; Ocean Motion, wave pool; Skull Island, adult activity pool; Tadpole Hole, children's area; lazy river; live entertainment; food service; beach shop.

Admission is separate from amusement park. All day pass, under $20. A 2-day combination pass with amusement park available, under $25. The days do not have to be used consecutively. Open March through mid-September, 10:00 A.M. to 6:00 P.M.

Illinois

Racing Rapids, adjacent to Three Worlds of Santa's Village, Routes 25 & 72, Dundee, (708) 426–5525. 4 slides; lazy river; bumper boats; go-carts; Fun Island, children's area with slides and activity pool; adult activity pool; food service; games arcade.

Admission separate, under $10. Combination ticket available, under $15. Open daily Memorial Day through Labor Day, 11:00 A.M. to 8:00 P.M.

Michigan

Wild Water Adventure, inside Michigan's Adventure, 4750 Whitehall Road, Muskegon, (616) 766–3377. 10 slides and flumes; lazy river; action river; wave pool; children's area with slides and activity pools; all water heated.

Admission included in the amusement park's pay-one-price ticket, under $15. Open daily Memorial Day through Labor Day, mid-morning to dusk.

Minnesota

Liquid Lightning, inside Valleyfair, 1 Valleyfair Drive, Shakopee, (612) 445–7600. 5 slides and flumes; lazy river; food service; viewing area.

Requires admission in addition to amusement park's fee. Options include a 2-hour visit, under $5, and an all-day pass, under $10. Open daily Memorial Day through Labor Day, 11:00 A.M. to dusk. Opens at noon on Sunday.

Missouri

Oceans of Fun, adjacent to Worlds of Fun, Kansas City, 4545 Worlds of Fun Avenue, (816) 454–4545. 35 different attractions including 5 slides and flumes; Surf City Wave Pool; Caribbean Cooler, lazy river; Knee-Hai/Belly-Hai, children's area; Neptune's Lagoon, a sand-bottom activity pool; Castaway Cove, an adult-only activity pool featuring the swim-up Belly-Up bar where alcoholic beverages are available; food service; bath shop; all water is heated.

Admission is separate from Worlds of Fun amusement park. All-day pass, under $15. A 2-day, 2-park combination ticket is available, under $25. Open Memorial Day through Labor Day, 10:00 A.M. to dusk.

White Water, five miles from Silver Dollar City, West Highway 76, Branson, (417) 334–7487. 6 slides and flumes; Restful River, lazy river; live entertainment including dive-in movies and beach dance parties; wave pool; food service; games arcade; Squirt's Island, children's area with slides and activity pools; beach shop.
Admission is under $15. Open daily from Memorial Day through Labor Day, 10:00 A.M. to 9:00 P.M. Silver Dollar City also owns the White Water water park in Marietta, Georgia, adjacent to its American Adventure amusement park, 250 North Cobb Parkway, (404) 424–9283.

New Jersey

The Morey family, who owns Morey's Pier and Mariner's Landing on the boardwalk in Wildwood, owns the following two Raging Waters water parks plus two others in California and Utah.

Raging Waters at Morey's Pier, Boardwalk at 25th Street, (609) 622–5477. 9 slides and flumes; adult activity pool; lazy river; Little Dipper, children's area with slides and activity pool; large hot tub; food service; beach shop. Admission options include a 2-hour pass, under $10; a 3-hour pass, under $15; and an after-5:00 P.M. special, under $7.50. Open daily Memorial Day through Labor Day, 9:00 A.M. to 7:30 P.M.

Raging Waters at Mariner's Landing, Boardwalk at Schellenger Avenue, (609) 729–0586. 12 slides and flumes; Little Dipper children's area with slides and activity pool; lazy river; adult activity pool with nets, rings, crawls, and swings; food service; beach shop. Hours and admission prices are same as Morey's Pier.

New York

Barracuda Bay, inside Darien Lake, Route 77, Darien Center, (716) 599–4641. 15 slides and flumes; food service; beach shop.
Requires admission in addition to amusement park's pay-one-price ticket. Two hours, under $5. No longer time periods available. Open daily Memorial Day through Labor Day, 11:00 A.M. to dusk. (*Author's note:* The water park is designed for use primarily as a slide activity area to enjoy and then return to the rest of the attractions in the amusement park.)

North Carolina

Rip Tide Reef, inside Carowinds, Carowinds Boulevard, Charlotte, (704) 588–2606. 4 slides and flumes; TideWater Bay, wave pool; WaterWorks, children's area with activity pool and slides; food service; games arcade; beach shop.

Admission is included in amusement park's pay-one-price ticket, under $20. Open daily Memorial Day through Labor Day, 10:00 A.M. to 7:00 P.M. Open weekends in May and September.

Ohio

Boardwalk Shores, inside Geauga Lake, 1060 Aurora Road, Aurora, (216) 562–7131. 8 slides; The Wave, wave pool; Turtle Beach, children's area with 10 major elements including 4 slides and 2 different children's lazy rivers; beach shops; food service; games arcade.

Admission is included in amusement park's pay-one-price ticket, under $15. Open daily Memorial Day through Labor Day, 11:00 A.M. or noon to dusk. Open weekends in May and September, weather permitting. (*Author's note:* Turtle Beach is the largest and most advanced water park for children in the country.)

Soak City, adjacent to Cedar Point, Sandusky, (419) 626–0830. 10 slides and flumes; Main Stream, lazy river; Tadpole Town, children's area with activity pool and slides; limited food service; beach shop; viewing area; sandy sunning beach.

Separate admission: all day, under $10; also one- and two-hour admissions available. Two-day combo pass with amusement park, under $45. Open daily Memorial Day through Labor Day, 10:00 A.M. to 10:00 P.M. or midnight. Hours until mid-June and from mid-August are shortened to noon to 8:00 P.M.

WaterWorks, inside Kings Island, Kings Island Drive, Kings Island, (513) 398–5600. 15 slides; Kings Mills Run, lazy river; Rushing River, giant tube ride; Splash Island, children's area with 3 slides and splash play area; food service; beach shop; all water heated; games arcade.

Admission is included in amusement park's pay-one-price fee, under $25. Open daily Memorial Day through Labor Day, 10:00 A.M. to 9:00 P.M.

Pennsylvania

Sandcastle, 1000 Sandcastle Boulevard, West Homestead, 4 miles from Kennywood Park, West Mifflin, (412) 462–6666. 15 slides and flumes; lazy river; adult activity pool; three hot tubs; marina on the Monongahela River; kiddie pool with slides; food service; beach shop; volleyball courts; miniature golf; shuffleboard courts; 1,400-foot boardwalk along the river.

All-day slide and pool pass, under $15. All-day pool pass, no slides, under $7.50. Open Memorial Day through Labor Day, 11:00 A.M. to 7:00 P.M.

After 8:00 P.M. the park becomes an adult entertainment center for ages 21 and over. Five separate bars and clubs are open, as are all water elements except slides. Live entertainment. Admission is $1 during the week, $4 on weekends.

WaterWorld, inside Waldameer Park, Route 832, Erie, (814) 838–3591. 10 slides and flumes; children's area with heated pools; large heated spa pool with 94-degree water; lazy river; food service; beach shop.

All-day admission, under $10. Combination ticket available with ride park. Open daily Memorial Day through Labor Day, 11:00 A.M. to 5:00 P.M.

Wild Water Kingdom, adjacent to Dorney Park, 3830 Dorney Park Road, Allentown, (215) 398–7955. Total of 34 different elements including 14 slides; 2 lazy rivers; wave pool; activity pool with various adult activities; Lollipop Lagoon, children's area with activity pool and 7 slides; food service; beach shop.

Separate admission, under $20, or combination ticket with amusement park for $3 extra. Open daily Memorial Day through Labor Day, 10:00 A.M. to 9:00 P.M.

Texas

WaterWorld, adjacent to AstroWorld, 9001 Kirby Drive, Houston, (713) 799–1234. 7 slides and flumes; Breaker Beach, wave pool; Mainstream, lazy river; Lagoon, activity pool featuring slides, nets, rope, and swings; Squirt's Splash, children's area; food service; beach shop; games arcade; live entertainment including the Looney Tunes characters in swimsuits.

Admission is separate from amusement park. All-day pass, under $20. A 2-day combination ticket with amusement park available, under $25. Open daily mid-May through September, 10:00 or 11:00 A.M. to 7:00, 8:00, or 9:00 P.M.

Utah

Lagoon A Beach, inside Lagoon Park, I–15 & Lagoon Drive, Farmington, (801) 451–0101. 9 slides; adult activity pool; lazy river; children's play area with 3 slides and activity pool; all water heated; food service; games arcade; volleyball courts; beach shop.

Admission is included in amusement park's pay-one-price fee, under $20. Open daily Memorial Day through Labor Day, 11:00 A.M. to dusk. Open weekends in May and September, weather permitting.

Raging Waters, 1200 West 1700 South, Salt Lake City, (801) 973–4020. 9 slides and flumes, including the world's first H2O Roller Coaster; large hot tub; wave pool; Raging WaterWorks, children's area that features several activity pools and slides; games arcade; volleyball courts; beach shop. Admission is under $15. Open Memorial Day through Labor Day, 10:30 A.M. to 8:30 P.M. (See other Raging Waters parks under New Jersey and California.)

THE BEST OF THE REST

The following water parks are not associated with or owned by an amusement park but are worth listing because they are the best of the rest.

Florida

George Millay is known as the father of the American water park industry. He founded the Sea World parks, sold them, and then established Wet 'N Wild Orlando, considered the first water park in the United States. Today he has four Wet 'N Wild water parks.

Wet 'N Wild, 6200 International Drive, Orlando, (407) 351–1800. 15 slides and flumes, including the ultimate water slide, the Black Hole, a dark double-rider trip down an enclosed tube with sound and lighting effects; lazy river; Pepper Park, children's area; wave pool; food service; beach shops; live entertainment including beach dances; games arcade.

Admission is under $20. Open daily mid-February through January 1. Hours are 9:00 A.M. to 11:00 P.M. during summer; 10:00 A.M. to 5:00 P.M. in winter.

Nevada

Wet 'N Wild, 2601 Las Vegas Boulevard South, Las Vegas, (702) 734–0088. 13 slides and flumes; Willy-Willy, a carousel-type rapid water ride; wave pool; Pepper Park, children's area; Suntan Lagoon, adult activity pool; food service; beach shops; games arcade.

Admission is under $15. Open April through September, 10:00 A.M. to 8:00 P.M.

Ohio

The Beach, I–71 and Kings Mills Road (Exit 25), Mason, (513) 398–7946. 14 slides and flumes; Thunder Beach, wave pool; Lazy Miami, lazy river; 2 adult activity pools; Dolphin Bay and Penguins Bay, children's areas; sand volleyball courts; games arcade; gift shops; beach shop; food service; live entertainment.

An all-day admission is under $15, with a daily after-5:00 P.M. special discount. Open daily May through Labor Day, 10:00 A.M. to 9:00 P.M. (*Author's note:* This is one of the nation's finest water park facilities.)

Texas

Wet 'N Wild, 1800 East Lamar Boulevard., Arlington, (817) 265–3356. 14 slides and flumes, including a Black Hole (see Wet 'N Wild, Orlando, Florida); wave pool; Suntan Lagoon, adult activity pool; lazy river; Pepper Park, children's activity pool with net climbs, slides, and swings; food service; beach shops.

Admission is under $20. Open late April through mid-September, 10:00 A.M. to 9:00 P.M.

Wet 'N Wild, 12715 LBJ Freeway, Garland, (214) 271–5637. 13 slides and flumes; wave pool; lazy river; adult activity pool with diving boards, rings, and ropes; Pepper Park, children's area with water guns, net climbs, and slides; sand volleyball courts; shaded picnic areas; beach shop; food service; games arcade.

Admission is under $15. Open late April through mid-September, 10:00 A.M. to 9:00 P.M.

AMUSEMENT PARKS
BY STATE AND PROVINCE

United States

ALABAMA
Main Street Family Fun Park,
   Orange Beach, 3

ALASKA
Alaskaland, Fairbanks, 3

ARIZONA
Golf N' Stuff, Phoenix, 4
Metro Midway and Discovery
   Center, Phoenix, 4
Old Tucson Studios, Tucson, 4

ARKANSAS
Burns Park Funland,
   North Little Rock, 6
Dogpatch USA, Dogpatch, 6
Fun Spot, Eureka Springs, 8
Magic Springs Family
   Theme Park, Hot Springs, 8
War Memorial Amusement Park,
   Little Rock, 9

CALIFORNIA
Belmont Park's Giant Dipper,
   San Diego, 10
Castle Amusement Park,
   Riverside, 11
Disneyland, Anaheim, 11
Escondido Family Fun Center,
   Escondido, 13
Funderland, Sacramento, 13
Funderwoods, Lodi, 14
Golf N' Stuff, Norwalk, 14

Great America, Santa Clara, 14
Happy Hollow Park and Zoo,
   San Jose, 16
Hecker Pass: A Family Adventure,
   Gilroy, 17
Knott's Berry Farm,
   Buena Park, 17
Marine World/Africa USA,
   Vallejo, 18
Marshal Scotty's, San Diego, 19
Pixieland Park, Concord, 20
Santa Cruz Beach Boardwalk,
   Santa Cruz, 20
Santa Monica Pier,
   Santa Monica, 21
Santa's Village, Skyforest, 22
Sea World of California,
   San Diego, 23
Six Flags Magic Mountain,
   Valencia, 24
Tahoe Amusement Park,
   South Lake Tahoe, 25
Universal Studios Hollywood,
   Universal City, 25

COLORADO
Elitch Gardens, Denver, 27
Fun Junction, Grand Junction, 29
Funtastic Nathan's,
   Englewood, 29
Lakeside Park, Denver, 29
Lollipop Park, Westminster, 30
Santa's Workshop, North Pole, 30
Time Out on the Court,
   Thornton, 31

CONNECTICUT
Lake Compounce Festival Park,
  Bristol, 32
Quassy Amusement Park,
  Middlebury, 33

DELAWARE
Funland, Rehoboth Beach, 34

FLORIDA
Busch Gardens, Tampa, 34
Cypress Gardens,
  Winter Haven, 35
Fun 'N Wheels, Kissimmee, 36
Fun 'N Wheels, Orlando, 37
Lion Country Safari,
  West Palm Beach, 37
Lowry Amusement Park,
  Tampa, 37
Miami Metrozoo, Miami, 37
Miracle Strip Amusement Park,
  Panama City, 38
Old Town, Kissimmee, 39
Raceway Park,
  Ft. Walton Beach, 39
Sea World of Florida, Orlando, 39
Universal Studios Florida,
  Orlando, 40
Walt Disney World Resort,
  Lake Buena Vista, 42

GEORGIA
American Adventures,
  Marietta, 47
Lake Winnepesaukah,
  Rossville, 47
Six Flags Over Georgia,
  Atlanta, 48
Tybee Island Amusement Park,
  Tybee Island, 49

HAWAII
Fun Factory, Kahului, Maui, 50
Waimea Fall Park,
  Haleiwa, Oaho, 50

IDAHO
Julia Davis Fun Depot, Boise, 51
Silverwood, Athol, 51

ILLINOIS
Blackberry Historical Farm,
  Aurora, 52
Kiddieland, Melrose Park, 54
Knights Action Park,
  Springfield, 55
Rockome Gardens, Arcola, 55
Six Flags Great America,
  Gurnee, 55
Three Worlds of Santa's Village,
  Dundee, 56

INDIANA
Adventureland,
  North Webster, 57
Enchanted Forest Amusement
  Park, Chesterton, 58
Fun Spot Amusement Park,
  Angola, 59
Holiday World, Santa Claus, 60
Indiana Beach, Monticello, 61
Indianapolis Zoo,
  Indianapolis, 62
Old Indiana Fun Park,
  Thornton, 63
Redbrush Park, Seymour, 64
River Fair Family Fun Park,
  Clarksville, 64
Sauzer's Kiddieland,
  Schereville, 65

NEBRASKA
Peony Park, Omaha, 96

NEVADA
MGM Grand Movie Theme Park,
  Las Vegas, 97
Playland Park, Reno, 97
Riviera Amusement Pavilion,
  Las Vegas, 98

NEW HAMPSHIRE
Canobie Lake, Salem, 98
Story Land, Glen, 99

NEW JERSEY
Action Park, McAfee, 103
Bowcraft, Scotch Plains, 104
Captain Good Times,
  Turnersville, 104
Casino Pier, Seaside Heights, 100
Central Pier, Atlantic City, 105
Clementon Amusement Park,
  Clementon, 105
Fantasy Island, Beach Haven, 106
Fun City Amusement Park,
  Sea Isle City, 101
Fun Town Pier,
  Seaside Heights, 101
Hunts Pier, Wildwood, 108
Jenkinson's Pavilion,
  Point Pleasant Beach, 101
Keansburg Amusement Park,
  Keansburg, 107
Mariner's Landing,
  Wildwood, 108
Morey's Pier, Wildwood, 109
Nickel's Midway Pier,
  Wildwood, 109
Playland, Ocean City, 102
Six Flags Great Adventure,
  Jackson, 110
Storybook Land, Cardiff, 111

Tivoli Pier, Atlantic City, 112
Wonderland Pier,
  Ocean City, 102

NEW MEXICO
Amusement Village,
  Carlsbad, 113
Cliff's Amusement Park,
  Albuquerque. 113

NEW YORK
Adventureland,
  East Farmingdale, 114
Astroland, Brooklyn/
  Coney Island, 115
Darien Lake, Darien Center, 116
Deno's Wonder Wheel Park
  Brooklyn/Coney Island, 117
Enchanted Forest, Old Forge, 117
Falls Street Faire,
  Niagara Falls, 119
Fantasy Island, Grand Island, 119
Great Escape, Lake George, 120
Hoffman's Playland,
  Newtonville, 121
Kid's Kingdom, Medford, 122
Lake George Ride and Fun Park,
  Lake George, 122
Magic Forest, Lake George, 123
Midway Park, Maple Springs, 123
Nellie Bly Park, Brooklyn, 124
Playland, Rye, 125
Seabreeze Amusement Park,
  Rochester, 126
Sylvan Beach Amusement Park,
  Sylvan Beach, 127

NORTH CAROLINA
Carowinds, Charlotte, 128
Crystal Beach, White Lake, 129
Emerald Pointe, Greensboro, 130
Ghost Town in the Sky,
  Maggie Valley, 130

TEXAS

AstroWorld, Houston, 171
Clown Around,
 Grand Prairie, 173
Fiesta Texas, San Antonio, 173
Funland Amusement Park,
 Wichita Falls, 173
Joyland Amusement Park,
 Lubbock, 174
Jungle Jim's Playland,
 Houston, 175
Jungle Jim's Playland at Memorial
 City, Houston, 175
Jungle Jim's Playland,
 Richardson, 175
Jungle Jim's Playland,
 San Antonio, 176
Kiddie Park, San Antonio, 176
Neff's Amusement Park,
 San Angelo, 176
Penny Whistle Park, Dallas, 177
Sandy Lake Amusement Park,
 Dallas, 178
Sea World of Texas,
 San Antonio, 179
Six Flags Over Texas,
 Arlington, 179
Sunshine Park, San Antonio, 181
Western Playland, El Paso, 182
Wonderland Park, Amarillo, 182

UTAH

49th Street Galleria, Murray, 183
Lagoon Park, Farmington, 184

VERMONT

Santa's Land, , 185

VIRGINIA

Busch Gardens, The Old
 Country, Williamsburg, 186
Kings Dominion, Doswell, 188
Ocean Breeze Fun Park,
 Virginia Beach, 189

WASHINGTON

Fun Forest, Seattle, 190
Riverfront Park, Spokane, 191

WEST VIRGINIA

Camden Park, Huntington, 191

WISCONSIN

Bay Beach Amusement Park,
 Green Bay, 192
Circle M Corral Family Fun Park,
 Minocqua, 193
Circus World Museum,
 Baraboo, 193
Riverview Park,
 Wisconsin Dells, 193
Thumb Fun Park, Fish Creek, 194

WYOMING

Wyoming Territorial Park,
 Laramie, 195

Canada

ALBERTA
Calaway Park, Calgary, 197
Fantasyland, Edmonton, 197

BRITISH COLUMBIA
Flintstones Bedrock City,
  Rosedale, 198
Playland Family Fun Park,
  Vancouver, 199

NEW BRUNSWICK
Crystal Palace, Dieppe, 199

NOVA SCOTIA
Upper Clements Amusement
  Park, Upper Clements, 200

ONTARIO
Canada's Wonderland,
  Maple, 200
Centreville, Toronto, 201
Maple Leaf Village,
  Niagara Falls, 201
Marineland of Canada,
  Niagara Falls, 202
Ontario Place, Toronto, 203

QUEBEC
La Ronde, Montreal, 203

Water Parks

CALIFORNIA
Raging Waters, San Jose, 205

FLORIDA
Shipwreck Island,
  Panama City, 205
Wet 'N Wild, Orlando, 210

ILLINOIS
Racing Rapids, Dundee, 206

MICHIGAN
Wild Water Adventure,
  Muskegon, 206

MINNESOTA
Liquid Lightning, Shakopee, 206

MISSOURI
Oceans of Fun, Kansas City, 206
White Water, Branson, 207

NEVADA
Wet 'N Wild, Las Vegas, 211

NEW JERSEY
Raging Waters at Morey's Pier,
  Wildwood, 207
Raging Waters at Mariner's
  Landing, Wildwood, 207

NEW YORK
Barracuda Bay, Darien Center, 207

NORTH CAROLINA
Rip Tide Reef, Charlotte, 208

OHIO
Beach, The, Mason, 211
Boardwalk Shores, Aurora, 208
Soak City, Sandusky, 208
WaterWorks, Kings Island, 208

PENNSYLVANIA
Sandcastle, West Homestead, 209
WaterWorld, Erie, 209
Wild Water Kingdom,
   Allentown, 209

TEXAS
WaterWorld, Houston, 209
Wet 'N Wild, Arlington, 211
Wet 'N Wild, Garland, 211

UTAH
Lagoon A Beach, Farmington, 210
Raging Waters, Salt Lake City, 210

About the Author

As Southeast editor for *Amusement Business Newsweekly,* an international trade publication for the outdoor mass entertainment industry, Tim O'Brien travels the world's highways and byways for a living.

His interest in parks began early, having grown up across from Buckeye Lake Amusement Park, near Columbus, Ohio, and the love affair continued as he grew. For his Masters thesis in film production at Ohio State University, he produced a film documentary on the rides at Sandusky, Ohio's Cedar Point.

He calls his job a "great marriage," as it combines his previous experience as a news reporter and editor with his love of parks. As Tim says, "There's something special in writing about people whose main business is to make people happy."

Tim is also an accomplished photographer and a roller coaster "freak," having ridden many of the world's greatest coasters.